Another Way Home

And Other Sermons that Matter

Nancy I. Penton

Parson's Porch Books

Another Way Home
ISBN: Softcover 978-1-955581-85-1
Copyright © 2022 by Nancy I. Penton

Cover Photograph provided by G. Allen Penton. Location: San Jose Mission, San Antonio, Texas.

Parson's Porch Books is an imprint of Parson's Porch *&* Company (PP*&*C) in Cleveland, Tennessee. PP*&*C is an innovative organization which raises money by publishing books of noted authors, representing all genres. Its face and voice is **David Russell Tullock** (dtullock@parsonsporch.com).

Parson's Porch *&* Company *turns books into bread & milk* by sharing its profits with the poor.

www.parsonsporch.com

Another Way Home

Contents

Foreword

I first met Nancy at a church in Atlanta almost fifteen years ago. I was the worship leader, and she headed up the prayer ministry. Our overlap in those two areas was some of our first interactions, but our first really personal conversation is still framed clearly in my mind. It was a Sunday morning, and I was just about to head backstage to begin worship. As I turned to leave, Nancy came down the stairs from a prayer meeting with a troubled look on her face. I asked her what the matter was, and she replied that she just didn't know if she had a place at the church anymore and was ready to find somewhere else. I told her that would be an incredible loss to the church community. This exchange was the beginning of many more conversations in the months to come.

Not long after that, my family and I felt God's call to plant Liberty Vineyard Church. Nancy and her husband, along with several others, were part of the initial church planting team. For the nine years that I pastored the church, I was privileged to pastor, pray with and for, work alongside, and do ministry with Nancy on a weekly and sometimes daily basis. Along the way, I received prayer, wise counsel, pastoring and mentoring, and genuine Godly love and care from her and her husband. Nancy has a heart for ministry and a passion for studying, is dedicated to prayer, and deeply loves the church. She also has a mature and growing relationship with God and is now an associate pastor of Liberty Vineyard Church.

Nancy is also a board-certified chaplain who pastored, counseled, prayed with, and spoken to numerous grieving and hurting families over the years. I believe this role led to her pursuing spiritual direction training within the Vineyard (a process by which one person helps another seek the Holy Spirit's leading and guidance within a particular set of circumstances). She is now a trained and experienced spiritual director within the Vineyard movement.

Nancy has had the opportunity to speak at a few Society of Vineyard Scholars conferences. She has, indeed, continued to find her voice in ministry and within the church, crafting and honing her skills and developing healthy and sustainable rhythms through spiritual practices. Nancy holds a Doctorate in Ministry from Mercer and is currently an adjunct professor at Mercer School of Theology. She continues to pour her knowledge and passion into the next generation of ministry students.

She has truly found a home at the intersection of prayer, study, writing, and teaching. She has led countless prayer retreats at our church, using her creatively developed curriculum. Her book, Praying with Pictures, a collaboration with her husband, a professional photographer, is a delightful culmination of these experiences.

Nancy's scholarly research, work in spiritual direction, advocacy for chaplaincy, and dedication to prayer ministry have given her a growing voice within the Vineyard movement. She is a champion for women pastors, teachers, and leaders within the Vineyard church and beyond. She regularly teaches at church services Sunday mornings at Liberty Vineyard. Her sermons are always well-prepared, well-researched, well-reasoned, scholarly, and thorough. And her whimsical and heartfelt delivery makes them endearingly personal.

I hope you enjoy the following collection of sermons in print as much as I have enjoyed them in person.

Rev. Zac Weaver, Founding Pastor Liberty Vineyard Church, Tucker, GA, Children's Pastor and Associate Youth Pastor at Maryville Vineyard, Maryville, TN

Introduction

When I first received the invitation from Parsons Porch to submit 25-30 sermons for a series on Sermons Matter, I felt a holy nudge in my spirit. This invitation to submit sermons struck a chord in my soul. Since serving on a church planting team for Liberty Vineyard Church in 2013, I preached several times in a calendar year, sometimes on Mother's Day, Father's Day, Advent, and after Easter, or during our pastor's summer vacations. As an Associate Pastor, I preach on our Preaching Team monthly. Last year I audited a preaching class at the seminary where I teach as an adjunct professor. Auditing that class sparked my desire to improve my preaching moments. Since seminary classes in 2006 and graduation in 2007, I have grown as a preacher and a preaching student.

When we were not preaching a specific series of sermons, and I had the freedom to preach anything from the biblical text, I often gravitated toward biblical characters. I found Naaman and a turning point question his servants asked. I imagined what it might have been like to be Nicodemus visiting Jesus at night. I considered Mary, the mother of our Lord, and how she treasured things in her heart. In 2021, I preached a first-person sermon with the voice of Mary Magdalene on the Sunday after Easter. Recently, I preached "Redeeming Martha" since so many women need to hear the invitation of "Martha, Martha" instead of imagining Jesus's voice with tones of condemnation or accusation.

Please know that some of these sermons were originally forty-five minutes, and in the process of formatting them for this manuscript, I edited them down to fewer pages and points. You will hear the same sermons with more scriptures and examples if you listen online. I preached some of these sermons on Zoom and some in the parking lot when we met outdoors.

Vineyard sermons lead to Ministry Time, where those listening have opportunities to respond to the message, the worship time, and the prompting of the Holy Spirit. We have teams of people who pray with and for one another as we respond to the Lord's invitation to our souls. Some of the sermons have benedictions because we did that for a while. Some do not. Most have opening prayers. Preaching involves art and skill and editing sermons to be thirty minutes takes discipline. It is easier to preach a longer sermon than a shorter one.

Of all the sermons I have preached at Liberty Vineyard Church, I have selected twenty-seven, starting with Advent and the Magi finding "Another Way Home" and ending with the resurrection and the Ascension of "This Same Jesus." May you find encouragement, authenticity, humor, and invitations to your soul from the Lord as you read these sermons.

Rev. Dr. Nancy I. Penton
Liberty Vineyard Church
Tucker, Georgia
www.libertyvineyardchurch.com
August 2022

Another Way Home: The Magi
Matthew 2:12

January 3, 2016

Matthew 2:12 (NASB) *"And after being warned by God in a dream not to return to Herod, the magi left for their own country by another way."*

Prayer: Lord, Open our eyes to see You and our ears to hear You. Open our hearts to love You. May we willingly follow on the way You lead us. In Jesus's name. Amen.

Introduction. Have you ever lived in a place without traffic? It has been so wonderful this week to go to work and return home without traffic. All that will change tomorrow. Traffic is part of living in a big city. Here we have lots of opportunities to take different ways home. For the past year, I have tried to take another way home based on what the GPS says, based on what my eyes can see on the road ahead. Based on what I have experienced in traveling in Atlanta and working in Buckhead. Trying to get home at night. Home. Another way home. We even tried selling our house and buying another home. That would have been home by another way. But this sermon is not about Atlanta traffic and going home another way because of traffic. It is about the Wise Men, the Magi, the ones who went home another way after they met Jesus.

Another Way Home is upside down. Another way home is another way to see things. Another way to think about things. Another way to believe and be changed. It is not another home. It is another way to get home. It is upside down because the One who made the stars led others to find himself by a star. Christmas Carols. When you think of Christmas carols, can you remember any of them with Bethlehem or with stars or with wise men? What about We three Kings? "following yonder star. Star of wonder, star of night, star of royal beauty bright," O Little Town of Bethlehem, "Above thy deep and dreamless sleep the silent stars go by." The verse about the star in Silent Night, "Silent night, holy night, wondrous star, lend thy light."

Our message comes from Matthew. Matthew is the first gospel we come to in the New Testament. It is written to the Jews to testify the good news, the gospel, that Jesus was born King of the Jews in the lineage of David. And that Jesus died King of the Jews under Pontius Pilate. Jesus rose again and offers salvation to the Jews. And to all people. Matthew, Mark, Luke, and John all refer to Jesus as the King of the Jews at his death. Matthew's gospel is the only one that refers to Jesus as King of the Jews at his birth. Through the question of the Magi. Turn with me to read Matthew, Chapter 2:1-12 (NASB):

> *Now after Jesus was born in Bethlehem of Judea in the days of Herod, the king, behold, magi from the east arrived in Jerusalem, saying, "Where is He who has been born King of the Jews? For we saw His star in the east and have come to worship Him." When Herod the king heard this, he was troubled, and all Jerusalem with him. And gathering together all the chief priests and scribes of the people, he inquired of them where the Messiah was to be born. They said to him, "In Bethlehem of Judea; for this is what has been written by the prophet: 'And you, Bethlehem, land of Judah, Are by no means least among the leaders of Judah; For from you will come forth a Ruler Who will shepherd My people Israel.'" Then Herod secretly called for the magi and determined from them the exact time the star appeared. And he sent them to Bethlehem and said, "Go and search carefully for the Child; and when you have found Him, report to me, so that I too may come and worship Him." After hearing the king, they went on their way; and behold, the star, which they had seen in the east, went on ahead of them until it came to a stop over the place where the Child was to be found. When they saw the star, they rejoiced exceedingly with great joy. And after they came into the house, they saw the Child with His mother Mary; and they fell down and worshiped Him. Then they opened their treasures and presented to Him gifts of gold, frankincense, and myrrh. And after being warned by God in a dream not to return to Herod, the magi left for their own country by another way.*

Their question: Where is he who has been born? This is not a question of *if*. This is a question based on the knowledge that the King of the Jews had been born. They were just trying to locate him. Where is he? Where is he who has been born? Where is he who has been born King of the Jews? Astronomical Sign: Notice: Star. They had seen his star in the East and had come to worship. It does not say that they followed the star. It says they saw his star while they were in the East. Notice. A Star appeared at the birth of Jesus. A special star that would indicate that the King of the Jews was born. This star appeared, and the star was noticed by the wise men. This sign in the sky was enough to call them to make a pilgrimage to meet this one who was born King of the Jews. My quest to follow that star. Long before the musical "Man of la Mancha," with the words to the song, "The Impossible Dream,"[1] "This is my quest to follow that star no matter how hopeless no matter how far.to fight for the right without question or pause to be willing to march into hell for a heavenly cause."

Astronomers. In Genesis, we see God creating the heavens and the earth with the sun to rule by day and the stars by night. God takes Abraham for a walk and asks him to consider the stars. As the stars, so shall your seed be. Scientists and astronomers have studied the skies for thousands of years. Sailors used to wait for the night skies to set their instruments by the north star. Now we have GPS and satellites. Stars light the night. Those who study the stars do it at night. In the darkness, they see the light. Have you ever been to a Planetarium? I remember going to New York as a child. And going to Fernbank here as an adult. And sitting in those seats that tip back. And seeing the ceiling darken and become full of stars. It is an amazing sight to get out of the city lights and see the constellations. The beautiful stars God has created. Psalm 19 says that the heavens declare the glory of God. Psalm 19:1-2 "The heavens are telling of the glory of God; And their expanse is declaring the work of His hands. Day to day pours forth speech, And night to night reveals knowledge." God Makes a Special Light. The heavens declare the glory of God. The heavens declare the birth of Jesus, the one born King of the Jews. Those who study the stars see it. They see his star. They were looking at night. When it is the darkest, it is time to see the stars. The One who made the stars made a special light to indicate the birth of Jesus. It was His star. The One who made the stars, the One who is the Light of the World, made a star to shine to indicate his special birth. They want to meet this One who has been prophesied. They want to meet this One who was born King of the Jews.

Researcher Molnar. Several researchers have tried to determine what happened in the sky 2000 years ago. One is Michael Molnar. According to Michael R. Molnar, astronomer and author of *The Star of Bethlehem: The Legacy of the Magi*,[2] the ancients looked to Aries for signs related to Judea. He based much of his hypothesis upon discovering an ancient Roman coin depicting Aries, the ram looking back at a star above. From the symbols on the coin, Molnar has researched pertinent dates, which he has tied to celestial events during the era. Molnar writes that here are things agreed upon about the Star: It signified birth. It signified kingship. It had a connection to the Jewish

---

[1] "The Impossible Dream" Songwriters: Leigh Mitch / Darion Joseph The Impossible Dream lyrics © 1966. Helena Music Company, Andrew Scott Music.

[2] https://www.ubcpress.ca/michael-r-molnar.

nation. It rose in the east, like other stars (due to the rotation of the earth). It appeared at a precise time. Herod didn't know when it appeared. It endured over time. It was ahead of the Magi as they traveled south from Jerusalem to Bethlehem. It stopped over Bethlehem.

King of the Jews. The Magi asked the king about the King. They asked Herod, the King of the Jews, about one who was born King of the Jews. And this new king was not born in Herod's house. Threat to Herod. Threat to his throne. Threat to his power. Threat to his rule. Threat to his control. Threat to all he had built. The temple he had built for God. The honor he had received in building such a grand building. They came to worship a King that was not Herod and was not in the temple Herod had built. Matthew 1 Matthew Chapter 1 gives us the genealogy of Jesus coming from Judah by Tamar., 14 generations from Abraham to David, and 14 from David to the exile. And 14 from the exile to Jesus. When Allen and I were in Bethlehem last year, we saw the place where they say Jesus was born. It is decorated with a 14-point star for the 14 generations. We saw the road they call Star Road.

Worship. Not only did they want to know where. They had come to worship. The Magi suggest worship. Magi wanted to worship. "We have seen His star in the east and have come to worship Him" (Matt 2:2). Herod echoes the Magi's suggestion and uses their words to make a relational request. A friendly request, an insinuation. Herod says he wants to worship. And he sent them to Bethlehem and said, "Go and search carefully for the Child; and when you have found Him, report to me, so that I too may come and worship Him." Accounts in Scripture: Earlier Indicators. Matthew indicates in his gospel. "This was done to fulfill what was written in the prophets." When we look back, we can see some indicators in scripture that are clues at the time but not clear looking forward. Sometimes we can look back to see the hand of God weaving our lives together.

Consider Jacob blessing Judah in Genesis 49:10, "The scepter shall not depart from Judah, Nor a lawgiver from between his feet, Until Shiloh comes; And to Him shall be the obedience of the people." Here is a reference to the coming Messiah. Shiloh is coming. From the line of Judah. Now think about the time of wandering in the wilderness. The King of Moab hires Balaam to curse the Israelites, yet he does not. "And Balaam lifted up his eyes and saw Israel camping tribe by tribe, and the Spirit of God came upon him. He took up his discourse and said, "I see Him, but not now; I behold Him, but not near; A Star shall come out of Jacob; A Scepter shall rise out of Israel, And batter the brow of Moab, And destroy all the sons of tumult." (Numbers 24:2, 3, 17) Link Between Daniel and Balaam. This passage from Genesis refers to the coming Messiah, to be descended from Judah. Balaam in

Numbers 24:17 also refers to the coming Messiah. The treasures of the temple had been carried away to Babylon. Daniel might have known of Balaam's oracle. Daniel might have shared the wisdom he had from being an Israelite with those he had met in Babylon.

Daniel, the wise man. Daniel was in Babylon and was considered one of the wise men. One of the ones who could interpret dreams. Chapter 2: 16-18:

> *So Daniel went in and requested of the king that he would give him time, in order that he might declare the interpretation to the king. Then Daniel went to his house and informed his friends, Hananiah, Mishael and Azariah, about the matter, so that they might request compassion from the God of heaven concerning this mystery, so that Daniel and his friends would not be destroyed with the rest of the wise men of Babylon.*

It would also make sense that Daniel could have spoken to the other wise men about this, especially as Daniel himself prophesied much about the Messiah (Daniel 9:25-26):

> *So you are to know and discern that from the issuing of a decree to restore and rebuild Jerusalem until Messiah the Prince there will be seven weeks and sixty-two weeks; it will be built again, with plaza and moat, even in times of distress. Then after the sixty-two weeks the Messiah will be cut off and have nothing, and the people of the prince who is to come will destroy the city and the sanctuary. And its end will come with a flood; even to the end there will be war; desolations are determined.*

The Magi were held in awe as highly educated scientists and scholars who could interpret dreams. And have power over demons. They were adept at various occult arts, such as astrology, interpretation of dreams, fortune-telling, and magic. The Magi believed the rising of a star to be of historical significance, that signs in the heavens would accompany the birth and death of great persons. Whether or not the Magi knew the prophecy of Balaam, or they knew of Daniel and the wise men in Babylon. Whoever they were, they were probably Gentiles. God appeared to the Magi with a sign in the heavens. God appeared to the Magi in a language they understood. The star appeared to the Magi as an invitation to worship, to follow. And it took courage and fortitude to plan the trip and set off across the countryside on a pilgrimage to meet. And to worship. To bring gifts and to celebrate. The King. The King of the Jews. They knew to ask about the One who was born King of the Jews. They asked Herod.

Who is Herod? Herod, who was not of the house of Judah, nor of Jewish descent but of Edom, hence a foreigner, was made king over the Jews by the Romans to the great dissatisfaction of the Jewish people. He warred with them for thirty years before he silenced and subdued them. It has been recorded that Herod had two of his sons executed, one of his wives, and a number of rabbis. Herod was responsible for grand building projects, especially the expansion of the 2nd temple, known as Herod's temple. The western wall still stands. Alarm: Herod is troubled and all Jerusalem. So now the Magi come asking Herod, the appointed King of the Jews, where the new King of the Jews is to be born. Herod wants to protect his position and power. He is jealous. Herod wants to protect his turf.

What about us? Have you ever felt threatened in a job you have had? A new person shows up on the job and can do things better than you can. This person can say things more articulately, can write better, can make better excel spreadsheets, can be more productive, and can make more friends. You wonder. Will I even have my job after the boss sees what this one can do? What about us and our experiences of God? What happens when someone we meet claims to have had different experiences of God than we have had? Do we feel threatened because they do not share our perspectives or our ideas of who God is and how God appears to people? What about families? A new child is born in a family, and the attention is diverted from the eldest child or elder children to the new baby. What happens to the siblings? Jealousy, rage, and attempts to exact revenge on the parents. No one asked the elder child if they wanted to share the undivided attention of the parent. Can this rage and resentment have detrimental outcomes? Of course, some parents handle this well. Some children handle siblings well.

The new king threatens Herod. Herod does not want the new King of the Jews to take his throne away. He calls for the chief priests and the scribes. Herod gathers the leaders of the Jews, the chief priests, and scribes to inquire of them. Look at verses 3-4. "When Herod the king heard this, he was troubled, and all Jerusalem with him. Gathering together all the chief priests and scribes of the people, he inquired of them WHERE the Messiah was to be born."

Consult the Scriptures. Even though God did not appear to the Magi in a book. The words of the prophet Micah, written in the book, are the words that give insight and direction to the Magi on which way to go. Look at verse 5. They said to him, "In Bethlehem of Judea; for this is what has been written by the prophet: 'And you, Bethlehem, land of Judah, Are by no means least among the leaders of Judah; For out of you shall come forth a Ruler Who will shepherd My people Israel.'" Let's go back to Micah 5, not only where but more than WHERE. Micah 5:2-4,

> *But as for you, Bethlehem Ephrathah, Too little to be among the clans of Judah, From you One will go forth for Me to be ruler in Israel. His goings forth are from long ago, From the days of eternity." Therefore He will give them up until the time. When she who is in labor has borne a child. Then the remainder of His brethren Will return to the sons of Israel. And He will arise and shepherd His flock In the strength of the Lord, In the majesty of the name of the Lord His God. And they will remain, Because at that time He will be great To the ends of the earth.*

Appeal: Herod told the Magi he wanted to worship. Look at verses 7-8 of Matthew 1. "Then Herod secretly called the magi and determined from them the exact time the star appeared. And he sent them to Bethlehem and said, "Go and search carefully for the Child; and when you have found Him, report to me, so that I too may come and worship Him." Notice: When they start out from Jerusalem, the star once again appears and leads them to the place where Jesus is. In Bethlehem. The scribes and chief priests are six miles away in Jerusalem, and the Magi, the ones from far away, make the trip to Bethlehem. Verses 9-10, "After hearing the king, they went their way; and the star, which they had seen in the east, went on before them until it came and stood over the place where the Child was. When they saw the star, they rejoiced exceedingly with great joy."

Rejoiced exceedingly with great joy. This was their joy. They had followed their quest. They had followed the star. They had found the One for whom they had searched. This now is cause for Great joy. Great is our joy. JOY, JOY, JOY. This is the glory of God in the face of Jesus Christ. Psalms and Isaiah foretold. The coming of the Magi was foretold. "The kings of Tarshish and the Isles shall offer gifts, the kings of Arabia and Seba shall bring tribute. All kings shall pay Him homage, all nations shall serve Him" (Psalm 72:10-11).

Isaiah also prophesied the gifts: "Caravans of camels shall fill you, dromedaries from Midian and Ephah; all from Sheba shall come bearing gold and frankincense, and proclaiming the praises of the Lord" (Isaiah 60:6). Adoration Notice: Prophetic Gifts. There they worship Jesus and bow down. And offer gifts. Some scholars have suggested the significance of the gifts, as well as the Christmas Carol, "We three Kings." Gold: A gift for a king. Frankincense: This is incense, the burning of which represents prayer and used by priests, the priestly nature of Jesus. Myrrh: A fragrant perfume used in embalming bodies. The inclusion of this gift is a prophetic sign of the death of Jesus. The three gifts underline the Messiah's offices as prophet, priest, and king.

Some think there were three Wise Men because of the three gifts. The Wise Men were warned in a dream not to return the way they had come. God warned them in a way they could understand. Verse 12, "And having been warned by God in a dream not to return to Herod, the magi left for their own country by another way. THEY LEFT BY ANOTHER WAY." Home by another way. James Taylor. One application of this text is written by Mr. James Taylor in his 1988 song, "Home by Another Way."[3] He writes:

> They visited with Jesus, they sure enjoyed their stay. Then warned in a dream of Herod's scheme, they went home by another way. Steer clear of royal welcomes, avoid a big to-do. A king who would slaughter the innocents will not cut a deal for you. Time to go home another way. Home by another way. Me and you can be wise guys too and go home by another way. We got this far to a lucky star but tomorrow is another day. We can make it another way.

Legends of the Wise Men. What happens to them? We do not know from scripture. We have some legends. They were changed after they met Jesus. They went home by another way. Legends say they told the good news far and wide of what they had seen and heard. Legends say that they met the apostles years later and were baptized and became saints. Legends help celebrate the Feast of the Epiphany in many countries of the world. Who are the Magi? According to a tradition dating back to medieval times, their names were Balthasar, Gaspar (or Casper), and Melchior, sometimes in varied skin tones representing different races. The Bible says they came from the East, but exactly where is not known. Arabia, Babylon, and Persia are popular choices. According to one tradition, Balthasar was king of Arabia, Gaspar was king of India, and Melchior was king of Persia. An Armenian tradition identifies the "Magi of Bethlehem" as Balthasar of Arabia, Melchior of Persia, and Gaspar of India. According to Bede. An 8th-century saint, Bede the Venerable, described the kings this way: "The first was called Melchior; he was an old man, with white hair and a long beard; he offered gold to the Lord as to his king. The second, Gaspar by name, young, beardless, of ruddy hue, offered to Jesus his gift of incense, the homage due to Divinity. The third, of black complexion, with a heavy beard, was called Balthasar; the myrrh he held

---

[3] James Taylor (1988), "Home By Another Way," https://www.azlyrics.com/lyrics/jamestaylor/homebyanotherway.html.

in his hands prefigured the death of the Son of man."[4] All of us. The magi stand for all the nations, including all of us who would come to worship Jesus. Here is Jesus, the Messiah of Israel. Here is the manifestation of the glory of God in the face of Jesus Christ. (Psalm 72:10-11) (Isaiah 60:1-2; cf. John 1:14; 2 Corinthians 4:6).

Epiphany. Today is Epiphany Sunday celebrating the Magi and the Star and the manifestation of Christ to the Gentiles. The Magi represent the Gentiles. (Matthew 2:1–12). The festival commemorates the Epiphany on January 6. It was one of the three major feasts of the liturgical calendar around which early Christian communities organized the rhythms of their life: Epiphany, Easter, and Pentecost. Question: How do we leave the Christmas manger? It is not how we have come and approached the Christmas manger or the house where the magi found the Child. But how will we depart from that place of encounter that will define what we become as believers and followers of this Jesus? How will we be different when we leave here today? Will we have encountered Jesus? Will we have an Epiphany moment?

Application: How are we different? The wise men, the Magi, were different after meeting Jesus. They humbled themselves, bowed down, worshiped, and gave gifts. They were changed. They would not be the same after this. When we meet Jesus, we worship and bow down. When we are changed, we do not act the same way, think the same way, or respond the same way. We have met Jesus. And Jesus has changed us. Think of others. When Bartimaeus met Jesus, it says he followed him on the way.

The gospels have lots of accounts of those who followed on the way. We act differently. Because we have met Jesus, we treat one another differently. We are changed. We can stand up and know the Truth that has made us free and the Light that shines in our darkness. The Way that Jesus is to the Father. The Way Home. Standing at the Nativity Scene, we see the need for the light of the world when we realize just how dark the world is around us. In the next verses in Matthew, we see that innocents will suffer. And persons still suffer for the name of Jesus. We go home by another way when we see the light on the path ahead of us. The birth of Jesus brings both worship and hostility.

The birth of Jesus images the account of Moses. Jesus is the new Moses. Out of Egypt. Threatened with annihilation at birth. A new Joseph going to Egypt

---

[4] https://www.catholiceducation.org/en/culture/catholic-contributions/the-magi.html.

to protect Jesus. Jesus makes enemies and friends at his birth, his death, and his resurrection. Home by another way. The Magi did not betray Jesus. They did not surrender the real King of the Jews to the one who was appointed the King of the Jews by the Romans. One challenge of this message is the question, "Will we take the safe passage promised by those who ask us to surrender the gospel, the good news, for the sake of their kingdoms and their power, or will we follow the paths of God that call us out in ways that will give the gospel of Jesus Christ opportunities to save this world?

We will meet Herods. Along the way of following the signs, the spiritual signs, the scriptures, the circumstances, the holy nudges, we will meet Herods. Herods who ask us what we are doing and want to join us. Herods pretend that they want to worship Jesus, too. Herods are jealous, ruthless, and tyrannical. Herods want to destroy the One we worship. Herods are jealous of anyone who would be a threat to their power and rule in the vicinity. We might not recognize them at first. We might think that they can help us find the One we seek. Watch and Pray We can be aware and notice the Herods' form of injustice that seeks power "by any means necessary" wherever it appears: in the workplace, in schools, in local and national governments, wherever and whenever it appears. We can pray Kingdom prayers and invite Jesus to change us and change our world.

Wise Persons Still Seek. "But without faith it is impossible to please him; for he that cometh to God must believe that he is, and that he is a rewarder of them that diligently seek him" (Heb. 11:6). Indicators that we are seeking. Listening. Following God's word. Walking in God's paths. Walking in the light we have. Psalm 119:105 "Thy word is a lamp to my feet and a light to my path." Jesus is the Messiah. Jesus is the King of the Jews. Jesus needs to be honored by all of us. By the nations of the world. The good news is for ALL PEOPLE. God has woven events into history that, looking back, we can marvel at and see God's hand. Even if the way forward is not clear, we can trust the future because of God's faithfulness in the past. Jesus is troubling to those who do not want to obey him. The claims of Jesus as God, the Son, the One who took on flesh and came from heaven to earth. Worshiping Jesus requires us to bring all of us to offer all of us sacrificially.

The Way Home. The way home is not always clear. The way home may have detours. The way home may have a winding path. Sometimes it takes a dream to lead us home. Sometimes it takes a pigpen to awaken us to our need for home. Ultimately, Jesus is the way home. We remember the song that says, "He came from heaven to earth to show the way." We are born. We die. We go home to be with the Lord. We call it going home. We do not enter our mother's wombs again, as Nicodemus was trying to unravel the riddle of the new birth. We are born to go home another way. Another way than we came here.

Closing Prayer. Lord God, We thank You for Your faithfulness. For weaving events of history for Your honor and glory. Thank You for showing Gentiles at Your birth the way to the brightness of Your light. We know that wise persons still seek You. We are here to Seek You and Worship You. Meet us here today. Shine brightly, O Light of the World. Shine brightly in us and through us so that others might see Your light and follow You fully. In Jesus' name, Amen.

Anticipation: Simeon and Anna
Luke 2:25, 36-37

November 29, 2015

Luke 2:25, 36-37 (NASB) *"And there was a man in Jerusalem whose name was Simeon; and this man was righteous and devout, looking forward to the consolation of Israel; and the Holy Spirit was upon him." "And there was a prophetess, Anna, the daughter of Phanuel, of the tribe of Asher. She was advanced in years and had lived with her husband for seven years after her marriage, and then as a widow to the age of eighty-four. She did not leave the temple grounds, serving night and day with fasts and prayers."*

Opening Prayer: Lord, We come to You. We thank You for this day. We anticipate Your presence among us. We anticipate what You are going to do. We anticipate who You have called us to be and our response to You. Would you fill us now with ears to hear what the Spirit is saying to us individually and corporately? In Jesus' name, Amen.

Introduction. When you hear the word Anticipation, what do you think of? Immediately one might think of a Carly Simon song by that title. "Making me wait. Keeping me waiting." From a song that came out when I was in high school, "Anticipation" "We can never know about the days to come But we think about them anyway And I wonder if I'm really with you now Or just chasing after some finer day." [5]

Anticipation. Waiting in the ICU waiting room. Or the surgery waiting room for news. Groom is waiting for the bride to come down the aisle, all the attendants, and finally the bride. Public Transportation. Waiting for a train, feeling the rumble of the tracks, waiting for a bus, and checking the timetable to know when to expect its arrival. What about making a Christmas list and then not waiting for someone to purchase the gifts? Or do we wait with anticipation that someone will give us the suggestions on our list? What about opening birthday gifts or Christmas gifts? Ripping open packages or waiting

---

[5] Carly Simon (1971), "Anticipation," Carly Simon Lyrics © Universal Music Publishing Group.
https://www.lyricsfreak.com/c/carly+simon/anticipation_20027226.html.

with anticipation while someone carefully unwraps packages so that the wrapping paper can be saved and reused. There is an expectancy in anticipation as well as a kind of suspense. A not knowing.

Describe Anticipation. Walk into a house where there is cooking, and our sense of smell alerts us to the flavors in the air. Anticipation of a meal. Or cake, pie, cookies. Or here at church, when it is close to noon, and the dinner we are planning to eat sends aromas into the air, and we stop thinking about the sermon and start thinking about and anticipating the lunch. Anticipation in Psalms. Especially Psalm 119:148, "My eyes anticipate the night watches." In Proverbs 8:34, Wisdom says, "Blessed is the one who listens to me watching daily at my gates waiting at my doorposts."

Anticipation-Waiting. Scripture lesson today is for the 1st Sunday of Advent. Advent means "coming" It is the time and the season in the church calendar of anticipation of the coming of Christ. The Advent season of the church calendar has historically tied the first Advent (the coming of Christ in the manger at Bethlehem) to the second Advent described in 1 Thess. 4:13-18 and the coming of Christ to the earth in Rev. 1:7, 19:11-16).

Advent Wreath. The first Advent of Jesus Christ set up the hope of believers in the promised second Advent. A basic Advent wreath consists of a circle with four candle holders with one candle in the middle. Three of the candles in the circle are purple. Historically, this color has symbolized penance. Purple also suggests royalty. One candle in the circle is pink or rose, usually symbolic of the Rose of Sharon. Jesus Christ is the One who took upon Himself the penalty for our sins. The center candle is white and is called the Christ candle. Purple represents Christ's majesty. Pink, the hope of His appearance. And white, the promise that one day He will come again.

Advent Carols. Come, Thou Long-Expected Jesus. "Come to set thy people free." O Come O Come Emanuel, "And ransom captive Israel." Advent Season of the church calendar. Rehearsing the familiar stories and accounts of the characters in the narratives of the birth of Christ. Matthew and Luke are the ones we usually focus on. The account in the Gospel of Matthew has the wise men coming from the east. They were watching the star and anticipating the birth of the newborn king. Shepherds. Luke 2. Keeping watch. Waiting for the new day. Protecting the sheep from wolves. Anticipation. And suddenly, there was something they were not planning and not anticipating.

Gospel of Luke. Turn with me to the Gospel of Luke in the New Testament. The 3rd Gospel Matthew Mark Luke. Or if you are in John, turn left. Turn back to Luke, written in an orderly account to most excellent Theophilus. Themes of seeking and saving the lost. Those who are lost will become found. Those who are the least will be noticed, and the last will be first. Luke has included prayers and praying persons at many intervals in the gospel. Today we are going to focus on two persons who are persons of prayer, persons who live in anticipation of seeing the Lord's Christ.

Context of today's Scripture. We will be reading from Chapter 2 today, starting in verse 21. On our way to verse 21 of Chapter 2, Luke Chapter 1 has the account of the promise of John the Baptist being born. The angel appears to Mary. Mary goes to Elizabeth's house. Luke 2 starts with the account of the birth of Jesus. And then, we get to the account of Simeon and Anna in the temple.

Luke 2:21-35 Simeon:

> And when eight days had passed, before His circumcision, His name *was then called Jesus, the name given by the angel before He was conceived in the womb. And when the days for their purification according to the law of Moses were completed, they brought Him up to Jerusalem to present Him to the Lord. (as it is written in the Law of the Lord, "Every firstborn male that opens the womb shall be called holy to the Lord"), and to offer a sacrifice according to what was said in the Law of the Lord, "A pair of turtledoves or two young pigeons." And there was a man in Jerusalem whose name was Simeon; and this man was righteous and devout, looking for the consolation of Israel; and the Holy Spirit was upon him. And it had been revealed to him by the Holy Spirit that he would not see death before he had seen the Lord's Christ. And he came in the Spirit into the temple; and when the parents brought in the child Jesus, to carry out for Him the custom of the Law, then he took Him into his arms, and blessed God, and said, "Now Lord, You are releasing Your bond-servant to depart in peace, According to Your word; For my eyes have seen Your salvation, Which You have prepared in the presence of all peoples, A Light of revelation to the Gentiles, And the glory of Your people Israel." And His father and mother were amazed at the things which were being said about Him. And Simeon blessed them and said to Mary His mother, "Behold, this Child is appointed for the fall and rise of many in Israel, and for a sign to be opposed—and a sword will pierce even your own soul—to the end that thoughts from many hearts may be revealed.*

Luke 2:36-38 Anna.

> *And there was a prophetess, Anna the daughter of Phanuel, of the tribe of Asher. She was advanced in years and had lived with her husband seven years after her marriage, and then as a widow to the age of eighty-four. She never left the temple, serving night and day with fastings and prayers. At that very moment she came up and began giving thanks to God, and continued to speak of Him to all those who were looking for the redemption of Jerusalem.*

Notice some things. Verse 21 that Jesus was named at his circumcision at eight days. In Chapter 1:59, John the Baptist was named at his circumcision at eight days. And Zechariah could speak again when he named him John. Noticing the days for purification comes from Leviticus 12, Verses 2-3, 6, 8.

> *When a woman gives birth and bears a male child, then she shall be unclean for seven days, as in the days of her menstruation she shall be unclean. On the eighth day the flesh of his foreskin shall be circumcised. 6. "When the days of her purification are completed, for a son or for a daughter, she shall bring to the priest at the doorway of the tent of meeting a one year old lamb for a burnt offering and a young pigeon or a turtledove for a sin offering." 8. "But if she cannot afford a lamb, then she shall take two turtledoves or two young pigeons, the one for a burnt offering and the other for a sin offering; and the priest shall make atonement for her, and she will be clean. (NASB).*

Two Characters: Simeon and Anna. Watching and praying in the temple. Waiting for the redemption of Israel. Waiting for the consolation of Israel. Waiting for the promised Messiah. Waiting for the fulfillment of the prophecies. Both saw Jesus face-to-face. Two witnesses. Deut 19:15 says, "Only on the evidence of two witnesses or three witnesses shall a charge be established."

Simeon. Righteous and devout. Looking for the consolation of Israel. The Holy Spirit was upon him when he was led to the temple that day. Luke also has written that The Holy Spirit was upon Zechariah 1:67, Elizabeth 1:41, and Mary 1:35. Ready to depart in peace. Now I can depart in peace. In my work as a chaplain in a nursing facility, I have seen many depart in peace. Or desire to depart in peace. Some wait to leave until their children come. Some want to have reconciliation with estranged family members before they feel they can depart in peace.

Simeon's Song is called the Nunc Dimittis in church history and liturgy. The Song of Simeon (Luke 2:29–32) is used as a canticle in Christian liturgy, especially at compline and evensong. "Now Lord, You are releasing Your bond-servant to depart in peace, According to Your word; For my eyes have seen Your salvation, Which You have prepared in the presence of all peoples, A Light of revelation to the Gentiles, And the glory of Your people Israel." A light of revelation to the Gentiles.

Echoes of Isaiah. Isaiah 9:2 (NASB), "The people who walk in darkness Will see a great light; Those who live in a dark land, The light will shine on them." Isaiah 42:6 (NASB), "I am the Lord, I have called You in righteousness, I will also hold You by the hand and watch over You, And I will appoint You as a covenant to the people, As a light to the nations." Isaiah 60 (NASB), "Arise, shine; for your light has come, And the glory of the Lord has risen upon you. "For behold, darkness will cover the earth And deep darkness the peoples; But the Lord will rise upon you, And His glory will appear upon you. "Nations will come to your light, And kings to the brightness of your rising."

Simeon, at the Holy Spirit's prompting, proclaims this response to his anticipation. After this proclamation, Simeon blesses them and prophesies to Mary. Verses 33-35,

> *And His father and mother were amazed at the things which were being said about Him. And Simeon blessed them and said to Mary, His mother, "Behold, this Child is appointed for the fall and rise of many in Israel, and for a sign to be opposed—and a sword will pierce even your own soul—to the end that thoughts from many hearts may be revealed.*

Simeon prophesies that Jesus will be opposed and that Mary will feel the pain of a sword in her heart. The thoughts from many hearts will be revealed because of Jesus. Identifying with Jesus has consequences of rejection, persecution, and a sword piercing hearts.

Anna. Let us turn to Anna, the prophetess. She is set in a family. Her father is Phanuel. Of the tribe of Asher. One of the ten scattered tribes. Asher is one of the sons of Leah's handmaiden, Zilpah. Asher's name means Happy Gen 30:13. Anna is now 84. She has served in the temple since her widowhood began seven years after marriage. In the temple, there was a court of women. This court of women did not mean that men could not go there. Women could not enter the temple's interior, so Anna served with fastings and prayers. When she saw Jesus, she immediately began giving thanks to God. And she continued to speak of him to all who were looking for and waiting for redemption.

For all those who were living in anticipation of the redemption of Jerusalem. Luke 1:68 Zechariah prophesies: "For He has visited us and accomplished redemption for His people." Luke 21:28 "When these things begin to take place, straighten up and lift up your heads because your redemption is drawing near." Luke 2:25 "looking for the consolation of Israel." "Looking for the redemption of Israel," in Luke 2:38. Another example from Luke is Joseph of Arimathea in Luke 23:51, who was waiting for the kingdom of God. Anna is undoubtedly in a line of prophetic disciples who will speak about Jesus. And giving hope to 84-year-old women I work with as residents in the nursing home.

Anna is not the first one in the temple to minister to the Lord. Several references in the Old and New Testaments convey the idea of ministering to the Lord. Levitical Priests. 1 Chron 23:5 Four thousand for the temple. Ezekiel 44:15-16 "But the Levitical priests, the sons of Zadok, who kept charge of My sanctuary when the sons of Israel went astray from Me, shall come near to Me to minister to Me; and they shall stand before Me to offer Me the fat and the blood," declares the Lord God. "They shall enter My sanctuary; they shall come near to My table to minister to Me and keep My charge." Acts 13:2 (NASB), "While they were ministering to the Lord and fasting, the Holy Spirit said, "Set apart for Me Barnabas and Saul for the work to which I have called them." Romans 15:16 (NASB), "to be a minister of Christ Jesus to the Gentiles, ministering as a priest the gospel of God, so that my offering of the Gentiles may become acceptable, sanctified by the Holy Spirit."

Waiting takes patience for the promises to come. Henri Nouwen says, "Waiting patiently is suffering through the present moment, tasting it to the full, and letting the seeds that are sown in the ground on which we stand grow into strong plants. Waiting patiently always means paying attention to what is happening right before our eyes and seeing there the first rays of God's glorious coming."[6]

John the Baptist. Luke 7:18-19, "The disciples of John reported to him about all these things. Summoning two of his disciples, John sent them to the Lord, saying, "Are You the Expected One, or do we look for someone else?" What happens when we do not want to wait? Examples in scripture where we see persons who had a promise and did not wait. Look at Abraham. Genesis 12

---

[6] https://henrinouwen.org/meditations/waiting-with-patience/ 20 November 2018.

and following with Ishmael. Look at the children of Israel when they wanted to see God and Moses had disappeared. Exodus 32 with the golden calf.

Anticipation Instructions. 2 Peter 3:11-14:

> *What sort of people ought you to be in holy conduct and godliness, looking for and hastening the coming of the day of God, because of which the heavens will be destroyed by burning, and the elements will melt with intense heat! But according to His promise we are looking for new heavens and a new earth, in which righteousness dwells. Therefore, beloved, since you look for these things, be diligent to be found by Him in peace, spotless and blameless.*

Jude 1:21 "Keep yourselves in the love of God waiting anxiously for the mercy of our Lord Jesus Christ." 1 John 3:23 "everyone who has this hope purifies himself."

Eagerly Wait. Romans 8:19, "For the anxious longing of the creation waits eagerly for the revealing of the sons of God." Romans 8:23, "And not only this but also we ourselves, having the first fruits of the Spirit, even we ourselves groan within ourselves, waiting eagerly for our adoption as sons, the redemption of our body." Romans 8:25, "But if we hope for what we do not see, with perseverance, we wait eagerly for it." Philippians 3:20, "For our citizenship is in heaven, from which also we eagerly wait for a Savior, the Lord Jesus Christ."

What about Us? Maybe we have waited and waited for something. Maybe we have fasted and prayed for something to happen. Anna was 84 years of age before she saw the promise. We have examples in scripture we can learn from. If we do not wait, we could create an Ishmael. Like Abraham. If we do not wait, we could lose a position of honor and influence. Like King Saul, if we do not wait, we do not know what the consequences will be. What are we waiting for? What are we longing for? Maybe we have children away at school and anticipate their homecoming for the holidays. Or school breaks. Maybe we are still praying for prodigal children to wake up and come to their senses. To come home. Maybe we have someone with whom we are offended or who is distant from us. We are anticipating a reconciliation. And we are anticipating a crucial conversation with the anticipation of what it will cost us to humble ourselves.

Repent for Impatience. Perhaps we have been hasty. We may need to repent for impatience. Question to me recently: Are you willing to wait? As long as I hear "this is that." Acts 2: 16ff not drunk as you suppose. This is that. But this is what was spoken of through the prophet Joel. Ask for the Fruit of the

Spirit to grow in our lives. Gal 5:22-23 love, joy, peace, patience, kindness, goodness, faithfulness, gentleness, self-control.

Questions: Have you ever prayed and received answers to your prayers? Have you ever fasted and prayed, and have you ever seen a breakthrough? With this day and age of uncertainty we live in, what would it take for us to be ready to depart in peace? Do we have unfulfilled prophecies in our lives? When we awaken in the morning, do we think this might be the day we meet Jesus face to face?

Ministry Time. Just as we are waiting for the Lord, the Lord is also watching and waiting for us and waiting for us to call out to Him to invite Him to be the Lord of our lives. An old invitation hymn says: "Jesus is waiting to enter your heart. Why don't you let Him come in? There's nothing in this world to keep you apart. What is your answer to Him? Time after time, He has waited before, and now, he is waiting again to see if you're willing to open the door. What is your answer to Him?"[7] We need to wait for God in anticipation of what God will do. We are here for you to pray with you. Come as I pray this closing prayer, and we listen to the closing song. We are here to pray for you. And if you are listening online and need prayer. Write to us on our website or on social media. Let us pray.

Closing Prayer: Lord God, We thank You that You do all things well. Thank you for Your words in scripture today. We invite and anticipate Your work in our lives. Hear us and answer our prayers, Lord. Let Your kingdom come, and Your will be done in our hearts, in our lives, in our families, in our churches, in our nation, in our world, Lord. We wait for you in anticipation today. Fill us with Your Holy Spirit for Jesus' sake. Amen.

---

[7] Ralph Carmichael (1958), "The Savior is Waiting," Source: The New National Baptist Hymnal (21st Century Edition) #192.

Awakening
Romans 13:11

June 21, 2015

Romans 13:11(NASB) *"Do this, knowing the time, that it is already the hour for you to awaken from sleep; for now salvation is nearer to us than when we believed."*

Prayer: God, our Father, on this Father's Day, we honor You. We worship You, Almighty God. There is none like You. Teach us today, from Your word and the evidence of Your working in the past. Help us awaken to what You have for us. In Your Son, Jesus', Name, Amen.

Introduction: Have you ever been sleeping so soundly that the alarm clock could not awaken you? Some persons set their alarm very loudly because they have overslept and did not hear their alarm. Me? I keep my alarm clock across the room so that I actually have to get up out of bed to turn it off. Do we have any snooze button fans here? Just 10 minutes more. Just 10 minutes more until the last possible time to get up. It works better for me if I do not need the snooze button. When I set my alarm, I set it for the latest possible time, and then I trust that I will wake up before the alarm awakens me, and it usually works for me. What calls you to awaken in the morning? Alarm clock? Rooster? iPhone rooster ring tone? A voice calling your name? A gentle touch? Sun coming through the window? A rude awakening to something tragic or unexpectedly unpleasant? Elevator passenger at work quote: "Woke up on this side of the dirt." Patient at work: "Puppies and kittens opening their eyes and seeing the light for the first time."

Our sermon this morning is entitled Awakening. Last night was Movie Night for Thinkers and Seekers.[8] We watched a 1962 black and white film. The story is about Helen Keller, born in June 1880, who becomes blind and deaf in infancy. Anne Sullivan, from the Perkins School for the blind, arrives in Alabama to find Helen Keller locked in her blindness and deafness and unaware of the connections between words and objects, between words and concepts. Through fingerspelling and lots of discipline, Anne helps awaken the person of Helen to know and feel love. This movie with Anne Bancroft

---

[8] Karen Sculley, "Movie Nights for Thinkers and Seekers"
http://movienightsforthinkersandseekers.com/.

and Patty Duke arrives on the scene in America in 1962 when the Charismatic Renewal spread like fire across this nation.

You may have seen this movie, Awakenings, in 1990.[9] It is set in 1969, in the Bronx. The hospital ward is nicknamed "The Garden" because they feed and water the patients. The patients were victims of the great "sleeping sickness" epidemic of the 1920s, and after a period of apparent recovery, they regressed to their current states. Now, in 1969, the patients have many different symptoms, but essentially, they all share the same problem: They cannot make their bodies do what their minds desire. Sometimes that blockage is manifested through bizarre physical behavior, sometimes through apparent paralysis. One day, in a medical trial, L-Dopa, the drug for Parkinson's, works. One patient, Leonard, who is played by Robert De Niro, wakes up. The movie follows Leonard through the stages of his rebirth. He was a bright, likable kid until the disease took its toll. He has been on hold for 30 years. He looks in the mirror and touches his face. Now, in his late 40s, he is filled with wonder and gratitude to be able to move around freely and express himself and fall in love.

We are going to watch a scene from this movie now. Did you notice? It is like a rebirth from being frozen. Their bodies thaw, and they begin to move and talk once again, some of them after thirty years of self-captivity. But gradually, the medicine stops working, and all the patients return to sleep. This has been an awakening for the patients. But it has also been an awakening for Robin Williams, who plays the psychiatrist, Dr. Malcom Sayer, who has only worked with earthworms and has not worked with persons.

One of the ways we try to stay awake and aware as a church is in the Pray the News segment each week. In the last year, we have cried out to God for the situations facing us in our country and in the world, threats like ISIS, Boko Haram, martyring Christians in places hostile to Christians, earthquakes, floods, tornadoes, and hurricanes. Can anyone tell me some of the topics we have been aware of this week that would cause us to pray the news? What happened in the courtroom was a beautiful demonstration of forgiveness. What will the church do in response? Will we awaken? Or will we be lulled into a lethargic indifference, a sleep?

In our text for today, Paul had not yet been to Rome. The book of Romans contains many personal references, twenty-six persons greeted by name. Phoebe carried the Letter to the Romans to Rome. Sixteen-year-old Emperor

---

[9] "Awakenings," https://www.imdb.com/title/tt0099077/.

Nero had come to power three years earlier in 54 CE but would not make the Christians scapegoats until after the fire in Rome in 64 CE.

The context in Chapter 14 is about bearing with one another, not judging one another, and recognizing that we all serve one Lord and Savior, Jesus Christ, and we do not need to agree on certain disputable matters such as eating meat and eating only vegetables. Chapter 13 starts with our relationship with governmental authorities and paying taxes, and now look at our key verses starting Chapter 13, verse 11, "Do this, knowing the time, that it is already the hour for you to awaken from sleep; for now salvation is nearer to us than when we believed."

This morning, God is calling us to awaken from things we have been asleep to. God is calling us to awaken from sleep. God is using prophetic calls in every area of our lives. We are not just here to be passive participants in life. We are called to action. We are called to evidence the transforming work of Christ in us. We need to be awake and aware of God's work, God's voice, God's kindness, and God's invitations to us. While you are getting ready to share about persons who were sleeping and awakening, let's read a passage from the gospels.

Turn with me to the first gospel and read Matthew 26: 36-45:

> Then Jesus came with them to a place called Gethsemane, and said to His disciples, "Sit here while I go over there and pray." And He took with Him Peter and the two sons of Zebedee, and began to be grieved and distressed. Then He said to them, "My soul is deeply grieved, to the point of death; remain here and keep watch with Me." And He went a little beyond them, and fell on His face and prayed, saying, "My Father, if it is possible, let this cup pass from Me; yet not as I will, but as You will." And He came to the disciples and found them sleeping, and said to Peter, "So, you men could not keep watch with Me for one hour? Keep watching and praying that you may not enter into temptation; the spirit is willing, but the flesh is weak." He went away again a second time and prayed, saying, "My Father, if this cannot pass away unless I drink it, Your will be done." Again He came and found them sleeping, for their eyes were heavy. And He left them again, and went away and prayed a third time, saying the same thing once more. Then He came to the disciples and said to them, "Are you still sleeping and resting? Behold, the hour is at hand and the Son of Man is being betrayed into the hands of sinners.

When Jesus was in the Garden of Gethsemane, He invited the disciples with him to keep watch with him. Repeatedly, they fell asleep on their watch. One of the calls for intercession is to be available to pray when we become aware of a situation. We learn to "watch and pray." Some intercessors are crisis intercessors who can be awakened to pray when the Holy Spirit prompts them to cry out to God on behalf of a crisis in a family, a city, or a nation. Jesus awakened the disciples and asked them to keep watching and praying.

Your turn. Where are there some significant places in scripture where we see individuals who were sleeping and what happened when they awakened? Adam, Genesis 3. Jacob, "and it was Leah" Gen 29:25. Samson. "and he knew not" Judges 16:20. Jonah, Jonah 1. Peter, James, and John, Luke 9:28. Jesus in the boat, Mark 4. Philippian Jailor, Acts 16. Last week, we talked about being prepared for the future by noticing what has happened in the past. In the past, a flood of people came. What if people are coming again to churches all over the world? People who are thirsting for truth, God, and depth. Let's look at a few glimpses of the past in Awakening stories in history.

If you get me started, I could teach and teach about church history. Several times in history in our country and abroad, there have been what historians have called Awakenings. This morning we will mention some historical awakenings and touch down briefly on two awakenings. Let's turn back to the mid- 1730s to 1740s in the American colonies. It was a time called the Great Awakening. Two specific preachers are associated with the Great Awakening: George Whitefield and Jonathan Edwards. One of the major preachers in the Great Awakening was Jonathan Edwards. Jonathan Edwards was the president of Princeton when he died.

Effects of the Great Awakening: Swept through the Colonies, and many souls were saved. Churches of common persons grew in attendance. More divisions and denominations started. Persons could make decisions for themselves and question authority on the basis of God's authority. State rule was a contract with the people. The chain of authority was not deferential to the ruling authorities as much as it had been in the English government. This contributed to the political climate in asserting independence from England.

2nd Great Awakening. 1790-the 1830s with several different segments. Camp Meetings in Cane Ridge, KY, where 20,000 gathered with seven preachers on tree stumps and standing up in wagons, all preaching at the same time. A young man who attended the famous 20,000-person revival at Cane Ridge, Kentucky, in 1802 captures the spirit of these camp meetings activity:

"The noise was like the roar of Niagara. The vast sea of human beings seemed to be agitated as if by a storm. I counted seven ministers, all preaching at one time, some on stumps, others on wagons. Some of the people were singing, others praying, some crying for mercy. A peculiarly strange sensation came over me. My heart beat tumultuously, my knees trembled, my lips quivered, and I felt as though I must fall to the ground."[10] This young man was so moved that he went on to become a minister. Evangelical ministers reached their audience at an emotional level that powerfully moved large crowds. Concern about one's soul. Inquiry about "What must I do to be saved?" Anxiety and fear of damnation. Conviction of sin and nothing one could do to earn salvation. Free Will to Choose to surrender to Jesus and God's will fully, fully surrender.

Effects of the 2nd Great Awakening: spiritual equality before God, multiplication of unschooled and not formally educated preachers/pastors, affected a wide range of societal classes and spanned across racial divides. The converts during the Second Great Awakening were predominantly female. A 1932 source estimated at least three female converts to every two male converts between 1798 to 1826.[11] Young people (those under 25) also converted in greater numbers and were the first to convert.

Welsh Awakening.[12] It would be lovely to have time to recount the influence of intercessors on revivals and awakenings, the many thousands of souls that were saved, the women that participated, and Rees Howells, Intercessor.[13] During the Welsh Revival, there were trips from and to America, inviting persons to respond to the Holy Spirit, agonizing in prayer for souls to be saved, 1904—1905 the young people were involved. The revival preachers were Seth Joshua and Evan Roberts with Four Points of personal awakening and revival. Evan Roberts taught: You must put away any unconfessed sin. You must put away any doubtful habit. You must obey the Holy Spirit promptly. You must confess Christ publicly. Within six months, 100,000 souls were converted in Wales. Saloons closed. Courts had no cases to try. Coal miners stopped swearing at their animals.

Azuza Street, in California, 1906. William Seymour preached with Pentecostal power. This revival spanned racial divides. Women were involved before they

---

[10] Cane Ridge Revival quote, James Finley. https://www.pbs.org/wgbh/pages/frontline/godinamerica/people/james-finley.html.
[11] "Second Great Awakening," https://ipfs.fleek.co/ipfs/QmXoypizjW3WknFiJnKLwHCnL72vedxjQkDDP1m XWo6uco/wiki/Second_Great_Awakening.html.
[12] James A. Stewart, *Invasion of Wales by the Spirit through Evan Roberts* (Revival Literature, 1963).
[13] Norman Grubb, *Rees Howells, Intercessor*. Fort Washington: Christian Literature Crusade, 1952 *Also https://www.jhopdc.com/rees-howells-part-1.*

had the right to vote. Charismatic Renewal. Fast forward to the Latter Rain Movement in the 1940s and then an episcopal priest in 1960, Dennis Bennett in Duquesne University, led to the Roman Catholic Renewal.

Third Wave Renewal. 1970s Jesus People with signs and wonders. The Vineyard Movement came out of this Third Wave. There have been cultural awakenings in our society with all of the spiritual awakenings. We have seen advances in medicine, justice, and mercy. But we have also seen tragedies. When we are awake, we notice, and we do something about injustice, pain, and suffering. We invite God's kingdom to come, and we look for signs of what God is already doing. Jesus said in John 5 that His Father is always working.

The same God who raised Jesus from the dead still calls us to give our hearts and lives to him. Phil Strout, our national director, says God is in the "passionate pursuit of humans." What is new in the church is what has been since the beginning. God is passionately pursuing humans. Our Father, God, wants us to love and serve Him. Jesus came to show us the Father. If you have seen me, you have seen my Father.

The Lord is stirring another awakening in our day. This awakening is not just for the church. This will affect cultures and societies in the world. We need to have our hearts right, eagerly awaiting the Lord, praying and asking, seeking and knocking. We dare not be spiritually sleeping when Jesus is calling us to wake up. Turn to or just listen to Ephesians 5:13-14, "But all things become visible when they are exposed by the light, for everything that becomes visible is light. For this reason it says, "Awake, sleeper, And arise from the dead, And Christ will shine on you."

We are not called to be ZOMBIES. Zombies are undead creatures, typically depicted as mindless, reanimated human corpses with a hunger for human flesh. Zombies are most commonly found in horror and fantasy genre works. The term comes from Haitian folklore, where a zombie is a dead body animated by magic. We are called to be alive, not the walking dead. To be free on the inside, we need to invite the light of Christ to shine on us, to shine in us, to shine through us. Today is Father's Day. Luke 15:17 "But when he came to his senses." The prodigal son awakened. Challenge. Where are we personally noticing nudges, invitations, and attachments? Where might we be in a far country? Can we decide to come home? If we knew the Father was waiting for us to return, would it help us decide? Come home today. Father IS waiting.

Let's revisit and finish out the scripture in Romans 13:12-14:

> *The night is almost gone, and the day is near. Therefore let us lay aside the deeds of darkness and put on the armor of light. 13 Let us behave properly as in the day, not in carousing and drunkenness, not in sexual promiscuity and sensuality, not in strife and jealousy. 14 But put on the Lord Jesus Christ, and make no provision for the flesh in regard to its lusts.*

We are to behave properly intentionally. We are to put on the Lord Jesus Christ intentionally. We are to make no provision for our own selfishness intentionally. We are alive in Christ, empowered by the Holy Spirit. We have been buried with Christ in baptism, and we have been raised to the newness of life. For it is in Him we live and move and have our being. We need to awaken and put on the armor of light. God is calling us to awaken from those things we have been asleep to. We are light bearers. We walk in the light as God is in the light. We are love-bearers. We walk in love and love one another. We are grace-bearers. We walk in grace. We are good-news bearers. We are living epistles read by all. We are ambassadors for Christ. We represent and re-present Christ. We put off deeds of darkness, and we put on the armor of light. We behave properly. We rid ourselves of things that detract us from fully following Christ. Just as Jesus called dead Lazarus to "Come forth," so we are given power in prayer, power in word, power, and authority to heal the sick and awaken those headed for despair and death.

Closing Prayer: Awaken us, O Lord. Awaken Your church, O Lord. Call us with Your kindness. Call us to repentance. Call us to care. Call us to love. Call us to serve. Call us to be aware. Let us hear, "Awake, O sleeper," with Your kind and loving voice. Holy Spirit, living in us, call forth the dreams that have died, the visions that have died, the purposes that have died, the holy aspirations that have died. O God, awaken us, awaken us. Forgive us for any places we have been lethargic, apathetic, indifferent, uncaring, and unloving. Help us to come to our senses and come home to your waiting and forgiving arms. In Jesus' name. Amen.

Ministry Time. I have selected a worship song sung by Chris Tomlin called *Awakening. I* have asked that it be played while we listen and sing along softly if you know it. This is a time for prayer. If any of you want to have a prayer because something today touched your heart, this is a time to respond to God. If you want to sit quietly and quietly pray while we listen to this song, feel free. If you want someone to pray with you, we are here to pray with you. If you are listening online and want prayer, please contact us on our website. "In our hearts, Lord. In this nation. Awakening. For You and You alone.

Awake my soul and sing. For the world You love. Awake my soul." [14] Listen now.

---

[14] "Awakening" by Chris Tomlin, Reuben Timothy Morgan, 2010. https://www.youtube.com/watch?v=Ljr6lqu2-ec.

By Faith, Abel
Hebrews 11:4

February 27, 2022

Hebrews 11:4 (NRSV), *"By faith Abel offered to God a more acceptable sacrifice than Cain's."*

Let us pray: Lord, as we open the scriptures this morning, may we hear from You today. Teach us as we listen for what You will say to us through this message and through Your Holy Spirit. Fill us with faith and hope in Christ and what has been prepared for those who have faith that pleases You, Lord. Amen. Come, Holy Spirit.

Introduction: This morning, we are going to look at two brothers who brought sacrifices and offerings to God. When we hear the word sacrifice, we might think of several possibilities, and the dictionary gives us a few starting points. In sports, we see something called a sacrifice bunt in baseball where the batter takes the guaranteed out to get a runner from 3rd base home.

There are sacrifices parents make for their children to provide for their children. Parents work difficult and tiresome jobs to bring home enough to pay the bills, send their children to school, and have enough for groceries. Marriage involves vows of promising to love and serve one another. In marriage, spouses make sacrifices for one another, learning we cannot always have our own way, deferring to the other spouse in love, and caring for one another. In times of illness, in caregiving for a family member, we offer sacrifices of our time and energy.

Then there are sacrifices offered to a deity, to God. In Leviticus, we read about the elaborate preparations for offerings and sacrifices with burnt offerings, wave offerings, and various kinds of offerings, and how the priests offer acceptable sacrifices to God. What is acceptable to God? David shares insight about the heart of the offering, the broken heart, and the contrite spirit. When Nathan, the prophet, confronted David about David's adultery with Bathsheba, David wrote Psalm 51, one of the great penitential Psalms. Psalm 51:15-17 O Lord, open my lips, and my mouth will declare your praise. For you have no delight in sacrifice; if I were to give a burnt offering, you would not be pleased. The sacrifice acceptable to God is a broken spirit; a broken and contrite heart, O God, you will not despise. One worship song we sing says, A broken heart and a contrite spirit you have yet to deny. And the song, I'm coming back to the heart of worship, it's all about You, Jesus.

Today's sermon title comes from Hebrews 11 in our hall of heroes of the faith. By faith, Abel. By faith, Abel. The entire book of Hebrews is written like one sermon. Keywords in Hebrews are "better than." Jesus is better than the angels, better than the prophets, better than the priests of old. Jesus is better than. Jesus is the exact representation of God, who came from heaven to offer a sacrifice better than any sacrifice—Himself. Look for those words when you read your Bible at home. And this morning, we look at a man, Abel, who starts the list in the hall of heroes of the faith.

By faith, Abel. We will read what it says about Abel here in Hebrews 11:4 and then go to Genesis 4. Hebrews 11:4, "By faith Abel offered to God a more acceptable sacrifice than Cain's." Through this he received approval as righteous, God himself giving approval to his gifts; he died, but through his faith he still speaks. To understand this faith of Abel, we go back to the beginning in Genesis. Adam and Eve have been created and formed by God. After they transgressed, they sinned, they disobeyed God, they tried to cover themselves with fig leaves, and God gave them coverings of animal skins. Those animals who died to provide the skins for covering Adam and Eve foreshadow the theme of the shedding of blood for the remission of sins. In Genesis Chapter 4, Eve gives birth to two sons and names them. The first one is Cain, and the second one is Abel. These sons were born, not made in the way God made Adam and Eve.

In Genesis Chapter 5, we see that Adam and Eve had sons and daughters, and Adam lived to be 930, and Eve lived to be a certain age, and they had sons and daughters. And we only have the names of three of all the children they could have parented in Adam's 930 years, Cain, Abel, and Seth. Somewhere in the time before Seth was born, when Adam was 130, we see that Cain worked the ground, and Abel took care of the flocks.

We do not know how old Cain and Abel were when it was time to bring an offering to the Lord. Sometimes we tell this story in Sunday School like these boys were children with sibling rivalry with the moral of the story, Do not hate your brother, Do not harm your brother. Care for your brother. We read in Genesis 4: starting in verse 3

> *In the course of time Cain brought to the Lord an offering of the fruit of the*
> *ground, and Abel for his part brought of the firstlings of his flock, their fat*

> *portions. And the Lord had regard for Abel and his offering, but for Cain and his offering he had no regard.*

So, the younger son, Abel, brought the best portions of a lamb, the firstborn of his flock. Perhaps the idea is that Abel offered the first lamb, not knowing if there would be other lambs, and yet trusting that if he, Abel, offered the best to God in faith, God would accept his offering. If Abel offered a male lamb, Abel also offered all of the little lambs this male lamb would father in the future. And we see that God accepted Abel and Abel's offering.

And Hebrews 11:4 reiterates that by faith, Abel offered a better sacrifice. Cain brought some fruit that likely was not the best of the fruit. One possibility is that this could have been fruit that had fallen on the ground or blemished in some way. It was not the best Cain could offer. And the timing of the offering is in the course of time. In the course of time, Cain makes a choice to present an offering to God. Some theologians argue that Cain's offering did not have blood, which was why it was not accepted. Other theologians argue that Cain did not give God an acceptable offering because it was just some fruit and not the best of what Cain had to offer. We will not solve that theological question today.

Cain and Abel did not have the written Levitical law when they brought their offerings to the Lord, and yet, in some way that we do not have in writing, they knew that God wanted offerings and sacrifices for worship. We do not know what they were told to bring to offer to God, but we know how God responded to their offerings. God accepts Abel and Abel's offering and does not approve of Cain or Cain's offering. From God's response, Cain's offering did not reflect full devotion to the Lord. And there was a consequence for not offering the Lord the best, with a humble heart, with joy, with a heart of obedience, with a longing for God to be worshiped.

We see that God did not look with favor on Cain and his offering, and we see in verse 5, "The LORD looked with favor on Abel and his offering, but on Cain and his offering he did not look with favor" (4:5). "So Cain was very angry." (4:5). Verse 5 So Cain was very angry, and his countenance fell. Verse 6 The Lord said to Cain, "Why are you angry, and why has your countenance fallen? Verse 7. If you do well, will you not be accepted? God asks Cain a series of five questions in this text, and these questions help us see the character of Cain. The first and second questions: Why are you angry, and why has your countenance fallen? So, we see here Cain's reaction to God not accepting the sacrifice of some fruit. Cain got very angry, and his countenance fell. Cain was angry when God did not accept him (Verse 6). Cain chose to become angry, but this was not his only choice. He could have chosen to be contrite.

Cain's choice to become angry led to the choice to be downcast in his countenance. "…and his face was downcast" (4:5). Have you seen kids with a pouty face? We can sometimes tell what they feel because it is written on their faces. Adults can be that way, too. Just wondering, could it be that Cain's downcast face, and sadness, came from stewing in his murderous anger? Perhaps. We know that Cain's emotions appeared on his face. God noticed Cain's facial countenance. Third question: If you do well, will you not be accepted?

God offers Cain an opportunity to make it right in this question, "If you do right, will you not be accepted?" God's question helps us see that what Cain did could be corrected. God would allow Cain to make it right. Then the instructive warning in verse 7: "And if you do not do well, sin is lurking at the door; its desire is for you, but you must master it" (NRSV). But if you do not do what is right, sin is crouching at your door; it desires to have you, but you must rule over it" (NIV).

This is a word for all of us. Sin is lurking at the door. Sin is crouching at the door. What is the temptation to sin that lurks at our door? The enemy of our souls sends temptations to crouch at our door, and it is up to us to flee from the temptation and not yield to it. Sin's desire is for you. The enemy offers us lots of opportunities to miss the mark and lots of opportunities to get angry and act on our angry impulses. The enemy is like a roaring lion, seeking whom he may devour, Peter says.

God knew Cain was angry. God could see it in Cain's countenance. "Why are you angry, and why has your countenance fallen?" Sin's desire is for you, BUT you must master it. If Cain does not repent, turn away, and do what is right, Cain will fall into the same trap that his parents had fallen into and will become prey to sin. God warns Cain that sin is already crouching at Cain's door, seeking to devour him.

Cain had the power to master the sin that desired to overtake him. Cain could have asked God to help him overcome this temptation. Cain could have been contrite. Cain could have owned up to what he had done in bringing an unacceptable offering. Cain could have changed the course of history right there, but NO. Cain allowed his anger, jealousy, and murderous rage to get the best of him. Cain did not master the sin that was crouching, lurking, at his door. Cain did not repent. He acted upon the depth of his anger.

Cain chose to invite Abel, his brother, out into the field. Verse 8, Cain said to his brother Abel, "Let us go out to the field." And when they were in the field, Cain rose up against his brother Abel and killed him. The murderous anger took over, and Cain acted upon the temptation to sin against God, his brother, his parents, and humanity in generations to come. Then we hear God's fourth question: Verse 9, Then the Lord said to Cain, "Where is your brother Abel?" He said, "I do not know; am I my brother's keeper?" Cain lied to the Lord when Cain said, "I do not know." Cain continues to go down the path of wrong choices by denying and lying.

As parents, aunts, uncles, and teachers, how many of us have asked children, "Who did this?" only to hear, "I don't know?" It is as old as Genesis. We are hiding our sin and hiding shame and not owning up to what we have done.

God asked not because God did not know. God asked to hear Cain's answer. Cain could have confessed to the murder. Cain could have pleaded with God for mercy. Instead, in my imagination, Cain is flippant with God. I read this with sarcasm in my voice, "Am I my brother's keeper?" Where did that come from? Sin. True. God did not make Cain his brother's keeper in this sense. Psalm 121:5, "The Lord is your keeper; the Lord is your shade at your right hand." What does it mean to be our brother's keeper?

Cain used the phrase acting like his brother was not his responsibility. And yet we are called to love our brothers and sisters in so many places in scripture. Just a few: From Hebrews 13:1, "Keep on loving one another as brothers and sisters." From 1 John 4: 20-21, "Whoever claims to love God yet hates a brother or sister is a liar. For whoever does not love their brother and sister, whom they have seen, cannot love God, whom they have not seen. And he has given us this command: Anyone who loves God must also love their brother and sister." From Galatians 5:13, "For you have been called to live in freedom, my brothers and sisters. But don't use your freedom to satisfy your sinful nature. Instead, use your freedom to serve one another in love."

Back to Genesis 4 now with Cain. But, instead of owning up to what Cain had done, Cain tries to hide his sin. We read Chapter 4 Verse 10: Fifth and Last question: "And the Lord said, 'What have you done?'" Cain does not answer this question. When Cain does not answer, God presents the evidence for the answer. "Listen; your brother's blood is crying out to me from the ground!" Verse 11, "And now you are cursed from the ground, which has opened its mouth to receive your brother's blood from your hand." Verse 12, "When you till the ground, it will no longer yield to you its strength; you will be a fugitive and a wanderer on the earth."

God gives Cain the natural consequences of his choices: "Now you are under a curse…" (Verse 11). Here is a person who has acted in an entirely obstinate way. And God metes out consequences for Cain's choices. The story of the generations of Cain goes on. His generations have some interesting characters who dwelled in tents, made musical instruments, and forged weapons of war.

The apostle John gives us more insight into Cain's heart in 1 John 3:12: "Do not be like Cain, who belonged to the evil one and murdered his brother. And why did he murder him? Because his own actions were evil and his brother's were righteous." We see in 1 John that those who belong to the evil one will have evil actions, and those with evil actions will naturally hate those with righteous actions.

And this from Jude: In Jude 1:11, we read, "They have taken the way of Cain," a description that refers to the ones who were self-centered and greedy such as Balaam and Korah. Like Cain, they disobediently devised their own ways of worship, and they did not come to God by faith. Cain's offering was not acceptable to the Lord. Cain's heart was not right."

By faith, Abel. Abel's blood cries from the ground. God hears Abel's blood crying from the ground. Abel becomes the case for the blood of innocent victims. Abel's blood cries out for vengeance. Abel's blood cries out for a resolution. It was the same Hebrew word as the enslaved Israelites in Egypt cried out to God, and God heard their cries and sent Moses. Jesus, in Matthew Chapter 23, lists woes upon the religious leaders of his day when he says in verses 34-36: "

> *Therefore I send you prophets, sages, and scribes, some of whom you will kill and crucify, and some you will flog in your synagogues and pursue from town to town so that upon you may come all the righteous blood shed on earth, from the blood of righteous Abel to the blood of Zechariah son of Barachiah, whom you murdered between the sanctuary and the altar. Truly I tell you, all this will come upon this generation.*

Jesus is pronouncing woes on the religious leaders of his day who did not listen to the prophets, the sages, and scribes. Verse 35 "the righteous blood shed on the earth from the blood of righteous Abel to the blood of Zechariah." The prophets were disregarded. It cost them their lives. The more Jesus taught and healed and delivered and advanced the kingdom of God, the angrier the enemies of the kingdom became.

We spent an entire class period in seminary with the professor asking who killed Jesus. Was it the Romans? Was it the religious leaders who made the case? Did Jesus die as a martyr for a cause? Steven accused the religious leaders of betraying and murdering Jesus, the Righteous One. And then, If you read John's Gospel, you see Jesus in his own words, laying down his life for his friends and calling it love. "This is my commandment, that you love one another as I have loved you. Greater love has no one than this, that someone lay down his life for his friends. You are my friends if you do what I command you" (John 15:12-14 ESV).

Sacrifice. God sacrificed to have a relationship with us. Romans 5:8, "But God shows his love for us in that while we were still sinners, Christ died for us" (Romans 5:8 ESV). Mark 10:45, "For even the Son of Man came not to be served but to serve, and to give his life as a ransom for many" (Mark 10:45 ESV). And now turn back to Hebrews to chapter 12. Let's look at verses 22-24, "But you have come to Mount Zion and to the city of the living God, the heavenly Jerusalem, and to innumerable angels in festal gathering, and to the assembly of the firstborn who are enrolled in heaven, and to God the judge of all, and to the spirits of the righteous made perfect, and to Jesus, the mediator of a new covenant, and to the sprinkled blood that speaks a better word than the blood of Abel. See that you do not refuse the one who is speaking; for if they did not escape when they refused the one who warned them on earth, how much less will we escape if we reject the one who warns from heaven! See that in verse 24, the blood of Jesus "speaks a better word than the blood of Abel."

What does the blood of Abel speak? "Vengeance." What does the blood of Jesus speak? Redemption. Reconciliation. Both Abel and Christ were slain by wicked men. As the 16th-century theologian Erasmus commented, "The blood of Abel cried for vengeance; that of Christ for remission."[15] Here we see that the blood of Jesus, the mediator of a new covenant in his blood, the blood of Jesus speaks a better word than the blood of Abel.

The first chapter of Hebrews tells us that in these last days, God has spoken to us by God's Son, Jesus. Jesus fulfilled the law and the prophets and has become our high priest in the order of Melchizedek. Jesus once and for all paid the sacrifice for our sins and sat down on the right hand of God the Father. Jesus, our high priest, offers himself to God as a holy sacrifice without spot or blemish.

---

[15] https://biblehub.com/commentaries/hebrews/12-24.htm.

Jesus made atonement for us. Jesus, himself, ever lives to make intercession for us. Jesus is coming again. Jesus. The name above all names. Wonderful savior. Glorious Lord. Jesus is the name worthy to be praised, honored, and adored. How do we respond to Jesus and what we are called to do and be?

If we are like Cain, we bring what we want to bring, when we want to bring it and how we want to bring it. Instead of obeying God, we are serving ourselves. That is how we could be like Cain. Abel brought a more acceptable sacrifice. Jesus. Is calling us to sacrifice. What? Yes. Our lives are to be living sacrifices, holy and acceptable to God. This is our reasonable worship. This is the will of God in Christ Jesus concerning us. Romans 12:1-2 (ESV):

> *I appeal to you, therefore, brothers, by the mercies of God, to present your bodies as a living sacrifice, holy and acceptable to God, which is your spiritual worship. Do not be conformed to this world, but be transformed by the renewal of your mind, that by testing you may discern what is the will of God, what is good and acceptable and perfect.*

We are to offer our hearts, our lives, our worship, and our best to God in thanksgiving and praise for all that God has done for us in Jesus. For all that God has done to bring us to this point. As Jesus, the Good Shepherd, lay down his life for the sheep, We are called to devote our lives to the kingdom of God and whatever God has given us to do. Sometimes what God has called us to sacrifice is what we love the most. God asked Abraham to offer Isaac, the son of the promise. Oh. Wait. That is for another sermon later in this series. Today is By Faith, Abel.

By Faith, Abel. What kind of sacrifice is acceptable to God? We see two verses here in Hebrews 12:15 and 16 "Through him then let us continually offer up a sacrifice of praise to God, that is, the fruit of lips that acknowledge his name" (Hebrews 13:15 ESV). I remember a 1970s happy and clappy song, "We bring the sacrifice of praise into the house of the Lord"[16] and "Do not neglect to do good and to share what you have, for such sacrifices are pleasing to God" (Hebrews 13:16 ESV).

We bring our tithes and offerings when we come to worship God. We share the first fruits of what God has given us in the ways we offer our time, our talents, and our treasure. God loves a cheerful giver. We cheerfully offer and

---

[16] Kirk Dearman, "The Sacrifice of Praise," https://www.umcdiscipleship.org/resources/history-of-hymns-we-bring-the-sacrifice-of-praise.

surrender our lives with gratitude to God, who has given us life and breath. We offer our prayers and intercessions to God, knowing that through faith, God hears us and grants our petitions. Jesus ever lives to make intercession for us.

God requires that we come honestly in faith, believing that God is and that God is a rewarder of the ones who diligently seek God. Hebrews 11: 6, "And without faith it is impossible to please God, for whoever would approach him must believe that he exists and that he rewards those who seek him." We do not have the burnt offerings, the wave offerings, the sacrificial system of Leviticus, and the tabernacle and temple worship of the Old Covenant.

We have Jesus, the Author, and Finisher, of our faith, who made an atoning sacrifice for our sins, not just our sins but the sins of the whole world. 1 John 2:1-2, "My little children, I am writing these things to you so that you may not sin. But if anyone does sin, we have an advocate with the Father, Jesus Christ the righteous; and he is the atoning sacrifice for our sins, and not for ours only but also for the sins of the whole world."

What shall we do? "Therefore be imitators of God, as beloved children. And walk in love, as Christ loved us and gave himself up for us, a fragrant offering and sacrifice to God" (Ephesians 5:1-2 ESV). By faith, Abel. Yes. Amen.

Let us pray: Oh, Lord, You see us, and You know us. You see us when we wake up and when we sleep. You do not despise broken hearts and contrite spirits. Lord, we want to offer You acceptable sacrifices, the fruit of lips that confess Your great and mighty name, the doing good and sharing what we have. We offer ourselves to You in our time, our talent, and our treasure. We want to honor You with our lives. We are so grateful to You. Lead us not into temptation but deliver us from the evil one. O help us in places where sin is trying to take us captive and get a foothold in our lives. We confess we need you, O Lord, how we need You. Help us walk in faith to please You, Lord, in Jesus' name. Amen.

Ministry Time. After the benediction, If you would like to respond to the message this morning, we have a team who will pray with you. We have a place over up front over here on this side, and we have time to pray with you. For those of you listening online, feel free to contact us through our website prayer page, and we will pray for you.

Benediction: Hebrews 13: 20-21: "Now may the God of peace, who brought back from the dead our Lord Jesus, the great shepherd of the sheep, by the blood of the eternal covenant, make you complete in everything good so that you may do his will, working among us that which is pleasing in his sight, through Jesus Christ, to whom be the glory forever and ever. Amen."

Connecting to Jesus as the Bread of Life
John 6:51

Father's Day 2021

John 6:51 (NIV) *"I am the living bread that came down from heaven. Whoever eats this bread will live forever. This bread is my flesh, which I will give for the life of the world."*

Opening Prayer. O, Lord God, You loved us and sent Jesus to earth. Jesus, Your heaven-sent Son of God, walked among us and invited others to follow Him. As we seek to hear Your message to us today, help us to follow Jesus faithfully in the journey we call life. Jesus, we want to hear Your call to follow You in specific ways today. Help us to hear Your voice and follow You well to green pastures and cool waters. Holy Spirit, the One who inspired these holy scriptures, spark life in our hearts today as we open our Bibles and our hearts today to hear a word from the Lord. In Jesus's name, Amen.

Turn with me in your Bibles or on your devices to John 6:48-51 (NIV):

> *I am the bread of life. 49 Your ancestors ate the manna in the wilderness, yet they died. 50 But here is the bread that comes down from heaven, which anyone may eat and not die. 51 I am the living bread that came down from heaven. Whoever eats this bread will live forever. This bread is my flesh, which I will give for the life of the world.*

(Hold up Matzah bread.) Matzah is unleavened bread. Especially cooked in a way that is striped, it is pierced, and it is broken when we eat it. In church gatherings all over the world, they use various kinds of bread and wafers. We chose to use matzah because it is a visible reminder to us of the Lord Jesus, whose body was beaten with the stripes from the whips, it was pierced with a spear at his side, and his body was broken for us as he was crucified for our transgressions and sins. John 6:49 "Your ancestors ate bread in the wilderness." Let's turn to Exodus 16:4-35,

> *Then the Lord said to Moses, "I will rain down bread from heaven for you. The people are to go out each day and gather enough for that day. In this way I will test them and see whether they will follow my instructions. (Skip to 11). The Lord said to Moses, 12 "I have heard the grumbling of the Israelites. Tell them, 'At twilight you will eat meat, and in the morning you will be filled with bread. Then you will know that I am the Lord your God.'" 13 That evening quail*

came and covered the camp, and in the morning there was a layer of dew around the camp. 14 When the dew was gone, thin flakes like frost on the ground appeared on the desert floor. 15 When the Israelites saw it, they said to each other, "What is it?" For they did not know what it was. Moses said to them, "It is the bread the Lord has given you to eat. (Skip to 21) Each morning everyone gathered as much as they needed, and when the sun grew hot, it melted away. (Skip to 31) The people of Israel called the bread manna. It was white like coriander seed and tasted like wafers made with honey. 32 Moses said, "This is what the Lord has commanded: 'Take an omer of manna and keep it for the generations to come, so they can see the bread I gave you to eat in the wilderness when I brought you out of Egypt.'" (Skip to 35). The Israelites ate manna forty years, until they came to a land that was settled; they ate manna until they reached the border of Canaan.

Manna. What is it? Bread in the desert. Coriander seed. Dropped every day but the Sabbath from heaven. The Daily bread each day. God fed the multitudes of people with something they called what is it, manna. And on the day before the Sabbath, they could go out and pick enough for that day and the next day. If they did not pick enough for the Sabbath, it was not there to pick on the Sabbath. What do we learn? God provided the manna six days a week. God considered gathering the manna labor. On the sixth day, they had to gather enough for that day and the Sabbath day because to go out to gather it on the Sabbath was considered work. They had to go out early to gather the manna because, in the heat of the day, it would melt away. It was a way for them to see God's faithfulness because morning by morning, they had new mercies. New manna. Fresh supply. And so, Jesus is telling the story and making the connection that these are the descendants of those who ate the manna in the wilderness.

They tasted of the provision of the Lord. They had family stories of how God provided from the storehouses of heaven and rained down manna on the earth. They wanted Jesus to give them manna every day so that they would have their needs provided. Just as Jesus had blessed the little boy's lunch the day before and broke it, and as it was broken out, it multiplied, they were looking for someone to make life easier for them. Every day, they misunderstood the multiplying of the bread and the fish. Jesus makes a different connection. And now the connection is that just as manna was sent from heaven. Jesus has been sent from heaven to give them access through his body as the bread of life, broken and sacrificed for the sins of the people. When the crowds gathered, and they were listening attentively to Jesus, there was a need for bread from heaven.

And Jesus reveals himself as the Bread of Life. He satisfies their practical needs by inviting them to a spiritual encounter with Him as the one who would save them from their sinful and selfish ways of life. The title of the sermon this morning is Making the Connection to Jesus as the Bread of Life. How does Jesus teach this bread of life message? What is available? Jesus takes what is available. He takes a little boy's lunch and blesses it and breaks it, and it multiplies. As the food was passed around, the food multiplied. And there were leftovers. And nothing was wasted. Nothing was wasted. Jesus connected this bread from heaven with his purpose in coming. He called himself the Bread of Life. Jesus came down from heaven to be born of a virgin in Bethlehem. Bethlehem, when translated from the Hebrew, means the house of bread. In preparing for this sermon, I was drawn to these verses in 1 Peter. I will read them. 1 Peter 1:18-21. (NIV):

> *For you know that it was not with perishable things such as silver or gold that you were redeemed from the empty way of life handed down to you from your ancestors, 19 but with the precious blood of Christ, a lamb without blemish or defect. 20 He was chosen before the creation of the world, but was revealed in these last times for your sake. 21 Through him you believe in God, who raised him from the dead and glorified him, and so your faith and hope are in God.*

I saw the connection between the ancestors in the wilderness and the emptiness in their lives. Even though God fed them manna from heaven and provided water from a rock and kept them for the forty years that they were in the wilderness, they perished in the wilderness because they did not know the Lord. They grumbled against Moses, they wanted to go back to Egypt, and when they sent spies into Canaan, they did not believe they could conquer the land with the report of the ten spies that there were giants in the land. What really struck me in the verses was the EMPTY way of life handed down to you from your ancestors. The empty way of life had me thinking and processing. The empty way of life handed down from your ancestors.

Who was Peter writing to? How did he know that the ancestors had an empty way of life? It is possible that those Peter was writing to were first-generation believers and Christ-followers whose ancestors did not know the Lord, were not familiar with the scriptures, and had just come to faith in their generation. The empty way of life could simply be life without Christ. As I thought about it some more, I thought about the generations since Christ and how many persons have lived an empty way of life. How many persons have lived without Christ and without hope in the world? Then I thought of the generations before Christ and the ways of life of some we read about in the Hebrew Bible, our Old Testament. So many persons we read about had empty ways of life. Even Solomon, who had prayed for wisdom and discernment, as the presumptive author of Ecclesiastes, writes about how under the sun, everything is vanity, emptiness, a chasing after the wind.

Think about our own families. I do not know how many generations back I would have to go to find faithfulness to Christ as a way of life handed down. I might find church attendance. I might find ancestors upset with the church and church people. I know that my mother and grandmother and her mother were the ones who loved the Lord. Think about how many generations back you have to go to find faith. On Allen's side of the family, his mother and grandmother knew the Lord, and Allen's father came to faith when his father was 24 years of age and spent a lifetime loving the Lord and raising five children to know the Lord. The empty way of life was still very present in my thoughts when I started comparing the empty way of life to the full way of life. And what does the fullness of life look like? John 10:10 "The thief comes only to steal and kill and destroy; I have come that they may have life, and have it to the full." Jesus said I have come that you might have life and that to the full. Or abundant life. Jesus offers an ABUNDANT LIFE, a full life to those who follow him and believe in him with faith and obedience.

So how do we get this fullness of life? 1 Peter 1:8-9 "Though you have not seen him, you love him; and even though you do not see him now, you believe in him and are filled with an inexpressible and glorious joy, 9 for you are receiving the end result of your faith, the salvation of your souls." John tells us in Chapter 20:31, "But these are written that you may believe that Jesus is the Messiah, the Son of God, and that by believing you may have life in his name." Jesus is the Bread of Life, the Resurrection, and the life, and we have life in believing and having a relationship with him. We do not need to live with the empty way of life that Peter talks about "For you know that it was not with perishable things such as silver or gold that you were redeemed from the empty way of life handed down to you from your ancestors." What is it about our ancestors? The ones who are ancestors in our families and in our families of faith. Allen and I went to the tombs of the Patriarchs in the Holy Land. One side has an Islamic Mosque attached with windows for viewing the tombs of Abraham, Sarah, and Isaac. One side has a Jewish Synagogue attached. From the Jewish Synagogue, there are windows to view the enshrined cases of Abraham and Joseph, and Leah. Tourists line up to view glimpses of the places where the Patriarchs' bones are enshrined. Honoring the ancestors is a way of connecting with the faith of the fathers and mothers of the faith. And yet we cannot depend on the faith of our mothers and fathers to be enough to save our souls.

We Are Redeemed. 1 Peter 1:19-20, "but with the precious blood of Christ, a lamb without blemish or defect. 20 He was chosen before the creation of the world but was revealed in these last times for your sake." The life of salvation is a life of fullness of joy, of perseverance through suffering, of taking up our cross and following Jesus into dark places with the light of the gospel. What causes emptiness? Not just in the way of life of the ancestors but in emptiness in our way of life. We are filling our lives with substitutes for our relationship with God. Emptiness in our way of life could also be happening because of things that drain us of life, with all the things that drain us of life. Disappointments can drain us of life. Life circumstances can drain us. Suffering can drain us of life and our will to live. Greediness and sin can drain us, and lack of rest can drain us.

YET. And yet. We can be full of life when our faith and hope are in God and in Jesus. This Jesus who was chosen before the creation of the world and revealed in the fullness of time. This Jesus who came in the fullness of time to call disciples, to do miracles, signs, and wonders, and to teach us about God who sent him. This Jesus who came to help us see God as one who loved us so much that God gave the Son to us. This Jesus who said if you have seen me, you have seen the Father. This Jesus who said my father and I are One. And so, Jesus came to reveal God's love and care for us. Jesus came to invite us to participate in carrying the good news. Our good news is that Jesus came to lay down his life for his friends to reconcile us to God through his precious blood. 1 Peter 1:21, "Through him you believe in God, who raised him from the dead and glorified him, and so your faith and hope are in God." Our faith and hope are in God. Connecting with Jesus as the Bread of Life helps us honor our fathers. Father's Day is a day to celebrate and honor our fathers. We certainly want to honor the fathers among us today. We want to honor our own fathers, the fathers of children in our families. And especially God our Father, who loved us so much that he sent Jesus.

Jesus came to give us the fullness of life. So, wherever our fathers have let us down. Wherever our earthly fathers have been wonderful, none of our fathers are as wonderful as God the Father, who so loved the world that he gave his only son. Begotten, not made. Jesus of Nazareth. Jesus said he was going to his father, to our God. And he would not leave us orphans. And so, if we have a father alive today, honor our fathers. If we have sons who are fathers, honor them as they father their children. If we have husbands who are fathers and uncles who are fathers, too many Father's Day sermons could make fathers feel like they are not enough. Let's honor our fathers today. Jesus came to give LIFE, and that life is ABUNDANT. The storehouses of Heaven are full. We are called to live life with fullness. We have a choice. We can continue to participate, as 1 Peter writes. Empty way of life of your ancestors. Or fullness of joy.

Jesus prayed to his Father in heaven and taught us to pray, "Our Father, which art in heaven. Jesus taught us to pray. Give us this day our daily bread." This daily bread is the physical bread. It is also our daily manna from heaven when we can gather in prayer, reading, listening, and our circumstances. We notice what God is doing on earth when we receive refreshment for our bodies and souls, our minds, wills, and emotions. We have a wonderful God who is Father to us. Father's Day is a great day to ask to be filled with the Holy Spirit. The Apostle Paul talked about the filling of the Spirit in the verb tense, which means continuing to be being filled with the Holy Spirit.

We leak. Unless we are fasting, we have to eat every day. We brush our teeth every day. We get emptied in our spirits when we pour out what is in there every day. Look at what Jesus said, Luke 11:13, "If you then, though you are evil, know how to give good gifts to your children, how much more will your Father in heaven give the Holy Spirit to those who ask him!" If you being evil, know how to give good gifts to your children, how much more will your Heavenly Father give the Holy Spirit to those who ask? "Ask, and you shall receive. Seek, and you shall find. Knock, and the door shall be opened. For whoever asks receives whoever seeks, finds whoever knocks, the door shall be opened." We have Jesus, who came as the light of the world. We have Jesus, who came as the shepherd of the sheep. We have Jesus who came to show us the Father. We have Jesus who came that we might have abundant life. We have Jesus who came to set at liberty those who are oppressed, to give sight to the blind, to proclaim the year of the Lord's favor.

We can ask God to fill us where we are empty in our spirit. We can give up the empty way of life that lives to gratify the desires of the flesh. There are deeper desires, desires of the heart. Our deepest desires long to please God, live in a relationship with God and honor God as our Heavenly Father. We have a father who is aware of our needs, what will supply our needs, and the vast storehouses in heaven ready to pour out good gifts.

Practical needs. Health, employment, school, funds. Sometimes what we need to give is practical. We provide school supplies to a local middle school. We pick up trash along the roadway. We volunteer at a community pantry or food bank. We knit prayer shawls for those who will feel the comforting touch of the love poured into the stitching. Yes. Practical things. Feed the hungry. Clothe the naked. Visit the sick. Visit those in prison. And in doing all these good things, we have a heavenly storehouse. We can go in prayer to our Father.

Ask for good things. We can ask for wisdom, guidance, direction, protection, provision, and vision for each day. Every day. We can meet with the Lord in the morning in the scriptures and through prayer. We can go about our day noticing where God is at work and inviting us to join in the work of God. What is the work of God? Heal the sick. Bring good news to the poor. Help blind eyes to see and deaf ears to hear. And, of course, the salvation of souls for the glory of God. The angels in heaven rejoice when one sinner repents. When we stop living for ourselves and start living for God, we make a conscious choice to accept the BREAD OF LIFE, the great salvation that God offers. We make a choice to take up our cross and follow Jesus. We make a choice to dedicate our lives to Christ. We make a choice to repent and be baptized and let the whole world know that we love the Lord who came to give us eternal life.

Jesus, who came to seek and save that which was lost. We were lost in our sins and selfish ways. Jesus came and gave us abundant life. Jesus gave us himself. THE BREAD OF LIFE. Jesus' body was broken for us. His blood was shed for us. He was despised and rejected by men. He saw that we were all going astray. We needed a shepherd. We needed someone to lead us to green pastures and living waters. If you want to meet Jesus in a renewed way today, we will be here to pray with you. If you want to be filled with the Holy Spirit to give the Lord your places of emptiness and receive his fullness, we will be here to pray with you. If you want to serve the Lord in practical ways, we are here to pray with you.

Closing Prayer. Lord, come and fill our emptiness with Your fullness. Come meet us in the depths of our deepest desires. Fulfill Your plans for us in us and through us. God, our Father, God the Son, God the Holy Spirit, we honor You in our midst today. We know You are ever present with us whether we experience Your presence or not. Today, we want to experience Your presence. Today, Holy Spirit, come in ways we can experience Your presence and Your power. Fill us today with Your goodness. Help us to be filled to overflowing with love for Jesus and to want to share our love for Jesus in our communities. Amen.

Ministry Time. After the Benediction, we will have ministry time over here on this side of the room if you would like to respond to the message, pray with us, or receive prayer for a particular need.

Benediction: 1 Peter 4:7-11: The end of all things is near. Therefore be alert and of sober mind so that you may pray. Above all, love each other deeply, because love covers over a multitude of sins. Offer hospitality to one another without grumbling. Each of you should use whatever gift you have received to serve others, as faithful stewards of God's grace in its various forms. If anyone speaks, they should do so as one who speaks the very words of God. If anyone serves, they should do so with the strength God provides. so that in all things, God may be praised through Jesus Christ. To him be the glory and the power for ever and ever. Amen.

Distant Promises: These Died in Faith
Hebrews 11:13-16

April 3, 2022

Hebrews 11:13-16 (NRSV) *"All of these died in faith without having received the promises, but from a distance they saw and greeted them. They confessed that they were strangers and foreigners on the earth, 14 for people who speak in this way make it clear that they are seeking a homeland. 15 If they had been thinking of the land that they had left behind, they would have had opportunity to return. 16 But as it is, they desire a better country, that is, a heavenly one. Therefore, God is not ashamed to be called their God; indeed, he has prepared a city for them."*

Let us pray. O God, as we open the Scriptures today, we want to learn from You and what You want to teach us. Holy Spirit, You who inspired the writers, come to breathe life into us today as we consider what You will say to us. In Jesus' name, Amen.

Introduction. Has anyone seen an overlay in the middle of the anatomy book? I may be dating myself. My father had a huge anatomy book with many chapters of explanations. In the middle of the book, there were clear pages with cross-sections of the human body that overlapped one another with different body systems on each page. It started with a picture of the front of a person with skin. Then, turn the page, and under the skin was a page of muscles and tendons in the musculoskeletal system, then the circulatory system, the digestive system, the layers and layers built upon one another, and the last page was the back side of a person with the skin again. Skin, muscles, veins and arteries, bones, internal organs, heart, lungs, and so on, and then the picture of the back side with skin on. Layers and layers we can see all build upon one another. On the outside, we see people sitting here in church with us. On the inside, there are hearts beating, lungs breathing, muscles and bones holding our bodies in position.

The book of Hebrews reminds me of the layers in the anatomy book. In Chapter 1 we see Jesus as the way God speaks to us. In times past, God spoke to us by the prophets. In these last days, God spoke by the Son. Jesus is better than the angels. Jesus is a merciful high priest. By the time we get to Chapter 12, Jesus is the Author and Finisher of our faith. In Chapter 11, we have heard messages about how faith is the substance of things hoped for and the evidence of things unseen. We have touched on some of the heroes of the faith, exemplars, and examples for us to see. We have heard about Abel, Enoch, Noah, and Abraham. And today, we start in verse 13. Read along in your Bibles or on your devices, verses 13-16 (above).

So now we will consider the verses section by section. Hebrews 11:13-16, "All of these died in faith." Who are these? These. The ones mentioned before the present verse. Who are these? When we see the word these, it refers to referring to specific persons, things, or situations just mentioned. Look back at verse 2. "Indeed, by faith, our ancestors received approval. By faith, our ancestors received approval." What happened when our ancestors received approval? They had faith that they demonstrated through their obedience. So, in Verse 13. "They died in faith without having received the promises, but from a distance, they saw and greeted them." Verse 6. "And we know that faith is the substance of things hoped for and the evidence of things not seen."

In winter, when we see daffodils pushing up through the earth in January or February, we have evidence of spring even though spring is not fully here. When we get past the point where it might snow, and the temperatures rise, we enjoy the promise of spring and spring itself. The evidence of spring came in the early flowers before we saw the winter go away and the pollen arrived. The kingdom of God is like that. We see signs of the inbreaking of the kingdom, and it gives us hope to continue in faith, believing that the kingdom of God will fully come on earth as it is in heaven.

Next, "They confessed that they were strangers and foreigners on the earth." The Greek is translated here as a pilgrim, stranger.[17] one who comes from a foreign country into a city or land to reside there by the side of the natives, a stranger sojourning in a strange place, a foreigner. The NT metaphor references heaven as the native country, one that sojourns on earth.

Who confessed they were strangers and foreigners on the earth? In the verses just prior to this, Abraham, "By faith Abraham obeyed when he was called to set out for a place that he was to receive as an inheritance; and he set out, not knowing where he was going. 9 By faith he stayed for a time in the land he had been promised, as in a foreign land, living in tents, as did Isaac and Jacob, who were heirs with him of the same promise." Abraham did not own the land, he sojourned there. Next Verse 14. "for people who speak in this

---

[17] "*Xenos*," Strongs G3581
https://www.blueletterbible.org/lexicon/g3581/kjv/tr/0-1/.

way make it clear that they are seeking a homeland." They are seeking a homeland.

This homeland is not in this world. This homeland is with God in the place God is preparing. You might remember the song "I'm just a poor wayfaring stranger"[18] "I'm just a poor wayfaring stranger Traveling through this world below There is no sickness, no toil, nor danger In that bright land to which I go I'm going there to see my Father And all my loved ones who've gone on I'm just going over Jordan I'm just going over home. Or "Guide me O thou Great Jehovah[19] pilgrim through this barren land. I am weak, but thou art mighty. Hold me with Thy powerful hand."

Peter encourages the believers living through persecution times to remember that they are sojourners on the earth. 1 Peter 2:11, "Beloved, I urge you as aliens and exiles to abstain from the desires of the flesh that wage war against the soul. 12 Conduct yourselves honorably among the Gentiles, so that, though they malign you as evildoers, they may see your honorable deeds and glorify God when he comes to judge."

Next, Hebrews 11 verse 15, "If they had been thinking of the land that they had left behind, they would have had opportunity to return." Abraham obeyed God when God told him to get up and go to a place that God would show Abraham. Abraham and Sarah did not want to go back.

On the journey with Abraham was Lot, Abraham's nephew, who pitched his tent near Sodom. When Lot and his family were rescued from the destruction of the cities of Sodom and Gomorrah, they were instructed not to look back. And we remember what happened with Lot's wife. She looked back and became a pillar of salt. So, Lot and Lot's wife are not included in this list of faith. "If they had been thinking of the land they left behind they would have the opportunity to return, and that would not have been acting in obedience or in faith. Lot and his wife are not mentioned here.

Compare this verse 15 with verse 10 we read of Abraham in verse 10, "For he looked forward to the city that has foundations, whose architect and builder is God."

We see that Abraham looked forward to the city whose architect and builder is God. In Scripture, we see places of worship. God instructed Moses in the tabernacle building, the tent of meeting in the wilderness. God met with

---

[18] https://hymnary.org/text/i_am_a_poor_wayfaring_stranger (public domain).
[19] https://hymnary.org/text/guide_me_o_thou_great_jehovah (public domain).

Moses there, and Moses built the tabernacle according to the pattern God had given him. David wanted to build a temple for the Lord, and Solomon built the temple where the Lord's presence and glory came and manifested in Jerusalem. The tabernacle and the temple were earthly places of worship, and yet God has a city in the heavens where God is both the architect and builder of that great city. Ezekiel saw visions of it. The apostle John saw visions of it. Abraham looked forward to that great city.

Look at verse 16, "But as it is, they desire a better country, that is, a heavenly one." Desire a better country, a heavenly one. Better. So, we see the better word. Better, in Hebrews, is one of the keywords. Just a few places of better in Hebrews, better things, a better hope, a better covenant, better promises, something better. Hebrews 6:9, "Even though we speak in this way, beloved, we are confident of better things in your case, things that belong to salvation." Hebrews 7:19, (for the law made nothing perfect); "there is, on the other hand, the introduction of a better hope, through which we approach God." Hebrews 7:22, "accordingly Jesus has also become the guarantee of a better covenant." Hebrews 8:6, "But Jesus has now obtained a more excellent ministry, and to that degree he is the mediator of a better covenant, which has been enacted through better promises." Hebrews 10:34, "For you had compassion for those who were in prison, and you cheerfully accepted the plundering of your possessions, knowing that you yourselves possessed something better and more lasting."

Next to verse 16. "Therefore, God is not ashamed to be called their God; indeed, he has prepared a city for them." The "therefore" is there for a reason. "Therefore" invites us to look at what comes before this verse. 16 But as it is, they desire a better country, that is, a heavenly one. Therefore, God is not ashamed to be called their God; indeed, he has prepared a city for them.

They desire a better country, that is a heavenly one. Therefore, God is not ashamed to be called their God; indeed, he has prepared a city for them. God is not ashamed to be called their God. Who? Those who desire a better country, a heavenly one. Who? Those who died in faith without receiving the promises. Who? Those for whom God has prepared a city, a better one, a heavenly one. Enter in. Enter in. There yet remains hope for the people of God. God has prepared a city. Before Jesus departed, in his Farewell Discourse in John 14, Jesus said, "I am going to prepare a place for you." Jesus did not leave us as orphans. Jesus came to us in the Holy Spirit.

Remember in verse 13, "These pleased the Lord." How? By faith! By faith. Without faith, it is impossible to please the Lord. Look at Hebrews 2: 10,

> *It was fitting that God, for whom and through whom all things exist, in bringing many children to glory, should make the pioneer of their salvation perfect through sufferings. 11 For the one who sanctifies and those who are sanctified all have one Father. For this reason, Jesus is not ashamed to call them brothers and sisters.*

Here are some other verses about not being ashamed. Paul in Romans 1:16, "For I am not ashamed of the gospel; it is the power of God for salvation to everyone who has faith, to the Jew first and also to the Greek." And three places in 2 Timothy. 2 Timothy 1:8, "Do not be ashamed, then, of the testimony about our Lord or of me his prisoner, but join with me in suffering for the gospel, relying on the power of God." And 2 Timothy 1:12, "and for this reason I suffer as I do. But I am not ashamed, for I know the one in whom I have put my trust, and I am sure that he is able to guard until that day what I have entrusted to him." And 2 Timothy 2:15, "Do your best to present yourself to God as one approved by him, a worker who has no need to be ashamed, rightly explaining the word of truth."

Before Adam and Eve sinned, they were naked and not ashamed. After they transgressed God's commandment, they knew they were naked, and they became ashamed. In their shame, they hid. Shame will do that to us. When we have acted shamefully, we tend to want to hide. In our hiding, we start out hiding from God and then from one another since we do not want others to know the shameful chapters of our lives. We cover our shame and hide from God, from one another, and from ourselves. When we pretend that we do not have those chapters common to all of us, we become fake, false, and disingenuous, putting on a good front to try to impress other people and to try to impress God. We all have sinned, and we all have missed the mark, and we all have suffered things common to being human.

We are all greatly loved. It is God's kindness that leads us to repentance. It is God who so loved the world that God gave Jesus, God's only begotten Son, so that whoever believes in Jesus will not perish but have everlasting life. It is Jesus who came into the world to show us the Father and what the Father is like. It is Jesus who is not ashamed to call us brothers and sisters. It is Jesus who understands our humanity and was tempted in all the ways we are tempted and yet Jesus did not miss the mark. Jesus is the one who calls us out of our shame into acceptance. Jesus calls us out of fear into love. Perfect love casts out fear. Perfect love displaces fear.

When we read, "God is not ashamed to be their God." Can that be said of us? Yes. God is not ashamed of us. All our sin, all of our shame, was nailed to the cross. We have been given new life, abundant life, and everlasting life. Where the enemy wants to keep us bound up in our shackles and chains of shame and fear, the Lord appears and breaks the chains that once bound us. The Lord Jesus has not given us the spirit of fear but of power and love and a sound mind. Again Verse 16, "God is not ashamed to be called their God."

What is shame? Shame is a noun: a painful feeling of humiliation or distress caused by the consciousness of wrong or foolish behavior. Shame is a verb: (of a person, action, or situation) make (someone) feel ashamed.[20] "I tried to shame him into giving some away." Shame usually follows a pattern. In the pattern of shame, we experience an intensely painful event. Then we believe the lie that our pain is who we are, and our failure is who we are — not just something we have done or have had done to us, and then we experience shame. And then our feelings of shame act like a trap and a snare. We start thinking that we can never recover — or that we do not deserve to recover. Shaming persons does not produce good fruit. Shaming sends us into hiding. When we confess our sins, "God is faithful and just to forgive us our sins and to cleanse us from all unrighteousness." (1 John 1:9). We have no need to stay ashamed.

Maybe some people would think that once they have messed up or missed the mark, and there was no way back to a relationship with Jesus. We all have chapters of our lives we do not want to read aloud. I wrestled with this text this week when I came to verse 16, which says God is not ashamed to be their God. I went back through my life and the places where God met me, forgave me, restored me, gave me another chance, and spoke kindly to me. We know that it is the kindness of God that leads us to repentance. We do not need to live lives of private defeat, condemnation, or self-recrimination. God so loved us that nothing can separate us from the love of God in Christ Jesus. God wants us to embrace our salvation and shine like lights in the darkness of this world.

We are not equal to our sins. We are not our sins. We are not what we have done or failed to do. We are not what others have done to us or failed to do for us. God is not the parent who in public shames a child for misbehaving or the parent who shames us when we miss the mark. If we have shame, we do not need to stay ashamed. The prodigal son went away to a far country and spent his inheritance on riotous living. When all was gone, and he was

---

[20] https://www.dictionary.com/browse/shame.

eating what he fed the pigs, he woke up. He came to his senses. He went back to his father and offered to be treated like a servant instead of a son. And the father ran to him, welcomed him home, and celebrated the homecoming of his son with a party. (Luke 15).

God in Christ raised us up from shame and dishonor to a place of value and honor. We are seated with Christ in heavenly realms. Paul writes about how we were once dead and the mercy of God that saved us in Ephesians 2:1-7:

> *All of us once lived among them in the passions of our flesh, following the desires of flesh and senses, and we were by nature children of wrath, like everyone else. 4 But God, who is rich in mercy, out of the great love with which he loved us 5 even when we were dead through our trespasses, made us alive together with Christ— by grace you have been saved— 6 and raised us up with him and seated us with him in the heavenly places in Christ Jesus, 7 so that in the ages to come he might show the immeasurable riches of his grace in kindness toward us in Christ Jesus.*

But what if you are ashamed of God? If you are ashamed of God, you will deny knowing God. You will not allow God to be your highest aim, and you will be swayed by the pleasures of sin and sinfulness. You will prefer to stay stuck in sin compared to accepting the richness of God's mercy. And if you are ashamed of God, Jesus said he would be ashamed of those who are ashamed of Him. Jesus in Mark 8:38, "Those who are ashamed of me and of my words in this adulterous and sinful generation, of them the Son of Man will also be ashamed when he comes in the glory of his Father with the holy angels." Jesus said for those who are ashamed of him; he will be ashamed of them before the Father. Now, If any of us have been ashamed of Christ, we can repent of where we have been ashamed of Christ so that we may be forgiven and persevere in faith until the very end.

Let's look at Peter, the great apostle. Peter, the apostle, made bold declarations of Jesus as the Christ. Peter walked on water, healed the sick, cast out demons, and walked with Jesus. And on the night Judas betrayed Jesus for thirty pieces of silver, Peter denied knowing Jesus three times before the cock crowed in the early morning light. Peter was ashamed of Christ, and Luke 22:61 says Jesus looked at him in the courtyard. What was in that look? "The Lord turned and looked at Peter. Then Peter remembered the word of the Lord, how he had said to him, "Before the cock crows today, you will deny me three times." 62 And he went out and wept bitterly." After Jesus rose from the dead and was cooking fish for breakfast on the beach, Peter recognized Jesus, left his fishing boat, and swam to shore. We find this in John's Gospel Chapter 21. Remember what Jesus asked him? Do you love me? Three times Jesus asked Peter if Peter loved him. Peter was restored that day. Even though Peter was ashamed of Jesus and denied Jesus, denied knowing Jesus, swearing that he did not know Jesus, it was the kindness of Jesus that restored Peter. Peter repented and received the restoration. Peter went on to boldly proclaim the gospel of Christ, the death and resurrection of Jesus, and the message of salvation through Jesus the Messiah.

God is not ashamed to be the God of Peter. If we have messed up, if we have denied Christ and loved the world and the things of the world more than looking forward to the heavenly city whose architect and builder is God, we have an opportunity to repent. We have an opportunity to shift our focus from ourselves and the things that keep us bound up in this world. We have an invitation in Hebrews 12:1-2,

> *Therefore, since we are surrounded by so great a cloud of witnesses, let us also lay aside every weight and the sin that clings so closely, and let us run with perseverance the race that is set before us, 2 looking to Jesus the pioneer and perfecter of our faith, who for the sake of the joy that was set before him endured the cross, disregarding its shame, and has taken his seat at the right hand of the throne of God.*

We can look unto Jesus, who came to bring good news to the poor, set the captives free, heal the blind eyes, preach liberty to the oppressed, and proclaim the year of the Lord's favor. (Luke 4) Jesus is the pioneer and perfector, the author and finisher, the Alpha and Omega, the beginning and the end. Jesus is not ashamed to call us brothers and sisters.

Hebrews 2:10-12,

> *It was fitting that God, for whom and through whom all things exist, in bringing many children to glory, should make the pioneer of their salvation perfect through sufferings. 11 For the one who sanctifies and those who are sanctified all have one Father. For this reason, Jesus is not ashamed to call them brothers and sisters, 12 saying, "I will proclaim your name to my brothers and sisters, in the midst of the congregation I will praise you.*

Brothers and sisters, God is not ashamed of you. Jesus is not ashamed of you. When we prize God above all else, we have faith that pleases God, and we look forward to the city whose architect and builder is God. This world pales in comparison to the greatness of the riches of the glory of Christ Jesus. Hebrews 9:26b-28:

> *But as it is, he has appeared once for all at the end of the age to remove sin by the sacrifice of himself. 27 And just as it is appointed for mortals to die once, and after that the judgment, 28 so Christ, having been offered once to bear the sins of many, will appear a second time, not to deal with sin, but to save those who are eagerly waiting for him.*

Jesus will appear a second time, not to deal with sin. He did that in his first coming when he suffered and died on the cross for our sins and the sins of the whole world. What does it say in Chapter 9, verse 28? He is coming to save those who are eagerly waiting for his. Are we eagerly waiting for Jesus, for his appearing, for his glory, for his rule and reign to come in fullness? Are we fixing our eyes on Jesus, the author, and finisher of our faith? Are we among those who love the Lord and are expectantly watching and waiting?

Are we living in faith and dying in faith? Whether or not we see the promises fulfilled before we die here, we have a confident expectation that God loves us. Jesus went ahead to prepare a place for us. Jesus will come again to gather us up into the heavenly city prepared for us, the new Jerusalem. Jesus is standing ready. Jesus is interceding for us. One day, the gathering of all the earth, every tribe, and every tongue will glorify God in the heavenly places where worship continually takes place. Night and day, the worshippers cry Holy, Holy, holy is the Lord God Almighty who was and is and is to come. Holy, Holy, Holy. Glorious things await us for those who live in faith and die in faith. Glorious things await us who eagerly await the restoration of all things, the kingdom of God coming in fullness and glory and power and might.

What do we see in these verses from Hebrews 11:13-16? They died in faith without having received the promises. From a distance, they saw and greeted the promises. They confessed that they were strangers and foreigners on the earth. They were seeking a homeland. They were not looking to return to the land they left behind. They desired a better country, a heavenly one. God is not ashamed to be called their God. God has prepared a city for them. What about us? Do we see and greet the promises of God from a distance? Do we consider ourselves pilgrims, sojourners, passing through this present age with hope and faith that this is not all there is? Are we seeking a homeland to truly call home, a better country, a heavenly country? Are we looking forward to the city God has prepared for us, those who love God? Are we rejoicing that God is not ashamed to be called our God? Are we grateful that Jesus is not ashamed to call us brothers and sisters? These all died in faith with distant promises. Will we be faithful to the end?

Closing Prayer: Lord God, You have prepared a city for those who live and die in faith, believing Your promises from afar. Jesus, You said to Your disciples that You were going to prepare a place for them, and You are still waiting to return for Your bride. Help us to live lives of faith, believing You, believing Your promises, believing in hope and faith that You are able to complete the good work You started in us. Where we have missed the mark, help us to notice it, to confess our sins, to repent, and walk in new ways of obedience to You and Your plans for us. We love You and set our affections on You, Lord. You are worthy of all our praise, honor, and worship. Even so, come, Lord Jesus. Maranatha. Amen.

Ministry Time: If you would like prayer, if you would like to respond to the message, please find someone near you to pray with you or come up here, and we will have a team to pray with you here. If you are listening online and want prayer, we have a place to request prayer on our website.

Benediction: Hebrews 13:20-21: Now may the God of peace, who brought back from the dead our Lord Jesus, the great shepherd of the sheep, by the blood of the eternal covenant, make you complete in everything good so that you may do his will, working among us that which is pleasing in his sight, through Jesus Christ, to whom be the glory forever and ever. Amen.

Go in Peace. Peace to You: Two Daughters
Mark 5:21-34

January 2, 2022

Mark 5:21-34 (NRSV), *Then one of the leaders of the synagogue named Jairus came and, when he saw him, fell at his feet and begged him repeatedly, "My little daughter is at the point of death. Come and lay your hands on her, so that she may be made well, and live." So he went with him. And a large crowd followed him and pressed in on him. Now there was a woman who had been suffering from hemorrhages for twelve years. 26 She had endured much under many physicians, and had spent all that she had; and she was no better, but rather grew worse. She had heard about Jesus, and came up behind him in the crowd and touched his cloak, for she said, "If I but touch his clothes, I will be made well."*

Let us pray: O Lord God, dear Jesus, we come to You this morning with hope for a New Year. We long for the true peace of Your presence and the overwhelming joy of Your salvation. Come, Lord Jesus, Come Holy Spirit. Teach us with Your wisdom today. Amen.

Introduction. When neighbors make noises that jar us from our sleep, we call that disturbing the peace. Some neighborhoods shoot off fireworks. Some shoot guns on New Year's Eve. If it disturbs our peaceful sleep, we awaken with a startle and may find it difficult to return to sleep. If we hear a thunderstorm approaching, it may be difficult to feel peaceful until we know the storm has passed us by. When we hear disturbing news, our peace can be shaken. *Peace to you.*

Think of other times that challenge our peace: What about sending a young adult out of the driveway with their driver's license? Sending a child away to school or away to college? When children play at a friend's house, and we are not there? Watching your children leave home to get married? Relational bumps and breakups? Friends who were once close who have distanced themselves? Persons, who are sick and dying? The title of the sermon this morning is "Peace to you. Go in peace."

Peace is especially important if it is real peace and not fake peace. When arguments cease, we call that peace. It may be a truce, but it seems peaceful. When wars end, we call that peace. But just because a war ends, the peace may be very fragile. About the wicked, Isaiah says in 59:7-9:

Their feet run to evil, and they rush to shed innocent blood; their thoughts are thoughts of iniquity, desolation and destruction are in their highways. The way of peace they do not know, and there is no justice in their paths. Their roads they have made crooked; no one who walks in them knows peace. Therefore justice is far from us, and righteousness does not reach us; we wait for light, and lo! there is darkness; and for brightness, but we walk in gloom.

The way of the wicked does not have peace. The Lord knows we live lives where dissension, arguing, bickering, and soul-disturbing news challenge our peace. We hear of failed businesses, poverty, wars, rumors of wars, climate challenges, storms, tornados demolishing cities, ravages, and trafficking of persons. Peace to you. Go in peace. Really? Yes.

When Zechariah prophecies about John the Baptist in Luke 1:76:

And you, child, will be called the prophet of the Most High; for you will go before the Lord to prepare his ways, to give knowledge of salvation to his people by the forgiveness of their sins. By the tender mercy of our God, the dawn from on high will break upon us, to give light to those who sit in darkness and in the shadow of death, to guide our feet into the way of peace."

When Jesus leaves the glories of heaven to be born as a baby, The angels announce to the shepherds: Luke 2:14, "Glory to God in the highest heaven, and on earth peace among those whom he favors!"

Isaiah calls the Messiah the Prince of Peace in Isaiah 9:6, "For a child has been born for us, a son is given to us; authority rests upon his shoulders; and he is named Wonderful Counselor, Mighty God, Everlasting Father, Prince of Peace." As I mentioned earlier, the sermon is entitled Go in Peace. Peace to You. It sounds backward, like maybe it would be better to say Peace to you, now Go in peace. The scriptures we are considering this morning have the order in this other way with Go in peace first, and then peace to you.

Our lesson today comes from the book of Mark, Chapter 5. The gospel of Mark is the shortest of the gospels, with 16 chapters. Chapter 5 has a parallel in Luke 8. Turn in our Bibles to Mark 5:21. Jesus had just healed the Gadarene demoniac and delivered him from a legion of demons who went into the pigs and over the edge of the cliff. The man was clothed and in his right mind and wanted to follow Jesus, but Jesus asked him to stay and tell his neighbors what good the Lord had done for him. Jesus delivered him from the torment of the demons, and the Gadarene demoniac was clothed in his right mind and had peace from the torment. And then skip to verse 21. We will read verses 21-34:

> *When Jesus had crossed again in the boat to the other side, a great crowd gathered around him; and he was by the sea. Then one of the leaders of the synagogue named Jairus came and, when he saw him, fell at his feet and begged him repeatedly, "My little daughter is at the point of death. Come and lay your hands on her, so that she may be made well, and live." So he went with him. And a large crowd followed him and pressed in on him. Now there was a woman who had been suffering from hemorrhages for twelve years. 26 She had endured much under many physicians, and had spent all that she had; and she was no better, but rather grew worse. She had heard about Jesus, and came up behind him in the crowd and touched his cloak, for she said, "If I but touch his clothes, I will be made well." Immediately her hemorrhage stopped; and she felt in her body that she was healed of her disease. Immediately aware that power had gone forth from him, Jesus turned about in the crowd and said, "Who touched my clothes?" And his disciples said to him, "You see the crowd pressing in on you; how can you say, 'Who touched me?'" He looked all around to see who had done it. But the woman, knowing what had happened to her, came in fear and trembling, fell down before him, and told him the whole truth. He said to her, "Daughter, your faith has made you well; go in peace, and be healed of your disease.*

Go in peace, Jesus said to the woman. Here we have the case of a woman who had been sick as long as Jairus' daughter had been alive. Jairus' daughter was twelve years of age and lay dying. Jesus responded to Jairus' request to come to Jairus' house. Jairus, the text says, was a leader in the synagogue. Jairus humbled himself at the feet of Jesus and begged him repeatedly to heal his daughter.

Jesus is on his way with Jairus when Jesus stops to ask, "Who touched me?" What was Jairus thinking at this point? Why are you stopping, Jesus? We have to hurry! As we read the scriptures, it is good to immerse ourselves in them and look around and consider what is going on here from various perspectives. What would it be like to be Jairus, a leader of the synagogue? What would it be like to be one of the disciples walking along each day? What would it be like to be in the pressing crowd?

Jesus stopped to tend to a woman. We do not know her name. We know she had faith. She could not approach Jesus from the front and converse with this rabbi, Jesus, like Jairus did. An incurable bleeding disorder plagued this woman for twelve years, and that had cost her social status and money to pay for physicians. She was considered untouchable because she was ceremonially unclean. In this state, she heard about Jesus and his miraculous work. She knew the crowds were following Jesus, and she got into the back of the crowd and made her way up from behind. She could see a glimpse of him, and I wonder how we imagine it.

If I am trying to get through a crowd, I say excuse me, excuse me, excuse me, and keep pressing my way forward. Allen knows I can move forward in a crowd when I want to, so I just keep pressing in. There was no social distancing here. The press of the crowd was real. Maybe you have seen artistic depictions of her sliding on the ground in between muddy feet, tasting dust to get to Jesus. The text says nothing about sliding on the ground with dust in her mouth.

The text says she came up from behind, and she was talking to herself. She had heard about Jesus and came up behind him in the crowd and touched his cloak, for she said, "If I but touch his clothes, I will be made well." In her conversation with herself, she said, "If I but touch his clothes, I will be made well." (How do we talk to ourselves? Do we have faith in our self-talk?) It took such faith to press in from behind and reach out and touch the edge, the hem of his garment. And it says that Jesus felt the power go out of him. "Immediately aware that power had gone forth from him, Jesus turned about in the crowd and said, "Who touched my clothes?" And his disciples said to him, "You see the crowd pressing in on you; how can you say, 'Who touched me?'"

Jesus knew someone had touched him. He knew that power had gone out of him. Have you ever laid hands on someone and felt the Holy Spirit move through your hands to touch someone and see them get healed? We sometimes experience that in prayer ministry when we lay hands on the sick, and they recover. We know it is the Lord, not us, but we can feel our hands get hot or feel power moving through us as we pray and touch in faith, believing the Lord for healing. Jesus did not reach out and touch this woman. She reached out and touched him. The disciples did not understand and thought this was preposterous. Of course, Jesus was in a crowd, and people were all around him. Of course, he was touched. There is a difference between bumping into someone and intentionally reaching out for a meaningful touch.

Notice: This unnamed woman, Jesus called "Daughter" in verse 34. Jesus called her daughter. The only place where Jesus calls a woman daughter. "Daughter, your faith has made you well; go in peace, and be healed of your disease." DAUGHTER is a relational term. Jesus called her Daughter, meaning daughter of God, acceptable to God. In the middle of the journey with the daughter of Jairus, Jesus acknowledges this woman who reached out and touched his clothes approaching from the back of the crowd, "Daughter."

If you have reached out in faith and you have not been healed, please know that healing will happen one day. Do not believe the lie that you did not have enough faith to be healed. Your healing is delayed. The kingdom of God is here now, but it is not fully present with us now. It is not fully here yet. We pray thy kingdom come and thy will be done in the Lord's prayer because it is not fully here yet.

We all could have our faith increased. In Mark 9, The man with the son who had a tormenting demon said, Lord I believe help my unbelief. (Mark 9:19-24):

> *"Bring him to me." And they brought the boy to him. When the spirit saw him, immediately it convulsed the boy, and he fell on the ground and rolled about, foaming at the mouth. Jesus asked the father, "How long has this been happening to him?" And he said, "From childhood. It has often cast him into the fire and into the water, to destroy him; but if you are able to do anything, have pity on us and help us." Jesus said to him, "If you are able!—All things can be done for the one who believes." Immediately the father of the child cried out, "I believe; help my unbelief!*

If we have unbelief, we can ask for help. But what often happens is we ask once, and we do not see any results, and then we stop asking. Some of us need to have the encouragement to keep asking. Keep speaking life. Keep believing that healing will come. It is too easy to listen to the lie of the enemy that the reason you were not healed was that you did not have enough faith. If you have the desire to be healed, listen to the deep desire and surrender your thoughts and desires to the Lord.

We have a promise in Proverbs 3:5-6, "Trust in the Lord with all your heart and lean not to your own understanding, in all your ways acknowledge him, and he will direct your paths." Psalm 37:3-5, "Trust in the LORD, and do good; so you will live in the land, and enjoy security. Take delight in the LORD, and he will give you the desires of your heart. Commit your way to the LORD; trust in him, and he will act."

What are your true desires? Your deepest longings? We know people who have had faith to touch Jesus who were not healed in ways we could see. It does not mean that we stop trying to reach out and touch Jesus. This woman heard, "Daughter. Go in peace." The coming kingdom still breaks through.

Miracles still happen. While he was still speaking, some people came from the leader's house to say, "Your daughter is dead. Why trouble the teacher any further?" But overhearing what they said, Jesus said to the leader of the synagogue, "Do not fear, only believe."

Pause to consider. What was Jairus thinking? Perhaps, If only we had hurried and had not stopped to tend to that woman, my daughter would be alive. Maybe, "Why did you not hurry, Jesus, when I begged you to come?" Mark 5: 37-43:

> *He (Jesus) allowed no one to follow him except Peter, James, and John, the brother of James. When they came to the house of the leader of the synagogue, he saw a commotion, people weeping and wailing loudly. When he had entered, he said to them, "Why do you make a commotion and weep? The child is not dead but sleeping." And they laughed at him. Then he put them all outside, and took the child's father and mother and those who were with him, and went in where the child was. He took her by the hand and said to her, "Talitha cum," which means, "Little girl, get up!" And immediately the girl got up and began to walk about (she was twelve years of age). At this they were overcome with amazement. He strictly ordered them that no one should know this, and told them to give her something to eat.*

The unnamed woman was healed when she touched Jesus in faith in a public crowd of people. Jairus's daughter was healed when Jesus privately took her by the hand and said, "little girl, get up," inside a house when everyone had to leave except the parents and Peter, James, and John. Two daughters that day received healing—the daughter who had faith and the daughter of Jairus. And now the "Peace to You" portion. When Jesus met with his disciples in the Farewell discourse in John, Jesus gave them his peace. John 14: 26-27 (NRSV):

> *But the Advocate, the Holy Spirit, whom the Father will send in my name, will teach you everything, and remind you of all that I have said to you. Peace I leave with you; my peace I give to you. I do not give to you as the world gives. Do not let your hearts be troubled, and do not let them be afraid.*

John 20, after Mary Magdalene's encounter, verses 18-23 (NRSV):

> *Mary Magdalene went to the disciples with the news: "I have seen the Lord!" And she told them that he had said these things to her. On the evening of that first day of the week, when the disciples were together, with the doors locked for fear of the Jewish leaders, Jesus came and stood among them and said, "Peace be*

> *with you!" After he said this, he showed them his hands and side. The disciples were overjoyed when they saw the Lord. Again Jesus said, "Peace be with you! As the Father has sent me, I am sending you." And with that he breathed on them and said, "Receive the Holy Spirit. If you forgive anyone's sins, their sins are forgiven; if you do not forgive them, they are not forgiven.*

How do we have peace in a troubled world? We have peace through Jesus Christ. Colossians 1:20 (NRSV), "and through him, (Jesus,) God was pleased to reconcile to himself all things, whether on earth or in heaven, by making peace through the blood of his cross." Romans 5:1-5 (NRSV):

> *Therefore, since we are justified by faith, we have peace with God through our Lord Jesus Christ, through whom we have obtained access to this grace in which we stand; and we boast in our hope of sharing the glory of God. And not only that, but we also boast in our sufferings, knowing that suffering produces endurance, and endurance produces character, and character produces hope, and hope does not disappoint us, because God's love has been poured into our hearts through the Holy Spirit that has been given to us.*

Romans 14:7 "The kingdom of God is righteousness, peace, and joy in the Holy Spirit." Galatians 5:22, "The fruit of the Spirit is love, joy, and peace." The apostles who wrote epistles greeted their readers with peace to you. "Grace and peace to you from God our Father and the Lord Jesus Christ." In this world, we will have trouble, Jesus said. But, "Be of good cheer. I have overcome the world!" Peace enters our hearts by the Holy Spirit. We do not have life without sorrow. In life's journey, we weep with anguish, pain, and suffering.

And yet we have this promise in Philippians 4:7 and 9 (NRSV): "And the peace of God, which surpasses all understanding, will guard your hearts and your minds in Christ Jesus. Keep on doing the things that you have learned and received and heard and seen in me, and the God of peace will be with you." We are not just asking for peace for ourselves without being willing to care for our neighbors. This peace is not only for us to receive without passing along the blessings of peace in practical ways. Romans 12, As much as it depends on us, we are to live at peace with all.

Share the Story of Dirk Willems with compassion for the enemy. Dirk Willems (1569) was a famous Anabaptist martyr who was in prison in the Netherlands when it was under Spanish rule by the Duke of Alva. Dirk was able to escape the prison onto the ice below the tower. When his captor tried to follow him, the captor was heavier than Dirk and fell through the ice. Instead of Dirk letting his pursuer drown in the broken ice, Dirk went back and rescued his captor. The rescued guard was less than grateful and arrested Dirk Willems again, and this time, he was locked in wooden leg stocks until they took him outside and burned him to death. He remains a folk hero in that town of Asperen.

Listen to the lyrics of this hymn, "Wonderful Peace"[21] "Far away in the depths of my spirit tonight Rolls a melody sweeter than psalm; In celestial-like strains, it unceasingly falls O'er my soul like an infinite calm. Refrain: Peace, peace, wonderful peace, Coming down from the Father above! Sweep over my spirit forever; I pray. In fathomless billows of love! What a treasure I have in this wonderful peace, Buried deep in the heart of my soul, So secure that no power can mine it away, While the years of eternity roll! I am resting tonight in this wonderful peace, Resting sweetly in Jesus' control; For I'm kept from all danger by night and by day, And His glory is flooding my soul! And I think when I rise to that city of peace, Where the Author of peace I shall see, That one strain of the song which the ransomed will sing In that heavenly kingdom will be: Ah soul are you here without comfort and rest, Marching down the rough pathway of time? Make Jesus your friend ere the shadows grow dark; Oh, accept this sweet peace so sublime!"

Ministry Time. As we come to the end of this service, you may pray right where you are for this peace to flood your soul. If you want to go to the front to pray, we will have a team over here to pray with you. If you need peace, deep peace in your soul today; if you want to ask the God of peace to give you peace in your heart and soul, ask in prayer, believing. Reach out and touch Jesus and receive that overwhelming peace. I am going to read these benedictions from scripture with peace in them. Listen as I read them and receive these words from the Hebrew Bible and from the epistles in the New Testament

Benedictions: From Numbers 6: "The Lord bless you and keep you; the Lord make his face to shine upon you, and be gracious to you; the Lord lift up his countenance upon you, and give you peace." From Romans 15:13, "May the God of hope fill you with all joy and peace in believing, so that you may abound in hope by the power of the Holy Spirit." From 2 Corinthians 13:11, "Finally, brothers and sisters, farewell. Put things in order, listen to my appeal, agree with one another, live in peace; and the God of love and peace will be with you." From 1 Thessalonians 5:23, "May the God of peace himself

---

21 WD Cornell. "Wonderful Peace," 1889 hymn in the Public Domain.

sanctify you entirely; and may your spirit and soul and body be kept sound and blameless at the coming of our Lord Jesus Christ."

Closing: Dear Friends, Now, May the Lord bless you and keep you. And give you peace. Peace to you. Go in peace. Amen.

Guard Your Heart
Proverbs 8:23

September 12, 2018

Proverbs 8:23 (NIV), *"Above all else, guard your heart, for everything you do flows from it."*

Opening Prayer: O Lord, meet us here today as we consider our hearts. Amen.

Introduction. Physical pump. Our hearts are physical pumps that pump the blood through our hearts into the rest of the body and deliver oxygenated blood to the tissues through the arteries. And remove the wastes and deoxygenated blood through the venous system. Our hearts are powerful pumps, and the balance of pressure needs to be just right for our hearts to work properly. Cardiologists keep watch over our hearts to guard them against beating too fast, too slowly, too much pressure. Extra bleeding.

Illustration of circulation and oxygenation. Do not want our blood pressure to get too high. Just right. Too much stress, salt, and other factors contribute to high blood pressure which, in turn contributes to heart trouble and kidney trouble. Need to Beat about 72 times a minute. Blood flows and brings life. Oxygen and nutrients to the tissues. Scripture repeats, "the life is in the blood." The heart is the pump at the center of the physical distribution of the blood. Their blood pressure is normal at 120/80—many ways to check the health of our physical hearts. Medical science has cardiograms, echocardiograms, stress tests, and blood tests for cardiac enzymes. Several years ago, with multi-system organ failure, the cardiologist was called to try to get the heart out of arrhythmia so that the blood could flow to all of the tissues. The bacteria that was walling itself off from the circulation was killing the tissues that could not get the blood. The cardiologist was trying to guard Allen's heart.to watch over it because there is life in the blood and all of the tissues needed to receive the life flow from the heart if it could work well.

What are some ways to monitor the health of our spiritual hearts.? What about the measures of wisdom and folly we have studied so far? The measures of righteousness and unrighteousness. What are we feeding our hearts? What is flowing out of them? Proverbs and one particular verse about our heart. In Hebrew, the heart is the inner person, mind, will, heart, understanding midst (of things), heart (of humans), soul, heart (of humans), mind, knowledge, thinking, reflection, memory inclination, resolution, determination (of will).conscience heart (of moral character) as the seat of appetites as the seat of emotions and passions as the seat of courage.

This is only one proverb about the heart. It is found in Chapter 4 of Proverbs. So far in Proverbs, we have been introduced to wisdom literature. We have seen the personification of Lady Wisdom contrasted with Folly. The two voices that call for our attention. We have been challenged with a healthy Fear of the Lord. And walking in wisdom and righteousness.

Making good choices. (NIV) 8:23, "Above all else, guard your heart, for everything you do flows from it." (NASB) 8:23, "Watch over your heart with all diligence, For from it flow the springs of life." (NKJV) 8:23, "Keep your heart with all diligence, For out of it spring the issues of life." Guard your heart with all diligence, for out of it flow the issues of life. My son, give attention to my words; Incline your EAR to my sayings. 21 Do not let them depart from your SIGHT; Keep them in the midst of your HEART. 22 For they are life to those who find them And health to all their BODY. 23 Watch over your HEART with all diligence, For from it flow the springs of life. 24 Put away from you a deceitful MOUTH And put devious SPEECH far from you. 25 Let your EYES look directly ahead And let your GAZE be fixed straight in front of you. 26 Watch the path of your FEET And all your ways will be established. 27 Do not turn to the right nor to the left; Turn your FOOT from evil.

Body parts. HEARING My son, give attention to my words; Incline your EAR to my sayings. VISION 21 Do not let them depart from your SIGHT; Keep them in the midst of your HEART. 22 For they are life to those who find them And health to all their BODY. HEART. Thinking. Feeling. Decisions. 23 Watch over your HEART with all diligence, For from it flow the springs of life. MOUTH 24 Put away from you a deceitful MOUTH And put devious SPEECH far from you. EYES 25 Let your EYES look directly ahead, And let your GAZE be fixed straight in front of you. FEET 26 Watch the path of your FEET, And all your ways will be established. 27 Do not turn to the right nor to the left; Turn your FOOT from evil.

Noun. When we think of a guard, we might think of a noun. A person is posted in a position to ensure security and safety. Where do we post guards? We post guards on watch at military installations. We have guards on watch at banks.at stores.in prisons. Where else? An Honor Guard at a funeral. Changing of the guard at Buckingham Palace. At the tomb of the Unknown

Soldier. There were guards posted at the tomb of Jesus. There were guards posted for Peter in prison and for Paul and Silas.

Verb. To guard is to protect. To guard against dangers, to watch over. To defend with fidelity, to preserve. Some of the translations say keep watch over your heart while others say guard your heart. Our sermon title today is Guard Your Heart. The word for guard is translated as Keep, Preserve, Watch over. Psalm 25:10 "All the paths of the LORD are lovingkindness and truth To those who KEEP His covenant and His testimonies." Psalm 25:21 "Let integrity and uprightness PRESERVE me, For I wait for You." Proverbs 2:11, "Discretion will guard you. Understanding will WATCH OVER you." 3:1, "Do not forget my teaching but let your heart KEEP my commandments." 3:21, "Let them not vanish from your sight; KEEP sound wisdom and discretion. 13:3, "The one who GUARDS his mouth preserves his life; the one who opens wide his lips comes to ruin." In studying and preparing for this message, I noticed that There are some things we Guard Our Hearts against. There are some things we guard our hearts with. There are some things we guard our hearts for. Here we go.

SIN. Memory verse from childhood in King James Version. Psalm119:111 Against Sin. Guard with the WORD. "Thy Word have I hid in mine heart that I might not sin against thee." Updated version. (NIV) "I have hidden your word in my heart that I might not sin against you." Earlier in Proverbs 4:4,21 context. V. 4 "Then he taught me, and he said to me, 'Take hold of my words with all your heart; keep my commands, and you will live.'" .21 "Do not let them out of your sight, keep them within your heart;" Psalm 19:14, "Let the words of my mouth, and the meditation of my heart, be acceptable in thy sight, O LORD , my strength, and my redeemer."

Pride and Vanity. Prov 11:2, "When pride comes, then comes dishonor, But with the humble is wisdom." Prov 16:18, "Pride goes before destruction, a haughty spirit before a fall." Prov 22:8 (NASB), "He who sows iniquity will reap vanity, And the rod of his fury will perish." God resists the proud. God RESISTS the proud. God opposes the proud. God purposefully blocks the pride of the proud. God resists the proud. But gives grace to the humble. James.4:6 1Peter 5:5, "In the same way, you who are younger, submit yourselves to your elders. All of you, clothe yourselves with humility toward one another, because 'God opposes the proud but shows favor to the humble.'" Old hymn. "Years I spent in vanity and pride caring not my Lord was crucified. Knowing not it was for me he died. At Calvary. Mercy there was great, and grace was free. Pardon there was multiplied to me. There my burdened soul found liberty. At Calvary."[22]

Guard against pride and vanity with the cross of Christ. How much He loved and gave for us. Guard Your Heart against Deceptions, especially the ones that begin with "Hath God said?" and question the character and consistency of God. Allen says when you deceive yourself, you are really deceived because you have lost the measure of truth. Guard your heart against strongholds. Every vain thing that exalts itself against the knowledge of God.

Guard against deceptions and strongholds with the truth. Subtle lies and vain imaginations, but we all tell ourselves stories from our perspectives. And if we have a skewed perspective, the stories we tell ourselves will not be true. They are closely tied to deception. We might all know Someone who keeps telling themselves stories that have revised history from the way it was in our memory. Life has not been fair. The stories they tell themselves become their version of the truth without looking at all the blessings of shelter, clothing, family, and financial provision for them. We are not talking here about persons who definitely need justice and healing. This is about the perceived injustices with exaggerated imagination. Subtle lies focus on half of the truth without looking at the whole truth. We need to help these folks see options out of their plight. Often, they cannot see the way out. Because of their perspectives and totalizing language. All or nothing.

Guard your heart against vain imaginations with some serious soul care. And reframing life in terms of a healthy balance. 2 Corinthians 10:3-5, "Indeed, we live as human beings, but we do not wage war according to human standards; 4 for the weapons of our warfare are not merely human, but they have divine power to destroy strongholds. We destroy arguments 5, and every proud obstacle raised up against the knowledge of God, and we take every thought captive to obey Christ."

Lingering and lasting anger. Prov 15:1, "A gentle answer turns away wrath, But a harsh word stirs up anger." Prov 15:18, "A hot-tempered person stirs up strife, But the slow to anger calms a dispute." Do not let the sun go down on your anger. That was Allen's Dad's marriage advice to us when we got married in the 1970s. If you let the sun go down on your wrath with your anger, you leave room for the devil to get a foothold in your life. Eph 4:26-

---

[22] Hymn, "At Calvary,"
https://hymnary.org/text/years_i_spent_in_vanity_and_pride.

27, "Be angry and yet do not sin; do not let the sun go down on your anger,
27 and do not give the devil an opportunity."

Offenses are stumbling blocks to our souls. Offenses will come. Luke 17:1,
"Then He said to the disciples, 'It is impossible that no offenses should come,
but woe to him through whom they do come!'" Offenses come in various
ways. We personally get offended when someone or something does not
meet our expectations. We get offended, and we cause pain to ourselves when
we assign motives to actions. They did this BECAUSE. When we start
assigning the BECAUSE, then we are in danger of being and staying
offended. Proverbs 18:19, "A brother offended is harder to be won than a
strong city, And contentions are like the bars of a citadel." We borrow
offenses when we hear a story from a family member, friend, co-worker, or
news broadcast. When we borrow offenses, that is very dangerous. Two
persons can work out their offense without the one who heard the story in
the first place knowing about it. That borrowed offense, or even the original
offense. If it is not dealt with, this can lead to resentment. And resentments
can build upon one another. And become bitter in our souls.

Guard your heart against offenses with forgiveness. Up to seven times? No
seventy times seven. Matt 18:22, "Be on your guard against all kinds of
greed." Luke 12:15 (NIV), "A man's life, a person's life does not consist of
the abundance of their possessions." Lord of The Rings. Gollum. My
precious. Willing to steal, kill and destroy for the precious ring. How many
kinds of greed are there? As many as we can imagine. And more. Besides
money. Prestige. Position. Possessions. Property. Power. Guard your heart
against greed with intentional generosity. Eph 4:28 (NIV), "Anyone who has
been stealing must steal no longer, but must work, doing something useful
with their own hands, that they may have something to share with those in
need."

David and Bathsheba. David wanted a beautiful woman he saw bathing on a
rooftop and sent for her. But she belonged to another man. and David
plotted and planned to cover his sin. When Bathsheba was with child, David
sent for her husband from the battle, but Uriah slept at the door and did not
go into Bathsheba. Because he did not want to partake of the pleasures his
wife could offer while his soldiers were out in the field and not privileged to
be at home with their wives. So David arranged for Uriah to be up front in
the battle in a place where he would likely be killed. And it was all covered
up until God sent a prophet, Nathan, to tell David a story. Of a man with
one ewe lamb. David was angry with the man and ready to pronounce severe
judgment. Nathan said, "Thou art the man." David repented. The child died.

Psalm 51, "Create in me a clean HEART, O God. And renew a right spirit within me." We have a worship song like that. And it comes from this episode. After David does not guard his heart, he knows what he speaks when he is teaching his son, Solomon, and instructing Solomon to guard his heart with all diligence. To not let his heart wander. In the direction of gold, greed, or glory. And yet, Solomon was led astray by all of those. Amassing vast sums of gold, horses, and women.

Unhealthy Guarding. The Charles Dickens tale is now a Christmas movie about Scrooge. A Christmas Carol. We see Scrooge guarding his money, hoarding his money, one of the examples of stinginess with zero generosity. Dickens masterfully transforms this hardened heart into one that is generous. Through wake-up calls in night-time visitations. In contrast, on the other side, we have good guarding.

Good Guarding. Have a healthy view of self. Have the ability to say yes or no without feeling undue obligation or coercion. Have healthy relationships. Have a significant and genuine relationship with God through prayer and practicing the presence of God all throughout the day. A running conversation with God will do a lot to guard our hearts with diligence.

Guard your heart with wisdom. Discretion. Understanding. Guard your heart with the guidance of a friend or mentor. Guard your heart with the armor of God. Guard your heart with the promises of God. Having these promises let us. Encourage one another while it is yet today. Encourage one another to love and good deeds.

Flow. When we think of flow. Get in the flow. Go along with the flow. Rivers flow toward the ocean—the seas. If we float on a tube in North Georgia, we float down the river. We float downstream with the flow. Out of the heart flows the issues of life. What is flowing out of our hearts.? Out of the heart, the mouth speaks. Old country preacher saying. The mouth is the bucket that draws from the well of the heart. If your heart is not pure, neither will your mouth be. What do we desire to flow out of our hearts and mouths? 2 Corinthians 7:1 (KJV) "Having these (precious) promises, beloved, let us cleanse ourselves from all defilement of flesh and spirit perfecting holiness in the fear of God."

Issues of Life vs. Springs of Life. Issues. What are the issues? You have issues. I have issues. That is your issue. This is my issue. Emotional issues are a relatively new use of the term. Definition of Issue from Merriam Webster "1 issues plural revenue (such: proceeds from a source of as an estate) 2:the action of going, coming, or flowing out: egress, emergence[23] 3:a means or place of going out. Issues: A new visa or green card, A new stamp, A new coin. A new magazine, A new event in scripture. The woman with the issue of blood who was healed.

Military Illustration: Military Issue. Uniform, weapon, food, barracks. In the military, you need to be prepared to lay it all down for the good of the country. You may be told, "Here is your foxhole. If the enemy comes, you are going to die in place." But in peacetime or non-combat situations, you have some leave time and some weekends and nights off. Not drilling 24/7. Sometimes we are in crisis, and it is a 24/7 thing, but it does damage if that is a permanent situation. Damage may not be reparable. Example. John McCain. Years as a POW, and when he came back, he could not comb his own hair, and to the day he died, he could not comb his own hair. That damage was not reparable. But his heart was committed to serving his nation in whatever capacity as a statesman who had friends and colleagues on both sides of the aisle.

Issues are boundaries, Issues of life. Springs of life in some versions.

Guard with boundaries against intruders and encroachers. The issues of life in the Hebrew refer to boundaries, to borders. From here to there. We do not have to totally be enmeshed with another person to the detriment of our soul. We need to be able to feel free to say yes and to say no to invitations from persons in our sphere of ministry, sphere of family. The basic premise of healthy borders is that we can say yes. Sometimes and no, sometimes. This far and no further.

Guard against intruders and encroachers with healthy boundaries. Numbers 34:11-12, "Then the LORD spoke to Moses, saying, "Command the sons of Israel and say to them, 'When you enter the land of Canaan, this is the land that shall fall to you as an inheritance, even the land of Canaan according to its borders. This shall be your land according to its borders all around.'"

Have you ever had a reasonable request that became too much? Here are some questions you can ask yourself if a situation is bumping up against a boundary issue for you. Am I free to respond to this request or this person? Do I feel coerced or manipulated to respond to this request? Healthy boundaries say so far and no more. Of course, we need to submit all requests to God in prayer and ask the Lord if He is calling us to help to assist to say

---

[23] Emergence Definition & Meaning - Merriam-Webster.

yes or if there is another way to help this person OR answer this request without our time and treasure. And keeping our emotional health and emotional energy. Example: Last week, I spent a lot of emotional energy when a phone call rang. I prayed and asked the Lord if I needed to answer the call. I did not have the emotional energy for the call, so I texted the person and invited a conversation in the morning for the next day. A good night's sleep and a lot of prayers helped me to be ready to have the conversation the next day. Guard our hearts in expending emotional energy. We only have so much supply before we need to lie down in green pastures to restore our souls. Prayer and our continuing conversation with God will help us monitor our emotional energy output. Practice Sabbath.

Caregiver fatigue. Caregivers get fatigued. The tendency is to overcommit to the person in our care and spend ourselves over and above the resources we have. I see this in chaplaincy in many cases. And sometimes, adult children just cannot take care of their parents anymore, or parents are unable to take care of their medically challenged children without institutional assistance. Just like a monetary budget where we cannot spend more than we bring into the household for very long without overdraft fees, the emotional strength and energy only go so far before there is an overdraft .and we find ourselves overcommitted. Overstretched, out of gas on a lonely road, and burned out.

Guard our hearts against emotional and physical fatigue with prayer, rest, and restoration for our souls. We sometimes need to have strategic time off. Again, practice sabbath principles. Take time to seek the Lord, to pray. To lie down in green pastures, to restore our souls.

Humor pause. Do you remember the movie "What about Bob?"[24] Bill Murray plays a psychiatric patient, Bob Wiley, who is very lovable. But Bob oversteps his psychiatrist/counselor's boundaries when he follows the psychiatrist on the psychiatrist's family vacation. Despite how insulting Richard Dreyfuss, the psychiatrist, tries to be, Bob does not seem to be offended and keeps inserting himself into the family dinners and swimming. And other adventures. The psychiatrist was trying to have healthy boundaries by taking his family on vacation and finding rest for his soul. Still, instead, he was pushed over the edge emotionally, and he reacted in anger and plotted to rid himself of Bob. It is a comedy. But there is a lot of truth in comedy. We need to have healthy boundaries as we guard our hearts with all diligence. We all need a guard to say, "this far and no more." Old movie scenes come to mind. "Stop! Who goes there?" Perhaps we could have some wisdom

[24] "What About Bob?" https://www.imdb.com/title/tt0103241/.

parameters to teach ourselves and our children about Stop! Who goes there? And not allow increasing trespasses on our souls and spirits.

Hoover Dam. Facts on Hoover Dam. Strength under pressure. Compress two elephants in a shoe box. So many pounds per square inch. That it can fill 15 swimming pools in one second, this pressure is converted to powerful energy for the electrical grid for California, Nevada, and Arizona. But when a Dam is breached, destruction ensues. Some of us may have lived in Georgia when the Toccoa Falls dam failed. And many lost their homes, and close to 40 lives perished in the dam's collapse.

Diligence is a Virtue. It is a desirable quality. Verses on diligence. God rewards those who diligently seek Him. Moses gave instructions in Deuteronomy to keep the commandments and ordinances with diligence. Deut 4:9, "Only give heed to yourself and keep your soul diligently, so that you do not forget the things which your eyes have seen and they do not depart from your heart all the days of your life; but make them known to your sons and your grandsons. Joshua 23:11, "So take diligent heed to yourselves to love the LORD your God." Prov 8:17, "I love those who love me; And those who diligently seek me will find me. Prov 10:4, "Poor is he who works with a negligent hand, But the hand of the diligent makes rich." Prov 11:27, "He who diligently seeks good seeks favor, But he who seeks evil, evil will come to him." Isaiah 26:9 "At night my soul longs for You, Indeed, my spirit within me seeks You diligently; For when the earth experiences Your judgments The inhabitants of the world learn righteousness."

Diligence in NT. Romans 12:8 and 11, "or he who exhorts, in his exhortation; he who gives, with liberality; he who leads, with diligence; he who shows mercy, with cheerfulness. Not lagging in diligence, fervent in spirit. Serving the Lord." 2 Peter 1:5, "Now for this very reason, also, applying all diligence, in your faith supply moral excellence and in your moral excellence, knowledge." Hebrews. 6:11 "And we desire that each one of you should show the same diligence so as to realize the full assurance of hope unto the end." Hebrews11:6 (NKJV), "He who comes to God must believe that He is, and that He is a rewarder of those who diligently seek Him." Luke 21:34, "Be on guard, so that your hearts will not be weighted down with dissipation and drunkenness and the worries of life, and that day will not come on you suddenly like a trap."

What kind of person? We are called to be loving. We are called to be forgiving. We are called to bless one another. We are called to love one another fervently from a pure heart. If we see someone overtaken in a fault, we are to restore such a one with the spirit of gentleness. (Galatians 6:1-2). We are being formed and conformed to the image of Christ. The Holy Spirit is working to do something holy and beautiful in us. When we see something that is not Christ-like about our brother or sister, we can pray for them and trust that God, who began a good work in them, will complete it. Pray for one another that the Holy Spirit would continue to do the good work. God is the author and finisher of our faith.

When what is flowing out of us is pure and loving and compassionate and wise and grateful and peaceful. Then we are guarding our hearts with the diligence we need. We are harnessing the power, and we are becoming effective in life and ministry.

Check our Hearts. Do we have Relationships? We have people in the body of Christ we share the journey with who can speak into our lives. Do we have Persons who will ask us questions such as "How is it with your soul?" Persons who do life with us. Those who come alongside and care and love and help us, and we also have opportunities to help them. We have the Holy Spirit who convicts us of sins and transgressions and trespasses. And offers us the gift of repentance. True willingness to change our ways and walk in a new path. One who will renew our minds and our thinking and offer us another opportunity to make restitution and repair relational breaches. Are we seeking and asking forgiveness from God and one another? Are we praying with the psalmist, "Search me O God and see if there be any wicked way in me and lead me in paths of righteousness"?

Divine Exchange. Guard our hearts with diligence. Divine exchange opportunity today If we have found things issuing out of us that we know are not pleasing to the Lord. Suppose we are harboring anger, offenses, and residual resentments against family members or members of the body of Christ. Or against persons of any type, we do not have to be stuck in our impurities of thought. We do not need to be stuck in our judgments. Healing is available in wisdom. Gain wisdom. In righteousness.do the right thing. In relationships. Have healthy relationships. We can exchange our self-protection for God's protection In prayer. Pray for the peace of God.

Invitation. Maybe you have been having trouble guarding your heart with all diligence. Maybe you have been offended and have not resolved the offense. Maybe you have borrowed offenses. Maybe you have noticed that greed has a stronghold in your heart, that it got an inroad and set up camp in there. Maybe you want to repent of places in your life that you let in unhealthy things to your heart, and you want to confess and repent today for unhealthy things that have set up camp in your heart. Phil 4:7 (NIV), "And the peace of God, which transcends all understanding, will guard your hearts and your minds in Christ Jesus." Think of it, brothers and sisters. The PEACE of God. God's peace. Not like the peace the world offers. God's peace will guard our hearts and minds in Christ Jesus. Not just our hearts and our emotional centers but our minds, too. The way we think about things. The way we think determines who we are in our ways and our actions. If we remember as a man, as a woman, as a person, thinks in their heart .so are they. And we can have an overriding peace as our gift to guard our hearts and minds in Christ Jesus.

The GOOD NEWS is that because of Jesus, we can be free to be ALL that God wants us to be. We can be free. We are called to Liberty. In Christ Jesus. We are free to live and move and have our being in Christ. We are free to love and free to do right when we guard our hearts with all diligence. When the peace of God guards our hearts and minds in Christ Jesus, we can do justly, love mercy, and walk humbly with our God. Maybe you want to ask God to help you with boundary issues in your relationships. Places others have encroached on your generosity of time, talent, and treasure. Maybe you wanted to say no but did not feel that you could because you wanted to please them, or you did not want to cause offense, but it went against the way you wanted to guard your heart. It went against what you believed God was calling you to do.

Ministry Time. Whatever the reason. Whatever you need prayer for. We can begin the healing process in prayer. Some of us will be relieved and released through praying with and for one another. Caution. Do not be disappointed if this is not a "one prayer and done" process. Some of us will need more work after the prayer. We will need to spend time with the Lord alone, and we might need to talk with our small group leader or our pastor, or someone on the leadership team. Some of us have situations of over-commitment that we will need wisdom from one another to deal with. As we close this time, we will invite the Holy Spirit to come. We will invite those who will take time with one another to pray with and for one another.

Closing Prayer. O God, thank You for Your wisdom, for Your guidance, for Your direction, for Your instruction in righteousness. Search us, O God, and see our hearts. We confess our sins, our transgressions, our foibles, and our follies. We come to You today to ask Your forgiveness. Grant us new mercy today. Help us to heal from past wounds, offenses, and pain that have bound us and hindered us from freely flowing with You and Your ways. Let

Your word be a lamp to our feet and a light to our path. Lead us, O Lord, in paths of righteousness. Amen.

I Am There
Matthew 18:20

July 28, 2019

Matthew 18:20, *"For where two or three have gathered together in My name, I am there in their midst."*

Introduction: Thinking back to the days when we were raising our children, whenever we took a road trip, we would be on our way, we had left home, and predictably, one of the children would ask, "Are we THERE yet?" Sometimes when Allen and I are traveling I hear myself asking, Are we THERE yet? Am I the only one who wonders when we will be THERE? When we plan a trip we think of where we want to go. We leave a place called "here" and we go to a place called "there."

A couple of weeks ago three of us left Atlanta to go to Denver to the National Conference. We left "here" in Atlanta to go "there" to Denver. THERE had different sights to see different air to breathe, the elevation was different. When we were "THERE" in Colorado we were not "here" in Atlanta. When we left "here" to go "there" we were not here. We were THERE. Humans have a capacity to be in one place at a time. When we are "here" we are not "there." When we are "THERE" we are not here. I usually wait to post where I have been on social media until I get home. I write that I was THERE in the past tense but social media marks me present as if I were THERE THEN, at that time, it says I am HERE even though I am home. Last week we were privileged to offer some words of testimony about the conference when we returned from being THERE to being HERE.

Moon Anniversary. Recently, July 20th, the world celebrated the 50th anniversary of the Apollo 11 mission moon landing by Neil Armstrong, Buzz Aldrin, and Michael Collins, On 20 July 1969, the Eagle module from Apollo 11 landed at Tranquility Base. The moon landing marked the culmination of America's Cold War human spaceflight program and positioned itself as a global leader in science and technology. Apollo 11 represented the U.S. accomplishing a seemingly impossible goal on a seemingly impossible timeline. The astronauts left HERE on earth to go THERE to the moon and then they left THERE, the moon, to come back HERE, the earth.

C.S. Lewis Humor Moment. Parts of Speech, nouns and adverbs. C.S. Lewis from *That Hideous Strength.*

"There are no servants here," said Mother Dimble, "And we all do the work. The women do it one day and the men the next. What? No, it's a very sensible arrangement. The Director's idea is that men and women can't do housework together without quarreling. There's something in it. Of course, it doesn't do to look at the cups too closely on the men's day, but on the whole we get along pretty well."

"But why should they quarrel?" asked Jane.

"Different methods my dear. Men can't help in a job, you know. They can be induced to it: not to help while you're doing it. At least, it makes them grumpy."

The cardinal difficulty," said MacPhee, "in collaboration between the sexes is that women speak a language without nouns. If two men are doing a bit of work, one will say to the other, 'Put this bowl inside the bigger bowl which you'll find on the top shelf of the green cupboard.' The female for this is, 'Put that one in the other one there.' And then if you ask them, 'in where?' they say, 'in there, of course. There is consequently a phatic hiatus."

And then over100 years ago, the song "Over There." When I was growing up, my father used to sing around the house. One of the World War I songs I remember my father singing was called "Over There." We won't be back till it's over, over there. The premise was that the soldiers were leaving here to go THERE to fight and they would be back HERE after they fought OVER THERE. 1917 George M. Cohen

Over there, over there
Send the word, send the word over there
That the Yanks are coming
The Yanks are coming
The drums rum-tumming
Everywhere
So prepare, say a prayer
Send the word, send the word to beware
We'll be over, we're coming over
And we won't come back till it's over
Over there.

Songwriters have written songs about HERE and THERE. Perhaps you can think of titles of songs that have the word HERE in them or the word THERE in them. Almost 50 years ago, Michael Jackson had a huge hit in 1970 with "I'll be THERE," with the premise that if and when she needed him, he would be there. "Whenever you need me, I'll be there I'll be there to protect you, with an unselfish love I respect you Just call my name and I'll be there."

Mariah Carey in 2007 Lyrics. "You and I must make a pact. We must bring salvation back, Where there is love, I'll be there. (I'll be there). I'll reach out my hand to you. I'll have faith in all you do. Just call my name and I'll be there. (I'll be there)."

"You Meet Me Here," Is a new 2019 Vineyard worship song, "Where can I go from Your presence, where can I run from Your spirit, spirit You meet me there, Your love surrounds me, changing the atmosphere, you meet me here." This song has echoes of Psalm 139:7-8, "Where can I go from Your Spirit? Or where can I flee from Your presence? If I ascend to heaven, You are there; If I make my bed in Sheol, behold, You are there."

I am spending time this morning talking about HERE and THERE because our Bible verse this morning talks about a place where Jesus says, "I am there" and so we are going to look at the concepts of here and there just a bit. Here and There are adverbs. An adverb is a word or set of words that modifies verbs, adjectives, or other adverbs. Adverbs answer how, when, where, why, or to what extent—how often or how much. Here and there are both ADVERBS.

Sometimes I have found myself in a conversation with a person and I am diligently trying to be present with them, My intention is to be HERE with them, and then my mind wanders over THERE. My body is HERE and my mind is THERE. Am I the only one this happens to? It is a discipline to stay HERE and be with the person in front of us. When I am physically HERE and my mind wanders over THERE I need to return to the present HERE and not be preoccupied with my thoughts over THERE,

Our text today Matthew 18:20. "For where two or three have gathered together in My name, I am there in their midst." We have looked at and considered many of the I AM statements in the Bible in this series. Today we are looking at one more of the I AM statements. Today we are looking at the I am THERE statement of Jesus, This I AM THERE has to do with a promise of presence. Jesus promises to be THERE, to be present when two or three have gathered in His Name. In this verse, the presence of Christ is promised in the assemblies of those who gather in the name of Jesus. Every believer has the presence of Christ with him or her personally, but the promise here refers to the meetings where two or three are gathered in his name, Jesus promises that when two or three are gathered in His Name He is THERE.

When We talk about God, we can say "God is HERE" and mean that right now, right where we are, God is present. We can say "God is THERE" and mean that right now, somewhere else, somewhere other than HERE, God is THERE. When Jesus chose to limit himself to a human body while he was on earth, he could be physically present here OR there but not both HERE and THERE. One of the attributes of God, the Father, God the Creator, is that God is everywhere present, God is both HERE and THERE, immanent and transcendent. The Lord is "God in the heavens above (transcendent) and on the earth beneath (immanent)" (Josh 2:11). One of the attributes of God the Holy Spirit is that God the Holy Spirit is present generally and specifically.

We serve a God who is not absent from God's creation. God is present in the creation in specific ways. God acts in the creation. God acts in us and through us. One of the philosophers who helped me in my early 20s was Francis Schaeffer. He wrote a trilogy of books *Escape from Reason, The God who is THERE*, and *He is THERE and He is Not Silent*. Schaeffer had a ministry to youth backpacking through Europe asking difficult questions about meaning and purpose. Quote: "We are surrounded by a generation that can find 'no one home' in the universe. In contrast to this, as a Christian I know who I am; and I know the personal God who is there." In every age, this God continues to provide the anchor of truth and the power of love to meet the world's deepest problems.

The Holy Spirit is present in the Hebrew Bible, the Old Testament, We remember that the Spirit of God was moving over the surface of the waters in Genesis 1:2, "The earth was formless and void, and darkness was over the surface of the deep, and the Spirit of God was moving over the surface of the waters. Psalm 104: God and God's Creation. One of my favorite Psalms is Psalm 104 where we read in verse 30, "You send forth Your Spirit, they are created; And You renew the face of the ground." The Holy Spirit renews the face of the ground. God is involved with God's creation; the creatures are dependent upon the Creator, for food and breath,

God's Manifest Presence. God's presence was manifest with Adam and Eve in Eden. The garden of Eden was a dwelling place where the God the Creator and the ones created in the image of God related to one another before the fall. God is present in the Hebrew Bible, generally and specifically. In Exodus 29, part of the message Moses received on Mount Sinai when he went up into the presence of the Lord was about the Tabernacle. Exodus 29:43-46:

> *I will meet there with the sons of Israel, and it shall be consecrated by My glory. 44 I will consecrate the tent of meeting and the altar; I will also consecrate Aaron and his sons to minister as priests to Me. 45 I will dwell among the sons of Israel and will be their God. 46 They shall know that I am the Lord their God who brought them out of the land of Egypt, that I might dwell among them: I am the Lord their God.*

Notice: God enters God's creation to create a people and a place for God's presence. Placing God's Name and presence. After the Lord had met with the people of Israel in the tabernacle in the wilderness. Fast forward to the time they were in the promised land. David has brought the ark of the covenant back to Jerusalem with much worship and many sacrifices. It is in David's heart to build a temple for the Lord, but it is David's son, Solomon who builds the temple for the presence of the Lord. When the conditions were met for the temple and it was built and dedicated, God's presence filled the temple. The place where God said "There, I will place my name." 1 Kings 9:3, "The Lord said to him, "I have heard your prayer and your supplication, which you have made before Me; I have consecrated this house which you have built by putting My name THERE forever, and My eyes and My heart will be THERE perpetually.

God's presence filled the tabernacle/temple. This is a particularly special presence of the Lord, a manifest presence. 2 Chron 5:13-14, "When the trumpeters and the singers were to make themselves heard with one voice to praise and to glorify the Lord, and when they lifted up their voice accompanied by trumpets and cymbals and instruments of music, and when they praised the Lord saying, "He indeed is good for His lovingkindness is everlasting," then the house, the house of the Lord, was filled with a cloud, 14 so that the priests could not stand to minister because of the cloud, for the glory of the Lord filled the house of God."

God's presence came in the incarnation of Christ. When Jesus came, he was called Emanuel, "God with us" Isaiah 7:14, "Therefore the Lord Himself will give you a sign: Behold, a virgin will be with child and bear a son, and she will call His name Immanuel. Matthew 1:23, "Behold, the virgin shall be with child and shall bear a Son, and they shall call His name Immanuel," which translated means, "God with us."

The Ascension Promise. Matthew 28:20, "And lo, I am with you always, even to the end of the age." I am with you always, what a promise of presence, I am with you, I am with you, ALWAYS! Another promise, Hebrews 13:5, "For He Himself has said, "I will never desert you, nor will I ever forsake you."

Revelation and the new heaven and new earth. In Revelation we have the promise of dwelling with God, Revelation 21:3, "And I heard a loud voice from the throne, saying, "Behold, the tabernacle of God is among men, and He will dwell among them, and they shall be His people, and God Himself will be among them."

Death. When we die, we leave HERE and go THERE to be with the Lord and the saints who have gone before us. I have been to many funerals as a chaplain, I have had the privilege of watching persons transition from HERE to THERE. Where do persons go, another dimension of life, they leave HERE to go THERE.

Hebrews 10:24-25, "and let us consider how to stimulate one another to love and good deeds, 25 not forsaking our own assembling together, as is the habit of some, but encouraging one another; and all the more as you see the day drawing near." We are not to forsake the assembling of ourselves together. What happens when we assemble together in the name of Jesus? We have the promise of Jesus, "For where two or three have gathered together in My name, I am there in their midst." Gathering together in His Name, we are known by Him and by His name. Jesus is our point of gathering; we gather around the name of Jesus. And we have the promise of the presence of Jesus.

After Emmaus, Jesus appeared in the midst. Luke 24:36, "While they were telling these things, He Himself stood in their midst and said to them, "Peace be to you." In this case Jesus was physically in their midst, He appeared in their midst. They were gathered together in His name, and He appeared to them physically before He ascended into heaven. Context of Matthew 18:20. Look at verse 19, "Again I say to you, that if two of you agree on earth about anything that they may ask, it shall be done for them by My Father who is in heaven.

John 14:13, "Whatever you ask in My name, that will I do, so that the Father may be glorified in the Son. John 14:14, "If you ask Me anything in My name, I will do it." John 14:26, "But the Helper, the Holy Spirit, whom the Father will send in My name, He will teach you all things, and bring to your remembrance all that I said to you." John 15:16, "You did not choose Me, but I chose you, and appointed you that you would go and bear fruit, and that your fruit would remain, so that whatever you ask of the Father in My name He may give to you."

In the Name of Jesus. John 16:23-24, "Truly, truly, I say to you, if you ask the Father for anything in My name, He will give it to you. 24 Until now you have asked for nothing in My name; ask and you will receive, so that your joy may be made full." Prayer involves abiding, asking, and receiving. Jesus said, "If you abide in Me, and My Words abide in you, you shall ask what you will, and it shall be done" (John 15:7). "Whatsoever you shall ask in prayer, believing, you shall receive" (Matthew 21:22).

Early church gathering. Acts 2:46, "Day by day continuing with one mind in the temple, and breaking bread from house to house, they were taking their meals together with gladness and sincerity of heart." Acts 5:42, "And every day, in the temple and from house to house, they kept right on teaching and preaching Jesus as the Christ." They worshipped in the temple and brought the good news of Jesus the Messiah to the temple and then a shift happened, not only did they go to a physical temple; they became the temple of the Holy Spirit. When they were in one accord in the Upper Room, the Spirit filled them, and they became the temple of the Holy Spirit. Now, We are the temple of the Holy Spirit, we are the dwelling place of God.

The promise is "that if two of you shall agree on earth as touching anything that they shall ask, it shall be done for them of My Father which is in heaven. For where two or three are gathered together in My Name, there am I in the midst of them" Binding and Loosing Context "Truly, I say to you, whatever you bind on earth shall be bound in heaven, and whatever you loose on earth shall be loosed in heaven. Again I say to you, if two of you agree on earth about anything they ask, it will be done for them by my Father in heaven. For where two or three are gathered in my name, there am I in the midst of them" (RSV). As we look at these words about binding and loosing, we can see that though we do not understand all about them, nevertheless it is apparent that prayer is authority, an authority which operates in mystery.

Prayer is the link to that invisible world which is the control center of all human life. We stand between two worlds when we pray. James 5:16 (CEB), "For this reason, confess your sins to each other and pray for each other so that you may be healed. The prayer of the righteous person is powerful in what it can achieve."

When we pray, we are HERE, but we can be HERE and pray for something THERE. Our prayers are not limited to HERE. We can touch the world through prayer. Example: We can be HERE praying for the persecuted church THERE, and God who is THERE, and HERE, will take our prayers HERE and answer our HERE prayers over THERE. Intercession helps us agree together to see God's will be done HERE on earth as it is already being done in heaven.

Luke 12:34, "For where your treasure is, THERE your heart will be also." This is also true the other way, we are God's treasured people, His heart is with us and God is PRESENT HERE with us when we gather in His Name. When two or three are gathered together in My Name I am THERE, in their midst. If Jesus is our treasure, our hearts will want to be with Jesus, we will gather together, we will pray, we will worship, we will honor the Lord, and Jesus will be THERE with us.

Waiting for the wind. When we went to the Come, Holy Spirit Conference in Denver one of the lessons we learned was the importance of waiting. Speakers would delay delivering their message when they sensed the Holy Spirit wind was blowing. We saw waves of the manifest presence of God visibly touching persons. We saw persons trembling, hands quivering, bodies bending, tears flowing. In John 3:8 Jesus said "the wind blows wherever it pleases. You hear its sound, but you cannot tell where it comes from or where it is going. So is everyone who is born of the spirit. We cannot see the wind, but we can see the effects of the wind, when the Lord is in our midst, we can put up the sail to catch the wind, our worship, our prayers, our fellowship together, are all ways of sending up the sail to catch the wind.

Closing Prayer: Dear Lord, We thank You that You are HERE, that when we gather together You are THERE, that You ARE God, You exist, You are not some mere fable, You are God. We thank You for those who were eyewitnesses of Your majesty, who beheld Your glory. We thank You, Jesus, for becoming flesh and dwelling among us. Come, Holy Spirit. Come and minister Your life and love and healing power in our midst. Come and touch our lives with YOUR presence. In Jesus Name, Amen.

Ministry Time: And now we will offer ministry time, We will wait, If you see someone who is being touched by the Lord, wait, and then ask if you can pray with them, we will also have a place up front over THERE if you want to come forward for prayer.

Jesus in the Ordinary
Matthew 11:25

December 27, 2020

Matthew 11:25 (CEV), *"At that moment Jesus said: My Father, Lord of heaven and earth, I am grateful that you hid all this from wise and educated people and showed it to ordinary people."*

Opening Prayer: Lord, as we open the scriptures today, we want to hear from You to learn from You and to be encouraged with the good news of the gospel today. Teach us we pray, Amen.

Introduction. Holidays and Ordinary Days. Most of the days of the year are not holidays, which being translated means holy day, a day fixed by law or custom on which ordinary business is suspended in commemoration of some event or in honor of some person. Most of the days of the year are ordinary days. If we only served Jesus and celebrated Jesus on special occasions, we would only think about Jesus on Christmas and Easter/Resurrection Day, and that is sad. Jesus is with us on both the holidays and on the ordinary days. The sermon today is about Jesus in the Ordinary. It is about ordinary people serving Jesus with their ordinary lives. It is about Jesus using ordinary examples to teach spiritual lessons. It is about the supernatural infusing the natural, the ordinary, all around us and the treasure inside of us.

Let's start with a definition. Ordinary is a word that serves as both an adjective and a noun. Adjective, with no special or distinctive features; normal. Noun. That which is commonplace or standard. So, then, Ordinary is Normal, commonplace, standard. In the NT, it can also mean common, uneducated, or unskilled.

Ordinary Time. There is something in the Church Calendar called Ordinary Time. When is it? It is most of the year between Christmas and Lent preceding Easter. And Between Easter and Advent preceding Christmas. The color of ordinary time vestments is green. Green is the color of growth. It is in ordinary times that we continue to grow as we walk with Jesus.

Ordinary carpentry. Jesus worked with his father in the ordinary, skilled trade of carpentry in Nazareth, where he grew up. In Matthew 13:54-57:

He came to his hometown and began to teach the people in their synagogue, so that they were astounded and said, "Where did this man get this wisdom and these deeds of power? 55 Is not this the carpenter's son? Is not his mother called Mary? And are not his brothers James and Joseph and Simon and Judas? 56 And are not all his sisters with us? Where then did this man get all this?" 57 And they took offense at him.

Question: How many ordinary, commonplace, standard days did Jesus spend? We do not know from scripture. We have roughly 30 years of Jesus growing and living days and years of village life in Nazareth. We do know that In his ordinary days, he grew in wisdom and stature and favor.

Children Grow. Our children will grow year by year. Some houses have special places on the wall or the doorframe where children are measured against a yardstick, and a little mark is placed there at the top of their heads. The following year the mark is higher up the wall. Day by day, if they stood next to the mark, it would not make much difference, but year over year, it makes a big difference, children grow taller, and children learn about life along the way

Ordinary days. Many days of our lives seem filled with routines. We could say they were ordinary days. What happens on ordinary days? Ordinary routines. If making coffee happens every day, then making coffee is part of your ordinary day. If brushing your teeth happens every day, then brushing your teeth is part of your ordinary day. We could list ordinary things that happen on our ordinary days, but this year has not been an ordinary year.

This 2020 has not been an ordinary year. When we look back on a year ago, we could think our lives were ordinary compared to now. This year, routines have been interrupted. The ordinary has become very difficult for the world: food insecurity, job insecurity, financial insecurity, housing insecurity, and health insecurity.

We continue to pray prayers of lament. How long, O Lord? We cry out, O Come, O Come Emmanuel. God is with us in "both-and" of life. God is with us in the exceptions to the ordinary and in the ordinary.

Jesus called twelve ordinary people to follow Jesus in their ordinary lives. Luke 6:12-16 (ESV):

In these days he went out to the mountain to pray, and all night he continued in prayer to God. 13 And when day came, he called his disciples and chose from them twelve, whom he named apostles: 14 Simon, whom he named Peter, and

Andrew his brother, and James and John, and Philip, and Bartholomew, 15 and Matthew, and Thomas, and James the son of Alphaeus, and Simon who was called the Zealot, 16 and Judas the son of James, and Judas Iscariot, who became a traitor.

We read about the disciples Jesus chose, ordinary men, fishermen, tax collectors, a zealot, and an embezzler. He invested days and years into these ordinary people. Jesus walked among ordinary people. He was accused of eating with ordinary people, tax collectors, and sinners.

The reformer, Martin Luther, taught the concept of the "priesthood of all believers." Before the Protestant Reformation, and since the Protestant Reformation, many churches separated the clergy from the laity. Martin Luther taught that whatever we did for work was holy to the Lord. We were priests to the Lord whether we dug ditches, worked in a skilled trade, or had a clergy occupation.

This was not an either/or holy or ordinary dichotomy. God infuses the ordinary with the holy. We have daily opportunities to notice God in the ordinary and to see how God infuses the ordinary with the holy. Jesus taught parables with ordinary illustrations.

Ordinary examples of the garment and wine. Turn to Luke 5:36-39:

He also told them a parable: "No one tears a piece from a new garment and puts it on an old garment. If he does, he will tear the new, and the piece from the new will not match the old. 37 And no one puts new wine into old wineskins. If he does, the new wine will burst the skins and it will be spilled, and the skins will be destroyed. 38 But new wine must be put into fresh wineskins. 39 And no one after drinking old wine desires new, for he says, 'The old is good.'"

Ordinary Examples of the sawdust and plank. Luke 6:39-42:

He also told them a parable: "Can a blind man lead a blind man? Will they not both fall into a pit? 40 A disciple is not above his teacher, but everyone when he is fully trained will be like his teacher. 41 Why do you see the speck that is in your brother's eye, but do not notice the log that is in your own eye? 42 How can you say to your brother, 'Brother, let me take out the speck that is in your eye,' when you yourself do not see the log that is in your own eye? You hypocrite, first take the log out of your own eye, and then you will see clearly to take out the speck that is in your brother's eye.

Ordinary Examples of a Tree and its Fruit. Luke 6:43-45:

For no good tree bears bad fruit, nor again does a bad tree bear good fruit, 44 for each tree is known by its own fruit. For figs are not gathered from thornbushes, nor are grapes picked from a bramble bush. 45 The good person out of the good treasure of his heart produces good, and the evil person out of his evil treasure produces evil, for out of the abundance of the heart his mouth speaks.

Ordinary Examples: Building on a foundation. Luke 6:46-49:

Why do you call me 'Lord, Lord,' and not do what I tell you? 47 Everyone who comes to me and hears my words and does them, I will show you what he is like: 48 he is like a man building a house, who dug deep and laid the foundation on the rock. And when a flood arose, the stream broke against that house and could not shake it, because it had been well built. 49 But the one who hears and does not do them is like a man who built a house on the ground without a foundation. When the stream broke against it, immediately it fell, and the ruin of that house was great.

Ordinary examples: farmer, seed, and soil. Luke 8-4-8:

And when a great crowd was gathering and people from town after town came to him, he said in a parable, 5 "A sower went out to sow his seed. And as he sowed, some fell along the path and was trampled underfoot, and the birds of the air devoured it. 6 And some fell on the rock, and as it grew up, it withered away, because it had no moisture. 7 And some fell among thorns, and the thorns grew up with it and choked it. 8 And some fell into good soil and grew and yielded a hundredfold." As he said these things, he called out, "He who has ears to hear, let him hear."

The Purpose of the Parables. Explanation Luke 8:9-15:

And when his disciples asked him what this parable meant, 10 he said, "To you it has been given to know the secrets of the kingdom of God, but for others they are in parables, so that 'seeing they may not see, and hearing they may not understand.' 11 Now the parable is this: The seed is the word of God. 12 The ones along the path are those who have heard; then the devil comes and takes away the word from their hearts, so that they may not believe and be saved. 13 And the ones on the rock are those who, when they hear the word, receive it with joy. But these have no root; they believe for a while, and in time of testing fall away. 14 And as for what fell among the thorns, they are those who hear, but as they go on their way they are choked by the cares and riches and pleasures of life, and their fruit does not mature. 15 As for that in the good soil, they are those who, hearing the word, hold it fast in an honest and good heart, and bear fruit with patience.

Praying the parable of the soils. Praying the parable of the soils. Show me the places in my heart that are being choked by weeds, eaten away, and have shallow roots. Transform my heart to be good soil to receive and act on Your words. And pray for those who, hearing the word, will hold it fast in an honest and good heart and bear fruit with patience.

Other ordinary examples: lamp, light, darkness, lamps, lampstands, dark, light, fig tree, sheep, goats, treasure, and pearl.

We have this treasure. 2 Corinthians 4:7 (MSG), "If you only look at us, you might well miss the brightness. We carry this precious Message around in the unadorned clay pots of our ordinary lives. That's to prevent anyone from confusing God's incomparable power with us." The NRSV reads, "But we have this treasure in clay jars, so that it may be made clear that this extraordinary power belongs to God and does not come from us." A treasure is not ordinary. A treasure is amazing, wonderful, extraordinary. Our treasure is hidden in clay pots, the "unadorned clay pots of our ordinary lives."

Heroes who did not know they were heroes. When we think of a hero, we think of someone who did something special, outstanding, amazing, marvelous, something of notable memory. I think of history and the names of notable people who have been written about for notoriety in one way or another. The Bible is full of ordinary people who became heroes, who did exploits and genealogies of people in lists of names of ancestors. We might not know anything about the father or grandfather or mother, but we see that most of the ones highlighted in scripture had fathers and mothers.

God interrupts ordinary things and ordinary people with extraordinary circumstances. And sometimes we see it, and sometimes others see it. One person who became a hero is the little boy in the feeding of the 5000. A boy had his lunch. We do not know his name. We do not know his reason for being in the crowd. We can imagine that when the crowd was gathering, some people would be curious to see what was happening. The feeding of the 5000 is recorded in all four gospels. Only John's gospel tells us about the boy. John 6:8-9, "One of his disciples, Andrew, Simon Peter's brother, said to him, 9 "There is a boy here who has five barley loaves and two fish. But what are they among so many people?" God took an ordinary boy with an ordinary lunch and did an extraordinary thing. Jesus blessed it and broke the bread, and it multiplied, and there were twelve baskets left over. This miracle is the extraordinary kingdom breaking into this ordinary cosmos. We can imagine that The boy had a story to tell about what Jesus did with his lunch that day, and there were witnesses who saw it happen. We can believe that if Jesus could multiply the loaves and fishes, Jesus could also bring His extraordinary to our ordinary offering.

The Bible is also full of nameless ordinary people who were part of crowds, and nations, lived in cities, towns, and villages, and we do not know their names. We may be ordinary to someone who notices our love for them and our love for God in our everyday routines. When we look for and find and notice treasure in one another, we are in the ministry of encouraging one another.

(Segue to John Woolman) John Woolman lived in the 1700s. We know about him through his journal and persons who have read The Journal of John Woolman and have mentioned him in his writings. The Journal has been continuously in print since 1774, published in numerous editions; the most recent scholarly edition was published in 1989. John Woolman was known for his simple lifestyle, for treating persons with respect and dignity, for being an abolitionist among the Quakers in the north, the group of Christ-followers he was part of.

One chapter of his journal that I read aloud to Allen this past week describes a decision about traveling on a ship to England in 1772 and the length of time he spent discerning how he was to travel with what accommodations, and through prayer, his conscience troubled him about staying in a finely decorated cabin. He settled on having peace about traveling in the lower part of the ship, the steerage. And then, reading on, we can read of his adventures and what he noticed in the steerage of the ship, and his prayers for the sailors and young boys who were training to be sailors. He was an ordinary man with an ordinary life of prayer about ordinary things that he wrote about. And we know some of the fruit of his life even though, at the time, he did not know how God would use him and his example to touch so many lives and influence so many future generations.

When Jesus saw the people gathered, he called them to come and take his yoke, his yoke is easy, and his burden is light. He promised rest for their souls, and he prayed this about ordinary people in Matthew 11:25 (CEV) "At that moment Jesus said: My Father, Lord of heaven and earth, I am grateful that you hid all this from wise and educated people and showed it to ordinary people."

It is Christ in us, the hope of glory. Think about front-line workers the ordinary people who have become heroes in this pandemic. Here is a short list. Healthcare workers, EMTs, fire, police, grocery workers, and mail carriers. Stories are being told and will be told of ordinary persons who served God with their ordinary lives as a service to others.

We are praying for Daily Bread. Jesus taught us to pray for daily bread, and when we do, we are inviting God to provide, noticing the provision, and being grateful for it. When we feed the hungry, we are part of the kingdom coming, with daily bread for the ones who need sustenance.

Pray ask, seek, knock. Look at Luke 11:9-13 (ESV):

> *And I tell you, ask, and it will be given to you; seek, and you will find; knock, and it will be opened to you. 10 For everyone who asks receives, and the one who seeks finds, and to the one who knocks it will be opened. 11 What father among you, if his son asks for a fish, will instead of a fish give him a serpent; 12 or if he asks for an egg, will give him a scorpion? 13 If you then, who are evil, know how to give good gifts to your children, how much more will the heavenly Father give the Holy Spirit to those who ask him!"*

As a chaplain, I attended many funerals of ordinary people, hard-working, fun-loving, ordinary people who had families or no family members left. How their stories are told and remembered is significant here and in the history of Christ-followers. We are living examples of how Jesus can take ordinary people with ordinary days and infuse our ordinary with his love, grace, and mercy. "Who lives, who dies, who tells your story?" This is a line from the song in the musical Hamilton that muses about who lives, who dies, and who tells your story really matters in both who is remembered and how they are remembered.

Ask, seek, and knock. Story of George Mueller (27 September 1805 – 10 March 1898). He saw the need for orphanages after the worsening cholera epidemic left children without parents on the streets or who were forced into the workhouse. George Müller realized immediate action was required. In 1835 he called a public meeting with a view to opening an Orphan Home. And over the years, he opened more homes and served more children. Müller built five houses for orphaned children, where 10,000 young Victorians were cared for before his death. So many good stories of seeing God answer specific prayers. In the Daily Bread story, the baker could not sleep and awakened at 2:00 am to bake bread for the children.

Meanwhile, the milkman knocked, and his milk cart broke down outside the orphanage and wanted to unload the wagon so that he could repair it, donating the milk on the wagon to the children. In the Fog at Sea story, Mueller had an appointment to preach in Canada. He had not missed an appointment and took the captain aside to pray and had a sense that the fog was gone, and it was, and he preached on schedule in Canada. Asking, seeking, knocking, and doors were opened.

We are going to have some ordinary days and some very special days. Whether we are doing our usual routines or doing celebratory things, we can find Jesus in each day. Our challenge this week is to find a new way to notice what Jesus is doing this week. Pray specifically to see something, notice something, read something, or listen to something that is an invitation to prayer, to gratitude, to intercession, to praise.

We sing a song called "It's a Slow Kingdom Coming," that talks about waiting until the day that every knee will bow, and every tongue confess that Jesus Christ is Lord. We will wait for that day. We are called to have a long obedience in the same direction as Eugene Peterson wrote about in his book on the Psalms of Ascent to Jerusalem.

Two prayers from the 1200s we can still pray today. Francis of Assisi prayed where there is hatred, let me sow love, where there is darkness, let me sow light, and so on. Richard, Bishop of Chichester, prayed in 1253, Day by day, dear Lord, of thee three things I pray: to see thee more clearly, love thee more dearly, follow thee more nearly, day by day."

When we pray the prayer that Jesus taught his disciples, "Your kingdom come on earth as it is in heaven," we are praying for the furtherance of the kingdom of God to spread here on earth. We are inviting the noticing of the kingdom.

Ministry Time: We are here for you. We are so glad you joined us today or that you tuned in to listen later. At Liberty Vineyard Church, we have a Pastoral Care Team who will pray with you, meet with you, and listen to you. We endeavor to share the love and light we have received with those in our church family, in our community, and in the larger Body of Christ. You can send prayer requests and praise reports on our website and listen to our sermons there as well as see the various opportunities to serve the Lord with us.

Closing Prayer: Lord God, we are so grateful for who You are and for the opportunity to see another day. In each of our days, Lord, teach us to pray, to praise, to love well, and serve well. Give us today our daily bread, Lord. Yours is the kingdom and the power, and the glory forever and ever. Amen.

Benediction: May the Lord bless you and keep you in your ordinary comings and goings this week and give you peace.

John the Baptist: Prepare the Way of the Lord
Luke 1:13-17

November 27, 2016

Luke 1:13-17 (NRSV), *"But the angel said to him, 'Do not be afraid, Zechariah, for your prayer has been heard. Your wife Elizabeth will bear you a son, and you will name him John. You will have joy and gladness, and many will rejoice at his birth, for he will be great in the sight of the Lord. He must never drink wine or strong drink; even before his birth he will be filled with the Holy Spirit. He will turn many of the people of Israel to the Lord their God. With the spirit and power of Elijah he will go before him, to turn the hearts of parents to their children, and the disobedient to the wisdom of the righteous, to make ready a people prepared for the Lord.'"*

Introduction. When you hear the word prepare or preparing, what do you think of? What have you had to prepare for in your life? Coaches prepare teams for competition. In our house, we prepare holiday meals with family and friends. For vacations. Maps, arrangements. More prep for camping trips. More gear. Christmas with shopping lists, Christmas card lists, and decorations. This year we have spent the year preparing to move and moving from one house to another, and we are still in the process.

Preparation. In the Bible, we have a record of God's preparation of places, of purposes, and of people. From Creation to Revelation, we see the hand of God calling and preparing a people for His glory. Before the foundations of the world, Christ became the Lamb of God, willing to leave the glories of heaven and redeem a people who were caught in the mire of sin and death. God sent prophets to call people to repentance and to offer hope in times of oppression and exile. Prophets prepared the way of the Lord. In the Hebrew Bible, prophets were not popular. They were often ostracized from the community. Ezekiel was given a word that he was to preach to a people who would not hear him. Isaiah offered messages of judgment and hope. Jeremiah wrote a prophetic book that the king burned in the fire and put Jeremiah in the dungeon. The prophets are accountable to God for their message. Malachi 3:1 "Behold, I am going to send My messenger, and he will clear the way before Me. Malachi ends with a promise of one who would come.in Malachi 4:5-6, "Behold, I am going to send you Elijah the prophet before the coming of the great and terrible day of the Lord. 6 He will restore the hearts of the fathers to their children and the hearts of the children to their fathers, so that I will not come and smite the land with a curse."

John the Baptist comes as a fulfillment of the prophecy of Malachi. Similarities to Elijah: A prophet in the wilderness who spoke truth to the powerful leaders of his day. Elijah was described as a hairy man wearing a leather belt around his waist in 2 Kings 1:8. John the Baptist comes as a fulfillment of the prophecy in Isaiah 40:3-5:

A voice cries out:
"In the wilderness prepare the way of the Lord,
make straight in the desert a highway for our God.
4 Every valley shall be lifted up,
and every mountain and hill be made low;
the uneven ground shall become level,
and the rough places a plain.
5 Then the glory of the Lord shall be revealed,
and all people shall see it together,
for the mouth of the Lord has spoken.

John the Baptist comes as a fulfillment of Hosea 2:13-15:

I will punish her for the festival days of the Baals,
when she offered incense to them
and decked herself with her ring and jewelry,
and went after her lovers,
and forgot me, says the Lord.

14 Therefore, I will now allure her,
and bring her into the wilderness,
and speak tenderly to her.
15 From there I will give her her vineyards,
and make the Valley of Achor a door of hope.

There she shall respond as in the days of her youth,
as at the time when she came out of the land of Egypt.

Harbinger. A harbinger is one who signals the arrival of another. Like frost signals winter. Like buds on the tree signal spring, a harbinger is also one who prepares the way for another, like a company of persons sent to clear the obstacles out of the way for a visiting dignitary. Hosea was speaking of a harbinger of hope in the wilderness. John the Baptist is a harbinger of hope.

One who would initiate a major change. One who would prepare the way of the Lord. The Lamb of God.

All four Gospels. The gospel writers all record something about John the Baptist. We will be reading a lot of scripture this morning from Luke 1, Luke 3, Matthew 3, Mark 1, John 1, and others, but we will be skipping around because it takes several vantage points of the picture to paint the picture and each gospel writer is writing from a different lens, a different perspective.

Luke 1. Turn with me, if you will, to Luke Chapter 1, and we will read about the promise of the birth of John the Baptist to his parents. Zechariah and Elizabeth are both descended from priests. Elizabeth from Aaron and Zachariah from Abijah. And they have been praying. Both were advanced in years and barren and crying out to God for a son. Something is about to happen. Let's start with verse 5 of Chapter 1. Read the scripture: Luke 1:5-25, 36-45, 57-80.

> *In the days of King Herod of Judea, there was a priest named Zechariah, who belonged to the priestly order of Abijah. His wife was a descendant of Aaron, and her name was Elizabeth. 6 Both of them were righteous before God, living blamelessly according to all the commandments and regulations of the Lord. 7 But they had no children, because Elizabeth was barren, and both were getting on in years. 8 Once when he was serving as priest before God and his section was on duty, 9 he was chosen by lot, according to the custom of the priesthood, to enter the sanctuary of the Lord and offer incense. 10 Now at the time of the incense offering, the whole assembly of the people was praying outside. 11 Then there appeared to him an angel of the Lord, standing at the right side of the altar of incense. 12 When Zechariah saw him, he was terrified; and fear overwhelmed him.*

Luke 1, notice that Zechariah is fulfilling his duty according to his time on the calendar. It was his turn to offer the incense. He was not expecting to see an angel. It causes me to wonder. How many of us have been praying and then come to worship God and do not expect to see God or God's messenger there? Continuing with the angel's announcement in verses 13-17:

> *But the angel said to him, "Do not be afraid, Zechariah, for your prayer has been heard. Your wife Elizabeth will bear you a son, and you will name him John. 14 You will have joy and gladness, and many will rejoice at his birth, 15 for he will be great in the sight of the Lord. He must never drink wine or strong drink; even before his birth he will be filled with the Holy Spirit. 16 He will turn many of the people of Israel to the Lord their God. 17 With the spirit and power of Elijah he will go before him, to turn the hearts of parents to their*

children, and the disobedient to the wisdom of the righteous, to make ready a people prepared for the Lord.

The angel announces the fulfillment of the prophetic words of the prophets of old. The scriptures are now to be fulfilled. This is a time to praise and thank God for sending a wonderful and awesome angel with this magnificent proclamation! It is not every day that Zechariah goes to offer incense. And now he is slow to believe this message from the angel's mouth in the temple of the Lord. Continuing in verses 18-23:

> *Zechariah said to the angel, "How will I know that this is so? For I am an old man, and my wife is getting on in years." 19 The angel replied, "I am Gabriel. I stand in the presence of God, and I have been sent to speak to you and to bring you this good news. 20 But now, because you did not believe my words, which will be fulfilled in their time, you will become mute, unable to speak, until the day these things occur. 21 Meanwhile the people were waiting for Zechariah, and wondered at his delay in the sanctuary. 22 When he did come out, he could not speak to them, and they realized that he had seen a vision in the sanctuary. He kept motioning to them and remained unable to speak. 23 When his time of service was ended, he went to his home.*

And then we read that the angel's words were true. "After those days his wife Elizabeth conceived, and for five months she remained in seclusion. She said, "This is what the Lord has done for me when he looked favorably on me and took away the disgrace I have endured among my people."

The birth narratives of Jesus and John are intertwined in this chapter. Skip to verse 36, where Gabriel is telling Mary she has been chosen and about Elizabeth. Luke 1:36-45:

> *And now, your relative Elizabeth in her old age has also conceived a son; and this is the sixth month for her who was said to be barren. 37 For nothing will be impossible with God." 38 Then Mary said, "Here am I, the servant of the Lord; let it be with me according to your word." Then the angel departed from her. (Mary Visits Elizabeth) 39 In those days Mary set out and went with haste to a Judean town in the hill country, 40 where she entered the house of Zechariah and greeted Elizabeth. 41 When Elizabeth heard Mary's greeting, the child leaped in her womb. And Elizabeth was filled with the Holy Spirit 42 and exclaimed with a loud cry, "Blessed are you among women, and blessed is the fruit of your womb. 43 And why has this happened to me, that the mother of my Lord comes to me? 44 For as soon as I heard the sound of your greeting, the*

child in my womb leaped for joy. 45 And blessed is she who believed that there would be a fulfillment of what was spoken to her by the Lord.

Notice: Elizabeth is filled with the Holy Spirit and blesses and prophesies to Mary, the mother of MY LORD. There will be a fulfillment. The Birth of John the Baptist, Luke 1:57-66:

Now the time came for Elizabeth to give birth, and she bore a son. 58 Her neighbors and relatives heard that the Lord had shown his great mercy to her, and they rejoiced with her. 59 On the eighth day they came to circumcise the child, and they were going to name him Zechariah after his father. 60 But his mother said, "No; he is to be called John." 61 They said to her, "None of your relatives has this name." 62 Then they began motioning to his father to find out what name he wanted to give him. 63 He asked for a writing tablet and wrote, "His name is John." And all of them were amazed. 64 Immediately his mouth was opened and his tongue freed, and he began to speak, praising God. 65 Fear came over all their neighbors, and all these things were talked about throughout the entire hill country of Judea. 66 All who heard them pondered them and said, "What then will this child become?" For, indeed, the hand of the Lord was with him.

Notice: John's father, Zechariah, was mute until he corroborated the name Elizabeth gave, "John." Then, Zechariah prophesies in Luke 1:67-80:

Then his father Zechariah was filled with the Holy Spirit and spoke this prophecy:

68 "Blessed be the Lord God of Israel,
for he has looked favorably on his people and redeemed them.
69 He has raised up a mighty savior for us
in the house of his servant David,
70 as he spoke through the mouth of his holy prophets from of old,
71 that we would be saved from our enemies and from the hand of all who hate us.
72 Thus he has shown the mercy promised to our ancestors,
and has remembered his holy covenant,
73 the oath that he swore to our ancestor Abraham,
to grant us 74 that we, being rescued from the hands of our enemies,
might serve him without fear, 75 in holiness and righteousness
before him all our days.
76 And you, child, will be called the prophet of the Most High;
for you will go before the Lord to prepare his ways,
77 to give knowledge of salvation to his people

by the forgiveness of their sins.
78 By the tender mercy of our God,
the dawn from on high will break upon us,
79 to give light to those who sit in darkness and in the shadow of death,
to guide our feet into the way of peace."

80 The child grew and became strong in spirit, and he was in the wilderness
until the day he appeared publicly to Israel.

Luke places this ministry in an exact historical context. Let's turn now to Luke 3:1-20 where John the Baptist is a voice crying in the wilderness.

In the fifteenth year of the reign of Emperor Tiberius, when Pontius Pilate was governor of Judea, and Herod was ruler of Galilee, and his brother Philip ruler of the region of Ituraea and Trachonitis, and Lysanias ruler of Abilene, 2 during the high priesthood of Annas and Caiaphas, the word of God came to John son of Zechariah in the wilderness. 3 He went into all the region around the Jordan, proclaiming a baptism of repentance for the forgiveness of sins, 4 as it is written in the book of the words of the prophet Isaiah,

"The voice of one crying out in the wilderness:
'Prepare the way of the Lord,
make his paths straight.
5 Every valley shall be filled,
and every mountain and hill shall be made low,
and the crooked shall be made straight,
and the rough ways made smooth;
6 and all flesh shall see the salvation of God.'"

We remember this is the fulfillment of Isaiah 40:3-5. Continuing with John the Baptist in the Wilderness in verses 7-20:

John said to the crowds that came out to be baptized by him, "You brood of vipers! Who warned you to flee from the wrath to come? 8 Bear fruits worthy of repentance. Do not begin to say to yourselves, 'We have Abraham as our ancestor'; for I tell you, God is able from these stones to raise up children to Abraham. 9 Even now the ax is lying at the root of the trees; every tree therefore that does not bear good fruit is cut down and thrown into the fire." 10 And the crowds asked him, "What then should we do?" 11 In reply he said to them, "Whoever has two coats must share with anyone who has none; and whoever has food must do likewise." 12 Even tax collectors came to be baptized, and they asked him, "Teacher, what should we do?" 13 He said to them, "Collect no

> *more than the amount prescribed for you." 14 Soldiers also asked him, "And we, what should we do?" He said to them, "Do not extort money from anyone by threats or false accusation, and be satisfied with your wages." 15 As the people were filled with expectation, and all were questioning in their hearts concerning John, whether he might be the Messiah, 16 John answered all of them by saying, "I baptize you with water; but one who is more powerful than I is coming; I am not worthy to untie the thong of his sandals. He will baptize you with the Holy Spirit and fire. 17 His winnowing fork is in his hand, to clear his threshing floor and to gather the wheat into his granary; but the chaff he will burn with unquenchable fire." 18 So, with many other exhortations, he proclaimed the good news to the people. 19 But Herod the ruler, who had been rebuked by him because of Herodias, his brother's wife, and because of all the evil things that Herod had done, 20 added to them all by shutting up John in prison.*

Notice some highlights. John's message called for repentance and baptism. John's message called for generosity. John's message called for actions .to bear fruit worthy of repentance. He was hard on the Pharisees, calling them a brood of vipers. Jesus later called them a brood of vipers in Matt 12 and Matt 23. The reference to vipers could come from the farming community where farmers burned the stubble of their fields to get ready for the next season of planting. When the fires came, it was not unusual to see the snakes slithering away from the flames in the field. Calling the Pharisees a brood of vipers was calling their wickedness into account and offering an opportunity to repent from being devious, deceitful, and wicked like their father, the devil. Their venom is deadly.

We see the baptism of Jesus in Matt 3:13-17:

> *Then Jesus came from Galilee to John at the Jordan, to be baptized by him. 14 John would have prevented him, saying, "I need to be baptized by you, and do you come to me?" 15 But Jesus answered him, "Let it be so now; for it is proper for us in this way to fulfill all righteousness." Then he consented. 16 And when Jesus had been baptized, just as he came up from the water, suddenly the heavens were opened to him and he saw the Spirit of God descending like a dove and alighting on him. 17 And a voice from heaven said, "This is my Son, the Beloved, with whom I am well pleased."*

Fulfill All Righteousness. Jesus, in baptism, gave approval to the ministry of John. Jesus submitted to baptism by John to model humility and to identify with the people He came to save. In an honor and shame culture, Jesus relinquishes the honor in order to embrace the shame of others. Jesus, in the baptism of John, was set apart for His own ministry. After Jesus submits to this baptism, God the Holy Spirit descends as a dove, and the voice of God the Father from heaven honors Jesus declaring Jesus to be His Son.

Mark 1. Mark's gospel opens with John the Baptist. Matthew, Mark, and Luke all have a record of the voice from heaven at the baptism of Jesus saying, "You are my beloved Son in whom I am well pleased." and then all three of them record Jesus being led by the Holy Spirit into the wilderness to be tempted.

Let's look at the 4th Gospel, John, and see how John the Baptist is recorded there.

John 1:6-9, 19-34:

> *There was a man sent from God, whose name was John. 7 He came as a witness to testify to the light, so that all might believe through him. 8 He himself was not the light, but he came to testify to the light. 9 The true light, which enlightens everyone, was coming into the world. (Skipping to verses 19-34):*
>
> *This is the testimony given by John when the Jews sent priests and Levites from Jerusalem to ask him, "Who are you?" 20 He confessed and did not deny it, but confessed, "I am not the Messiah." 21 And they asked him, "What then? Are you Elijah?" He said, "I am not." "Are you the prophet?" He answered, "No." 22 Then they said to him, "Who are you? Let us have an answer for those who sent us. What do you say about yourself?" 23 He said, "I am the voice of one crying out in the wilderness, 'Make straight the way of the Lord,'" as the prophet Isaiah said. 24 Now they had been sent from the Pharisees. 25 They asked him, "Why then are you baptizing if you are neither the Messiah, nor Elijah, nor the prophet?" 26 John answered them, "I baptize with water. Among you stands one whom you do not know, 27 the one who is coming after me; I am not worthy to untie the thong of his sandal." 28 This took place in Bethany across the Jordan where John was baptizing. (The Lamb of God). 29 The next day he saw Jesus coming toward him and declared, "Here is the Lamb of God who takes away the sin of the world! 30 This is he of whom I said, 'After me comes a man who ranks ahead of me because he was before me.' 31 I myself did not know him; but I came baptizing with water for this reason, that he might be revealed to Israel." 32 And John testified, "I saw the Spirit descending from heaven like a dove, and it remained on him. 33 I myself did not know him, but the one who sent me to baptize with water said to me, 'He on whom you see the Spirit descend and remain is the one who baptizes with the Holy Spirit.' 34 And I myself have seen and have testified that this is the Son of God."*

The Thong of His Sandal. In ancient Mediterranean thought, a household servant's basest tasks involved the master's feet, such as washing his feet, carrying his sandals, or unfastening the thongs of his sandals. John thus claims to be unworthy to even be the Coming One's slave.

Jesus started his ministry and called his disciples while John the Baptist was in prison. Turn with me, if you will, to Matt 11, where John sends some disciples with a message for Jesus. [A similar account is Luke 7:18-35] but we will read this account in Matt 11:1-19:

> *Now when Jesus had finished instructing his twelve disciples, he went on from there to teach and proclaim his message in their cities. 2 When John heard in prison what the Messiah was doing, he sent word by his disciples 3 and said to him, "Are you the one who is to come, or are we to wait for another?" 4 Jesus answered them, "Go and tell John what you hear and see: 5 the blind receive their sight, the lame walk, the lepers are cleansed, the deaf hear, the dead are raised, and the poor have good news brought to them. 6 And blessed is anyone who takes no offense at me." (Jesus Praises John the Baptist). 7 As they went away, Jesus began to speak to the crowds about John: "What did you go out into the wilderness to look at? A reed shaken by the wind? 8 What then did you go out to see? Someone dressed in soft robes? Look, those who wear soft robes are in royal palaces. 9 What then did you go out to see? A prophet? Yes, I tell you, and more than a prophet. 10 This is the one about whom it is written, 'See, I am sending my messenger ahead of you, who will prepare your way before you.' 11 Truly I tell you, among those born of women no one has arisen greater than John the Baptist; yet the least in the kingdom of heaven is greater than he. 12 From the days of John the Baptist until now the kingdom of heaven has suffered violence, and the violent take it by force. 13 For all the prophets and the law prophesied until John came; 14 and if you are willing to accept it, he is Elijah who is to come. 15 Let anyone with ears listen! 16 "But to what will I compare this generation? It is like children sitting in the marketplaces and calling to one another, 17 'We played the flute for you, and you did not dance; we wailed, and you did not mourn.' 18 For John came neither eating nor drinking, and they say, 'He has a demon'; 19 the Son of Man came eating and drinking, and they say, 'Look, a glutton and a drunkard, a friend of tax collectors and sinners!' Yet wisdom is vindicated by her deeds."*

Jesus Honors John. Look at how Jesus honors John the Baptist as the greatest among those born of women. He corroborates John's message as valid. He says he is the Elijah to come. Now we turn to Mark 6 for one account of the death of John the Baptist. The Death of John the Baptist Mark 6:14-29.

King Herod heard of it, for Jesus' name had become known. Some were saying, "John the baptizer has been raised from the dead; and for this reason these powers are at work in him." 15 But others said, "It is Elijah." And others said, "It is a prophet, like one of the prophets of old." But when Herod heard of it, he said, "John, whom I beheaded, has been raised." For Herod himself had sent men who arrested John, bound him, and put him in prison on account of Herodias, his brother Philip's wife, because Herod had married her. For John had been telling Herod, "It is not lawful for you to have your brother's wife." And Herodias had a grudge against him, and wanted to kill him. But she could not, for Herod feared John, knowing that he was a righteous and holy man, and he protected him. When he heard him, he was greatly perplexed; and yet he liked to listen to him. But an opportunity came when Herod on his birthday gave a banquet for his courtiers and officers and for the leaders of Galilee. When his daughter Herodias came in and danced, she pleased Herod and his guests; and the king said to the girl, "Ask me for whatever you wish, and I will give it." And he solemnly swore to her, "Whatever you ask me, I will give you, even half of my kingdom." She went out and said to her mother, "What should I ask for?" She replied, "The head of John the baptizer." Immediately she rushed back to the king and requested, "I want you to give me at once the head of John the Baptist on a platter." The king was deeply grieved; yet out of regard for his oaths and for the guests, he did not want to refuse her. Immediately the king sent a soldier of the guard with orders to bring John's head. He went and beheaded him in the prison, brought his head on a platter, and gave it to the girl. Then the girl gave it to her mother. When his disciples heard about it, they came and took his body, and laid it in a tomb.

Quiet Place. In two of the accounts of John's death, we see Jesus withdrawing to a solitary place, a quiet place. Mark 6:31 and Matthew 14:13. I pay attention to that as a chaplain. Sometimes in grief, one needs to be with people for comfort, and sometimes one needs to be alone. Jesus was inundated with people all the time. And In both Mark and Matthew, Jesus takes time to be alone.

In the Book of Acts, Chapter 1 (The Promise of the Holy Spirit) Acts 1:1-5:

In the first book, Theophilus, I wrote about all that Jesus did and taught from the beginning until the day when he was taken up to heaven, after giving instructions through the Holy Spirit to the apostles whom he had chosen. After his suffering he presented himself alive to them by many convincing proofs, appearing to them during forty days and speaking about the kingdom of God. While staying with them, he ordered them not to leave Jerusalem, but to wait there for the promise of the Father. "This," he said, "is what you have heard from me; for John baptized with water, but you will be baptized with the Holy Spirit not many days from now.

Chapter 18, we meet Apollos who had been baptized by John the Baptist. Acts 18:24-25, "Now there came to Ephesus a Jew named Apollos, a native of Alexandria. He was an eloquent man, well-versed in the scriptures. He had been instructed in the Way of the Lord; and he spoke with burning enthusiasm and taught accurately the things concerning Jesus, though he knew only the baptism of John." And look at Acts 19:1-7. Paul in Ephesus.

While Apollos was in Corinth, Paul passed through the interior regions and came to Ephesus, where he found some disciples. He said to them, "Did you receive the Holy Spirit when you became believers?" They replied, "No, we have not even heard that there is a Holy Spirit." Then he said, "Into what then were you baptized?" They answered, "Into John's baptism." Paul said, "John baptized with the baptism of repentance, telling the people to believe in the one who was to come after him, that is, in Jesus." On hearing this, they were baptized in the name of the Lord Jesus. When Paul had laid his hands on them, the Holy Spirit came upon them, and they spoke in tongues and prophesied—altogether there were about twelve of them.

What have we learned? John the Baptist was a prophetic voice crying in the wilderness to prepare the way of the Lord. He called for repentance and baptized people who confessed their sins and repented. Jesus honored him. His ministry was widespread. He did what he was called to do to prepare the way of the Lord. Crying out against unrighteousness cost him his life.

Have you ever heard a message that cut you to the core? You thought your life was going along well, and then you heard something that invited you to get right with God. To adjust your life? To repent? The prophetic word is like that. True prophetic words are words from God that touch your heart in a surgical way. God sends messengers with messages to call people back to Himself. To live rightly. To love rightly. To change their ways.

What did they go out to see? A reed shaken in the wind? No? They heard the prophetic cry to make themselves ready. To Prepare. To get their hearts right. To stop doing things that would hinder their spiritual progress. To start doing things that would prepare the way of the Lord. The word Repent is a word that means a decision that results in a change of mind AND a change of action. Repentance. In Spiritual BIRTH, we repent and confess our sins, renounce our sins, and embrace Jesus Christ as our Savior. In Spiritual GROWTH, we are obedient to what Christ commands. We are responsive to the Holy Spirit and the word of the Lord in Scripture. Producing Spiritual

Fruit. We bear fruit worthy of repentance. We are willing to accept the guidance and correction of the Holy Spirit.

John Prepared the Way. John was announcing the rule of God's Kingdom would overthrow the power and rule of the evil in the world. The Kingdom was near because the King was HERE. Jesus is the Way. Even as John was sent to prepare the way of the Lord. We know that. Jesus is the Way to the Father. In John 14:6, Jesus said, "I am the Way the Truth and the Life. No one comes to the Father except through Me." John prepared the way for Christ Jesus and now. And Jesus promised in John 14 that He was going to prepare a place for us. And if He is preparing a place, He promised He would come again. So then, how shall we live? What do we need to do to be ready for His appearance?

Ministry Time: Questions: What prophetic word has cut us to the heart and called us to change our ways? What are we doing to prepare the way of the Lord in our own hearts? What are we doing to prepare the way of the Lord by removing obstacles in the path for others seeking the Lord? Is there something today that you would like one or a few of us to gather around you and pray with you?

Closing Prayer: Thank You, Lord, for John the Baptist. The one whose voice is crying in the wilderness prepared the way for You. Thank You, Jesus, for being the Way, the Truth, the Life. O, Lord, Jesus, we love You today and want to honor You in all we do and say. As the Christmas carol invites, Let EVERY heart prepare Him room and heaven and nature sing. And help us, Lord, with all our hearts, to continue to prepare the way for You. Help us to tear down the places of self-importance and pride. Help us to fill in the valleys of doubt with hope. Help us to seek forgiveness and offer forgiveness. Help us to remove obstacles and offenses for others to see You more clearly. O, come to our hearts, Lord Jesus, there is room in our hearts for You. In Your precious and holy Name, Jesus, Amen.

Lessons from Lydia
Acts 16:14

July 12, 2020

Acts 16:14 (NRSV) *"A certain woman named Lydia, a worshiper of God, was listening to us; she was from the city of Thyatira and a dealer in purple cloth. The Lord opened her heart to listen eagerly to what was said by Paul."*

Opening Prayer. Dear Lord, As we open the Scriptures today, teach us. Help us to hear Your encouragement to us today. Help us to listen and to love You more. Come, Holy Spirit. Open our eyes to see and ears to hear the message You have for us today. In Jesus' Name, Amen.

Introduction: Colors. Does anyone here have a favorite color? I have a friend whose favorite color is red. My favorite color is blue. Who likes purple? When we see clothes made out of fabric today, there are lots of colors, red, blue, yellow, pink, brown, green, and purple. In these days, chemists can make any color with chemical dyes, synthetic dyes, dyes that will hold their color, and some dyes that will wash out over time. I know that when I need purple, if I have some red paint and some blue paint, I can mix them together and get purple.

Nazareth Village. In Bible times, the clothes, the fabrics, were soaked in dye to make them colorful. On one of our traveling trips, Mr. Penton, Allen, and I went to Nazareth in the Holy Land of Israel. We went to see the town where Jesus grew up. In that town now, some people have designed a place called Nazareth Village. It has olive trees, sheep, goats, olive oil presses, a place to shear the sheep, and women who work there who dye the wool and weave blankets and shawls with the wool. They showed us how they use roots and vegetables to dye the wool. They were able to make a yellow dye, a green dye, and a red dye from different roots and leaves, and they soaked the wool in the dyes to make the wool different colors.

Purple. One of the most expensive dyes in Bible times was the purple dye. International Standard Bible Encyclopedia says Purple dye was manufactured by the Phoenicians from a marine mollusk, Murex trunculus. The shell was broken in order to give access to a small gland which was removed and crushed. The crushed gland gives a milky fluid that becomes red or purple on exposure to the air. Piles of these broken shells still remain on the coast at

Sidon and Tyre. The purple gland is found in various species of Murex and also of Purpura.

Purple dye was made in two ways, one by the madder root and one by a sea snail, a mollusk, called Murex trunculus. The shell was not purple itself. The pigment was secreted by a gland in the lining of the stomach. The shell had to be punctured, and the mollusk had to be removed in order to secure the dye. The juice, at first whitish, changed on exposure to yellowish or greenish and finally to red, amethyst, or purple, according to the treatment.[25]

Background for Seller of Purple Source: Smithsonian Institute. Marine snails were collected by the thousands to make Tyrian purple. They were then boiled for days in giant lead vats, producing a terrible odor. The snails, though, aren't purple, to begin with. The craftsmen were harvesting chemical precursors from the snails that, through heat and light, were transformed into valuable dye. The snails were collected by the thousands, and they were boiled in giant lead vats, and there was a terrible odor in making the dye.

Some Of The Places Of Purple In The Bible. Purple cloth was used in the furnishings of the tabernacle (Exodus 25:4, etc.), and The kings of Midian had purple raiment (Judges 8:26). Solomon's temple (2 Chronicles 2:14; 3:14); in the palanquin of Solomon (Song of Solomon 3:10); and in In Song of Solomon 7:5, the bride has hair like purple. The hangings of the palace of Ahasuerus (Esther 1:6). Mordecai was clothed with purple by Ahasuerus (Esther 8:15); the worthy woman of Proverbs 31:22 has clothing of fine linen and purple. In the parable of the rich man and Lazarus of Luke 16:19. Jesus was given a purple, royal robe garment by the Roman soldiers (Mark 15:17, 20; John 19:2, 5).

Today we are going to meet a seller of purple. We are going to turn in our Bibles to Acts 16 or locate Acts 16 on our devices and see how the Apostle Paul and his traveling companions came to meet Lydia, the seller of purple. Missionary Journey. Part of the Book of Acts is devoted to missionary journeys. A missionary journey involves traveling to a place that is not home to share the good news of Jesus. Missionaries are sent from home to a place where they are sent to preach the good news that Jesus is the King of Glory, the Savior of the world, the hope of the future, the way to peace with God,

---

[25] International Standard Bible Encyclopedia.

the way to knowing God. Through Jesus, we are forgiven for our sins, and we are made right with God when we repent and believe the good news.

Today we are looking at Paul's Second Missionary Journey. Time in the Book of Acts. When we read the Book of Acts, we might read through the chapters and not realize how much time this book covers. From the time Jesus was taken into heaven until the end of Acts Chapter 28, there are at least 30 years. We know that the Apostle Paul died in about the year 67, and he was alive in Rome at the end of Acts. The bible scholars estimate the time of the visit to Philippi that we will study today is between 49ad and 51CE, and the book of Philippians was written after 51CE, perhaps from his time of imprisonment in Rome around 62 CE. Let's read the scripture in Acts 16 today. I will be reading from the NRSV starting in verse 11. Acts 16:11-15 (NRSV):

(The Conversion of Lydia.)

> *We set sail from Troas and took a straight course to Samothrace, the following day to Neapolis, 12 and from there to Philippi, which is a leading city of the district of Macedonia and a Roman colony. We remained in this city for some days. 13 On the sabbath day we went outside the gate by the river, where we supposed there was a place of prayer; and we sat down and spoke to the women who had gathered there. 14 A certain woman named Lydia, a worshiper of God, was listening to us; she was from the city of Thyatira and a dealer in purple cloth. The Lord opened her heart to listen eagerly to what was said by Paul. 15 When she and her household were baptized, she urged us, saying, "If you have judged me to be faithful to the Lord, come and stay at my home." And she prevailed upon us.*

Notice The Map. 11 We set sail from Troas and took a straight course to Samothrace, the following day to Neapolis, 12 and from there to Philippi, which is a leading city of the district of Macedonia and a Roman colony. We remained in this city for some days. In the travels, we see a boat or ship to put out to sea from Troas and go straight to Samothrace. The next day they went to Neapolis and from there to Philippi. So, some of the travels included sailing, and some included walking. In Philippi, there was a Roman Road called the Via Egnatia that connected the port city of Neapolis to the city of Philippi and connected Philippi to Thessalonica, and ultimately connected Rome on the Adriatic to Asia Minor, Turkey.

History of Philippi. A little history. Philippi was a city in eastern Macedonia, established by Philip II in 356 BCE. Philip II was the father of Alexander the Great. Philippi was known for its gold, and Philip of Macedon offered it protection probably to access the available gold. The Romans took over in about 168 BCE, and it became a Roman colony. A Roman Road was built called the Via Egnatia. Mentioned in Acts 16:12 12 and from there to Philippi, a leading city of the district of Macedonia, a [Roman] colony; and we were staying in this city for some days. The present municipality is located near the ruins of the ancient city, and it is part of the region of East Macedonia and Thrace in Greece.

Notice "Some Days." We remained in this city for some days. We do not know how long some days are, but we can imagine that it was long enough to ask around to find out some things about the city. (So when they first went to the city, Paul and Silas, and the person or persons who made up the "we," some Bible scholars think the "we" scriptures include Luke, the physician who joined them in Troas, we set out, could also be Timothy in the "we" passages here.) We supposed that there would be a place of prayer. In the other cities Paul and Silas visited on this second missionary journey, they went to synagogues first to bring the good news. Most of the time, we notice that Paul went to the synagogue to preach. When Paul arrived in Philippi, there was no synagogue. For there to be a synagogue, a quorum of men had to be available in a city. Ten tithing men could support a synagogue. We can see in Chapter 17:1-4, the next chapter, that when Paul went to Thessalonica, there was a synagogue. In verse 10, the synagogue at Berea, In verse 17, the synagogue at Athens, and the marketplace. Chapter 18, verse 4 synagogue at Corinth. So it says they supposed there would be a place of prayer at the river.

Place of Prayer at the River. There are several songs I can think of about going down to the river to pray. Let's go down to the river to pray. Maybe you can think of some. Here is one traditional song from the 1800s that talks about going down to the river to pray. "As I went down to the river to pray" (Traditional) Lyrics. "As I went down in the river to pray Studying about that good ol' way And who shall wear the starry crown. Good Lord, show me the way. O sisters, let's go down. Let's go down, come on down O sisters, let's go down. Down in the river to pray."[26]

A Place Of Prayer. A place of prayer is a wonderful thing to have. Where would it be if you were to think of a place of prayer in your life? I used to have a place of prayer in a special chair. Now in this season, it is in the corner of my sofa. Where is your place of prayer? It is good to pray alone, and it is also good to pray with others in a place of prayer. When Jesus was leaving,

---

[26] "Down to the River to Pray,"
https://www.stlyrics.com/lyrics/obrotherwhereartthou/downtotherivertopray.htm
.

he sent the disciples to wait in Jerusalem in a place of prayer for the gift of the Holy Spirit. When they were in the place of prayer, the Holy Spirit came. There was a place of prayer at the river, and women were assembled there to pray. And Paul and his companions found the women assembled at the river. Verse 13 "And on the Sabbath day we went outside the gate to a riverside, where we were supposing that there would be a place of prayer; and we sat down and began speaking to the women who had assembled." Paul and his companions sat down and began speaking to the assembled women. And then, we are introduced to Lydia. Lydia was with the assembled women on the Sabbath at the place of prayer at the river.

What do we know about Lydia? We read that a certain woman named Lydia is from the city of Thyatira-where is that? Asia Minor, across the Aegean Sea from Philippi. Thyatira in Asia Minor was a city that had many crafts and craftsperson guilds. Thayer's Greek Lexicon Thyatira (Thoutera), a colony of Macedonia Greeks, situated between Sardis and Pergamos on the river Lycus; its inhabitants gained their living by traffic and the art of dyeing in purple. Thyatira was especially noted for the trade guilds, which were probably more completely organized there than in any other ancient city. Every artisan belonged to a guild, and every guild, which was an incorporated organization, possessed property in its own name, made contracts for great constructions and wielded a wide influence. Powerful among them was the guild of coppersmiths; another was the guild of the dyers, who, it is believed, made use of the madder-root instead of shellfish for making the purple dyestuffs.[27] A member of this guild seems to have been Lydia of Thyatira, who, according to Acts 16:14, sold her dyes in Philippi. The color obtained by the use of this dye is now called Turkish red. What do we know about Lydia?

Lydia is a seller of purple cloth fabrics or purple dye. What is purple dye? We have already mentioned that Purple Dye was the symbol of royalty and luxury. Because of its high price, due to the expensive method of obtaining it, only royalty and the rich could afford purple attire. There are Bible references to purple in the tabernacle, in the parable of the rich man and Lazarus, and in the color of the robe that the soldiers gave Jesus. What do we know about Lydia? A worshiper of God- perhaps like others who were noted God-fearers in the book. Cornelius, (Acts 10:2 says that Cornelius "was a devout man who feared God with all his household; he gave alms generously to the people and prayed constantly to God." Lydia was at the place of prayer at the riverside, and she was listening. The NRSV uses listening eagerly.

---

[27] International Standard Bible Encyclopedia.

What Do We Know About Lydia? The Lord opened her heart to respond (NASB). The Lord opened her heart to listen eagerly to what was said by Paul. (NRSV). Here is Lydia, a merchant, a worshiper of God, in a place of prayer on the Sabbath day, and she was listening to Paul and his companions. We can only imagine what good news they were sharing with the women. We imagine from other scriptures they shared the Good News of Jesus, God's Son, who came from heaven and did many miracles, signs, and wonders. We can imagine that they shared that Jesus came to give new life, abundant life and that Jesus called all who were weary to come to Him, and He would give them rest. This Jesus died for our sins and was buried and rose again on the third day, according to the scriptures and the witnesses, and now Jesus has ascended to heaven and has sent the Holy Spirit. We can imagine Paul inviting the women to become followers of Jesus and to be baptized right there in the river.

The inbreaking of the Kingdom Of God. And Lydia heard the good news and verse 14 says The Lord opened her heart to listen eagerly, to respond. The inbreaking of the kingdom of God comes at various times and places. God's kingdom is advancing, and the reign of God has now come to Lydia's heart and home. She was listening with discernment to what Paul was saying. She was a worshiper of God who had come to a place of prayer, and in that atmosphere, she heard the truth about Jesus the Messiah and how Jesus loved her and wanted her to follow Him as Lord and Savior. Jesus is the one who sent Paul to Macedonia to meet her and her friends at the river. Jesus was inviting her to know about Him and to know Him and the good news of the resurrection and new life in Him.

Reminiscent of the woman at the well: John 4 This part of the Lesson from Lydia reminds me of the woman at the well. John 4:28-29, "Then the woman left her water jar and went back to the city. She said to the people, 29 "Come and see a man who told me everything I have ever done! He cannot be the Messiah, can he?"

Jeremiah 29:11-14 NIV. One of the beautiful promises in Jeremiah says,

> For I know the plans I have for you," declares the Lord, "plans to prosper you and not to harm you, plans to give you hope and a future. 12 Then you will call on me and come and pray to me, and I will listen to you. 13 You will seek me and find me when you seek me with all your heart. 14 I will be found by you," declares the Lord.

Lydia went to a place of prayer. She sought and found the Lord, and the Lord was found by her. What do we know about Lydia? We see that Lydia and her household were baptized. Verse 15 "The Lord opened her heart to listen eagerly to what was said by Paul." When she and her household were baptized, not only was Lydia baptized, she went back and told everyone in her household. All the relatives and servants and everyone who lived in the household came and were baptized. Notice that she and her household were baptized. She was not alone with the good news. She went home and shared what she had seen and heard with her household. And verse 15, when she and her household had been baptized. Then she invited Paul and Silas to come. Lydia is considered to be the first convert in Europe, what is now Europe, Greece.

She prevailed upon us. Notice the "she prevailed upon us, she insisted. She urged us. The other time that expression in Greek is used was when Jesus was on the road to Emmaus and he was with two of his followers who had lost hope, and he was explaining how the Messiah must come and die and fulfill the prophecies. When it was dark, the travelers, Cleopas and his friend invited Jesus to stay. Luke 24:28-29 (NIV) "As they approached the village to which they were going, Jesus continued on as if he were going farther. 29 But they urged him strongly, "Stay with us, for it is nearly evening; the day is almost over." So, he went in to stay with them. "If you have judged me to be faithful to the Lord." She urged us (Paul and his companions) to discern and come with her to her house to stay. Notice that Lydia's invitation of hospitality was not on her merits as a seller of purple, as a wealthy businesswoman, as an important merchant in the town, as an important woman. No, her invitation was based on her devotion to the Lord. If you have judged me to be faithful to the Lord, come to my house and stay. She was a woman of means to be able to host Paul and his group of traveling companions. Lydia is apparently able to invite guests to the household. Possibly she could have been a widow. Come to my house and stay.

Lesson: Have a welcoming home or place to invite guests and practice hospitality with the generosity of spirit and resources. When Peter had the opportunity to go to the house of Cornelius, he saw the Gentiles, God-fearers, receive the Holy Spirit, and Peter was invited to stay in the house of Cornelius, a Gentile and now a baptized believer and Peter stayed. When Paul and Silas had the opportunity to go to the house of Lydia, a God-fearer and now a baptized believer, along with her household, Paul and Silas went to Lydia's house and stayed.

How did Paul get to Lydia? Look back at chapter 15, where the Jerusalem Council met and sent a letter along with Paul and Barnabas. Jewish Believers and Gentile Believers. Some of the Jewish followers were trying to convince the gentiles that the Gentiles needed to become Jewish, to follow circumcision, to follow dietary laws, in order to truly follow Jesus. And there were heated arguments in the church about what needed to happen to truly be believers in Christ and followers of Jesus. And so Paul and Peter and some leaders gathered in Jerusalem to have a meeting, a council in which they would decide what to do with these Gentiles and those who were trying to get the Gentiles to practice certain things from Judaism in order to be Christians, Christ-followers. And they came up with a few things on this list and wrote a document to be circulated. The next thing was to appoint apostles to take this decision document to the believers in towns across the world, to churches that had been planted and churches yet to be planted.

Acts 15:30-31 and 36-41:

> *So they were sent off and went down to Antioch. When they gathered the congregation together, they delivered the letter. 31 When its members read it, they rejoiced at the exhortation. 36 After some days Paul said to Barnabas, "Come, let us return and visit the believers in every city where we proclaimed the word of the Lord and see how they are doing." 37 Barnabas wanted to take with them John called Mark. 38 But Paul decided not to take with them one who had deserted them in Pamphylia and had not accompanied them in the work. 39 The disagreement became so sharp that they parted company; Barnabas took Mark with him and sailed away to Cyprus. 40 But Paul chose Silas and set out, the believers commending him to the grace of the Lord. 41 He went through Syria and Cilicia, strengthening the churches.*

So Paul sets out with Silas. And Paul and Silas travel together and find companions for the journey. Acts 16:4-8 (NASB):

> *Now while they were passing through the cities, they were delivering the decrees which had been decided upon by the apostles and elders who were in Jerusalem, for them to observe. 5 So the churches were being strengthened in the faith and were increasing in number daily. 6 They passed through the Phrygian and Galatian region, having been forbidden by the Holy Spirit to speak the word in Asia; 7 and after they came to Mysia, they were trying to go into Bithynia, and the Spirit of Jesus did not permit them; 8 and passing by Mysia, they came down to Troas.*

So if you look at the map, you can see the regions mentioned, Phrygia, Galatia, Mysia, Bithynia, and you can find Troas on the coast of the Aegean Sea and that is where Paul had a dream. Acts 16:9-10, "A vision appeared to

Paul in the night: a man of Macedonia was standing and appealing to him, and saying, 'Come over to Macedonia and help us.' 10 When he had seen the vision, immediately we sought to go into Macedonia, concluding that God had called us to preach the gospel to them."

Sometimes God speaks in dreams and visions. Other visions in Scripture. Acts 10 Cornelius. Acts 18 Paul. The vision God gave Ananias in Acts 9:10-19:

> *Now there was a disciple in Damascus named Ananias. The Lord said to him in a vision, "Ananias." He answered, "here I am, Lord." 11 The Lord said to him, "Get up and go to the street called Straight, and at the house of Judas look for a man of Tarsus named Saul. At this moment he is praying, 12 and he has seen in a vision a man named Ananias come in and lay his hands on him so that he might regain his sight." 13 But Ananias answered, "Lord, I have heard from many about this man, how much evil he has done to your saints in Jerusalem; 14 and here he has authority from the chief priests to bind all who invoke your name." 15 But the Lord said to him, "Go, for he is an instrument whom I have chosen to bring my name before Gentiles and kings and before the people of Israel; 16 I myself will show him how much he must suffer for the sake of my name." 17 So Ananias went and entered the house. He laid his hands on Saul and said, "Brother Saul, the Lord Jesus, who appeared to you on your way here, has sent me so that you may regain your sight and be filled with the Holy Spirit." 18 And immediately something like scales fell from his eyes, and his sight was restored. Then he got up and was baptized, 19 and after taking some food, he regained his strength.*

Acts 10:1-7 vision: Cornelius.

> *In Caesarea there was a man named Cornelius, a centurion of the Italian Cohort, as it was called. 2 He was a devout man who feared God with all his household; he gave alms generously to the people and prayed constantly to God. 3 One afternoon at about three o'clock he had a vision in which he clearly saw an angel of god coming in and saying to him, "Cornelius." 4 He stared at him in terror and said, "What is it, Lord?" He answered, "Your prayers and your alms have ascended as a memorial before God. 5 Now send men to Joppa for a certain Simon who is called Peter; 6 he is lodging with Simon, a tanner, whose house is by the seaside." 7 When the angel who spoke to him had left, he called two of his slaves and a devout soldier from the ranks of those who served him, 8 and after telling them everything, he sent them to Joppa.*

Paul's vision in Acts 18:9-11, "One night the Lord said to Paul in a vision, 'Do not be afraid, but speak and do not be silent; 10 for I am with you, and no one will lay a hand on you to harm you, for there are many in this city who are my people.' 11 He stayed there a year and six months, teaching the word of God among them."

God speaks in many ways. God speaks through the scriptures, prayer, circumstances, the church, creation, dreams, and visions to show us God's purposes and plans for us. We need to be ready to listen, to pay attention, to discern the voice of the Lord in our daily lives. God still invites us to Join Jesus in mission trips, in ministries, in encouragement visits.

Another Lydia. As I grew up in Hawthorne, NJ, I met Mrs. Lydia, my pastor's wife, who had a heart full of love and hospitality. She loved the Lord, could sing beautifully, and was the mother of two children, one a year younger than I was. Ms. Lydia got involved with the school system when prayer was taken out of schools in the 1962 and 1963 Supreme Court decisions. This Lydia appealed to the elementary school for permission to conduct an after-school Bible Club. I was one of the members of the Bible Club at Franklin School, along with Lydia's daughter. We were encouraged to carry our Bibles to school on club day and to memorize scripture and recite the scriptures aloud. I remember memorizing the entire chapter of Isaiah 53 in the Bible Club. Ms. Lydia is in heaven now, and I just messaged her daughter in the past week to let her know, again, how much her mom influenced me to love Jesus and to love scripture.

The name Lydia means travail. She is not mentioned by name elsewhere in the New Testament, only in Acts 16. Church History gives her credit for helping the church in Philippi to get started when all her household believed and were baptized, and she hosted Paul and his companions in her home. Even though we do not have any recorded words or any direct quotes from Lydia, her actions are described. Her actions remain in scripture as lessons for all of us.

Practical Lessons from Lydia. Here are some practical Lessons from Lydia. Go to a place of prayer. Have an open heart. Listen with discernment. Receive the Good News. Be obedient in Baptism, in the next steps in which God calls you to follow. Have a welcoming home or place to invite guests. Practice hospitality, generosity of spirit, and resources. One more we have not talked about. Be a safe place for those who have been imprisoned for the sake of the Gospel.

Later in Acts 16, Paul and Silas were imprisoned, and the Philippian jailer and his household became believers in Jesus. The famous verse "Believe on the

Lord Jesus Christ and you shall be saved, and your household" is in Acts 16:31 "Believe on the Lord Jesus, and you will be saved, you and your household." After Paul and Silas were released from prison, where did they go? Let's look at verse 40. "They went out of the prison and entered [the house of] Lydia, and when they saw the brethren, they encouraged them and departed." Of all the places Paul and Silas would go after prison, they went to Lydia's house, and there they encouraged the brethren in her household and then departed to continue on the journey.

Open Home/Open Heart. Lydia welcomed Paul and his companions into her home. She opened her heart to the message and opened her home with hospitality. What are some practical ways we can open our hearts and homes today? This week, intentionally pray and ask the Lord to show us ways to practice the hospitality of heart and home. In our lessons from Lydia today. We have learned about purple and how precious it was in Bible days. We have learned how God arranged circumstances and plans to give Paul a vision of a man in Macedonia calling, "Come help us." We have seen how God led Lydia to a place of prayer to meet Paul and his companions and to hear the good news of the gospel. We have learned how she opened her heart and home to welcome these missionaries who had brought the good news of the Kingdom of God to her. Lydia's open heart and open home were available and made room for the Church in Philippi to grow and flourish. As we open our hearts and homes with hospitality, we will continue to see the Kingdom of God expanding and growing in fruitfulness.

Ministry Time: If you need prayer. I am about to close in prayer and would like to invite those listening online to Let us know if you need prayer. We have a place on our website to write prayer requests. We have a team who will pray for you and with you.

Closing Prayer. O Lord, we come to You now with thankfulness and gratitude in our hearts for these examples from the early church. We thank You for the lessons from Lydia. Give us open hearts that we might continue to hear the words You speak to us. Give us open homes to welcome those whom You send us. In Jesus' Name, Amen.

Let Not Your Heart Be Troubled
John 14:1

November 26, 2017

John 14:1 *"Let not your heart be troubled."*

Opening Prayer. O Lord God, how excellent is Your Name in all the earth! We thank You for Liberty Vineyard Church. We thank You for the glory of Your Son, Jesus. We thank You for the fellowship of the believers. And we thank You for those who are listening online. Teach us from Your word today and help us to be even more devoted to our Lord Jesus Christ, in whose name we pray, Amen.

Introduction. On a scale from 1-10, how easy is it for us to get upset? That depends. Is the trouble far away? Is the trouble close by? The nearer we are to trouble, the easier it is to feel upset. When trouble in the news is far away, we could tend to have a sense that trouble is not imminent here. The internet has made it possible for us to see trouble on the other side of the world, another area of our country, another city in our state, another town in our county, just like it was next door. General trouble. We live in a fallen world. Wars are far away, with the capabilities of wars coming close by. Cities erupting with violence. Violence could come close by. Pollution. Unwanted chemicals in our food supply or our water supply. The trouble with addictions of many kinds. Family members and dear friends compromise their lives and health with addictive behaviors.

The trouble with family members who have gone astray or who have shunned us, or who have acted against us verbally and/or physically. The trouble with our health. Not feeling well. Bodies breaking down, injured, malfunctioning. The trouble with relationships in our workplaces or school environments or church relationships. Name the trouble you are facing. Any list of troubles is incomplete if it does not include the trouble YOU are facing. The trouble I am facing. Trouble is general. But it is also personal. In the Beatle's song from the 60s, "Let It Be," there are some lyrics, "When I find myself in times of trouble Mother Mary comes to me speaking words of wisdom Let it Be."[28]

---

[28] The Beatles (1970), "Let it Be," https://genius.com/The-beatles-let-it-be-lyrics.

Classic country songs are full of troubles and woes. One of the songs we have inherited from the spirituals born from enslaved peoples is "Nobody knows the trouble I've seen. Glory, Hallelujah. Sometimes I'm up, Sometimes I'm down. Oh yes Lord. Sometimes I'm almost to the ground. Oh, yes, Lord."[29]. We "pray the news" to cast our cares on the Lord and to lay our burdens down.

Illustration: The parade. Each year on Thanksgiving Day in New York City, there is a parade. Thousands of people crowd the sidewalk to catch a glimpse of what is going by. Bands, performers, floats, and huge balloons soar overhead. When a person is on the sidewalk, they catch a glimpse of the parade from their vantage point. On television, we have access to more of an aerial view. Blimps with cameras mounted high above the parade have a higher perspective. Beyond the blimps, God looks down from heaven and can see the beginning and the end of the parade lineup and who is in place, and how the parade is moving. So, when we are on the sidewalk, so to speak, as we look at the news, and we start to pray and take all of these items that could trouble us to the throne of grace, we can get a more heavenly perspective on how to pray and what God might be doing in the midst of the trouble we see.

So, not just praying the news. But in all of life. It helps me to think of time as God's creation. God sees the beginning of time. God sees the end of time. All of our ancestors were in the parade long before we were born. They will be rewarded, or they will suffer for the choices they made, and the consequences of those choices visit the next generations. And God sometimes chooses to intervene in our history. Sometimes God sends deliverers. Sometimes God sends helpers. God is busy writing redemptive history.

So whatever situation we see in the news that is troublesome, we can ask God to come down, send helpers, send deliverers, and breakthrough with miracles. Bring Glory into the mess we see.

Our Memory Verse today comes from the Gospel of John. Chapter 14: verse 1 "Let not your heart be troubled." This was one of the passages of scripture Pastor Larry McGill asked the first graders in summer Bible School to memorize. There would be a prize for the children who memorized John 14:1-6 by the end of the week. And I wanted the prize. Imagine. But whatever

---

[29] "Nobody Knows the Trouble I've Seen,"
https://hymnary.org/text/sometimes_im_up_sometimes_im_down_oh_yes.

trinket I received as a child is pale in comparison to the comfort I receive from praying these verses and sitting with these verses in my heart.

The first word is Let. Allow. Not. Allow not. Power. Gatekeeper power.to allow or not to allow. YOUR. I cannot do anything about someone else's heart in this process. This is about YOUR heart. My heart. Jesus is speaking personally. Let not YOUR heart. Be. Troubled. Stirred up. Anxious, worried, upset. Thayer's Greek Lexicon, "to cause one inward commotion, take away his calmness of mind, disturb his equanimity; to disquiet, make restless."

There is also a sense of agitation and stirring up. Other Greek words for trouble, but this is the one used here in John 14:1 and 27.

Acts 15:24, "Since we have heard that some of our number to whom we gave no instruction have disturbed you with their words, unsettling your souls" (NASB). 1 Peter 3:14. "But even if you should suffer for the sake of righteousness, you are blessed. And do not fear their intimidation, and do not be troubled" (NASB). The Psalms are full of cries amid troubles. The Psalmists would encourage themselves in the Lord. Psalm 42, "Why so downcast O my soul. Hope in God" (NASB). Psalm 37 "Fret not thyself. Fret not yourself because of evildoers; Fret not yourself; it tends only to evil. For the evildoers shall be cut off, but those who wait for the Lord shall inherit the land" (NASB). What encourages me is that Jesus was troubled and yet without sin.

Two times before Jesus instructed the disciples, the same Greek word was used. John 12:27, "Now My soul has become troubled; and what shall I say, 'Father, save Me from this hour? But for this purpose I came to this hour" (NASB). John 13:21, "When Jesus had said this, He became troubled in spirit, and testified and said, "Truly, truly, I say to you, that one of you will betray Me" (NASB). Trouble in our hearts does not have to be an indicator of lack of faith or sin. How we handle the trouble in our hearts either pleases God or creates distance between God and us.

Our Memory verse today is found during a discourse. Scriptures have recorded several discourses of Jesus. In Matthew, the term Five Discourses of Matthew refers to five specific discourses by Jesus within the Gospel of Matthew. The five discourses are the Sermon on the Mount, the Missionary Discourse, the Parabolic Discourse, the Discourse on the Church, and the Discourse on End Times.

Let's consider some Farewell discourses. Moses in Deuteronomy 32, Jacob in Genesis 49. Outside of the Bible, one of the most celebrated farewells is Socrates' farewell, found in Plato's Phaedo. Luke records a farewell of Jesus in Luke 22:14-36 and a farewell of Paul to the Ephesian elders in Acts 20:18-35.

If we knew we were dying, what would we say to our loved ones? Chaplains sometimes have opportunities to assist residents/patients who know they are dying to make amends with estranged family members, forgive, bless, and say kind words before the last breath. Other times, especially in sudden death, the intended last words often go unsaid. Every day in emergency rooms, folks did not plan to be there. They left their homes and somehow either caused an accident or were involved in an accident with injuries severe enough to cause trauma to their bodies.

Farewell of Jesus. We find Our Memory Verse in John 14:1 and 14:27 "Let not your heart be troubled." The Farewell Discourse of Jesus starts in Chapter 13 after the washing of the feet and after Judas leaves. John 13:31-17:26 is the Farewell Discourse. The Beloved Disciple is the only gospel writer who offers us an up close and personal conversation spanning several chapters of the New Testament. Whenever we wonder what will happen, what is in Jesus's heart toward us, we can sit down with Jesus on the night he was betrayed and read step by step—washing the disciples' feet, sending Judas out. Knowing Judas would betray him, talking to the eleven about heaven, the Father, the Holy Spirit, the vine and the branches, no more servants but friends, not leaving them as orphans, coming to them. What he required was obedience to the commands. And a new commandment to love one another. We hear Jesus praying to the Father and praying for us.

John 14 for Pastoral Care. After Psalm 23, with its promises of God making us to lie down in green pastures, leading us beside still waters, and restoring our souls, and the wonderful shepherd care depicted in that Psalm, the most requested scripture is John 14. John 14 offers hope that Jesus is preparing a place for us, Jesus will come for us and receive us to himself, Jesus is the way, the truth, and the life. And if we have seen Jesus, we have seen the Father.

Hebrews 1 says that Jesus is the exact representation of the Father. John 14 promises that Jesus and the Father will come and make their abode with us. We will not be orphans. We are not orphans. We are given a family. We are adopted into God's family.

Funerals. One of the most often quoted passages at funerals is John 14:1-6. Whether I am attending the funeral of a young person or an older person,

John 14 offers comfort and confidence in the midst of bereavement. Jesus knew He was going away. Jesus knew the cup that was before him. And he wanted to comfort the disciples. Later in the chapter, he reiterates. Let not your heart be troubled, neither let it be afraid. A prayer of the heart is some word or phrase that we offer in prayer that centers us on a promise of God, a name of God, or an attribute of God. In recent weeks I have had occasion in family situations to find my heart troubled. This verse has come to mind and come to my heart. And I have offered it up in prayer. Kardia, the heart, is that organ in our body that is the center of blood circulation and hence was regarded as the seat of physical and spiritual life.

More heart verses. Deuteronomy 4:29, "But from there you will seek the Lord your God, and you will find Him if you seek Him with all your heart and with all your soul." Deuteronomy 6:5-6, "You shall love the Lord your God with all your heart, with all your soul, and with all your strength. And these words which I command you today shall be in your heart." Psalm 27:14, "Wait on the Lord; Be of good courage, And He shall strengthen your heart; Wait, I say, on the Lord! Proverbs 2:2, "So that you incline your ear to wisdom, And apply your heart to understanding." Proverbs 3:5 "Trust in the Lord with all your heart, And lean not on your own understanding;" Proverbs 4:23, "Keep your heart with all diligence, For out of it spring the issues of life." Luke 12:34, "For where your treasure is, there your heart will be also." Ephesians 3:17, "So that Christ may dwell in your hearts through faith; and that you, being rooted and grounded in love." Ephesians 5:19, "Speaking to one another in psalms and hymns and spiritual songs, singing and making melody with your heart to the Lord." Philippians 4:7, "And the peace of God, which surpasses all comprehension, will guard your hearts and your minds in Christ Jesus. 1 Thessalonians 3:13, "So that He may establish your hearts without blame in holiness before our God and Father at the coming of our Lord Jesus with all His saints." 2 Thessalonians 3:5, "Now may the Lord direct your hearts into the love of God and into the patience of Christ."

History of John Bunyan[30] (28 November 1628 – 31 August 1688) was an English Christian writer and preacher, who is well-known for his book *The Pilgrim's Progress*. He was a Reformed Baptist. John Bunyan had very little schooling. John Bunyan was received into the Baptist church in Bedford by immersion in 1653. In 1655, Bunyan became a deacon and began with

---

[30] https://www.britannica.com/biography/John-Bunyan.
https://christianhistoryinstitute.org/magazine/article/john-bunyan-the-man-preacher-and-author.

success. In 1658 he was indicted for preaching without a license. The authorities were relatively tolerant of him for a while, and he did not suffer imprisonment until November of 1660, when he was taken to the county jail. Bunyan afterward became pastor of the Bedford church. In March of 1675, he was imprisoned for preaching publicly without a license, this time being held in the Bedford town jail. When he was freed six months later, he was not bothered again by the authorities.

Bunyan wrote, "It gave me no pleasure to see people drink in my opinions if they seemed ignorant of Jesus Christ and the value of being saved by Him. Sound conviction for sin, especially the sin of unbelief, and a heart set on fire to be saved by Christ, with a strong yearning for a truly sanctified soul-this was what delighted me; those were the souls I considered blessed."[31] Wrote *Heart's Ease for Heart Trouble*. The key is faith. Faith in Jesus who said he would come back and take us to himself. Wrote *Grace Abounding to the Chief of Sinners*. Tormented in his soul, thinking he had committed the unpardonable sin. Thinking he had, like Esau, sold his birthright for a mess of pottage. Bunyan thought he had missed the grace of God. The glorious revelation that God's grace was able to reach him and to give him the faith Bunyan needed to overcome the traps of the devil. Satan. He had a huge breakthrough in faith and wrote *Pilgrim's Progress*. This book was influential when I was a child.

Jesus did not end the sentence with "Let not your heart be troubled." No. Jesus invites the disciples to believe, trust, have faith, and have confidence. More than mental acknowledgment. A deep and abiding knowing faith and trust in both God and Jesus. What will our belief in God, and Jesus as the representation of God, result in for us? Our hearts do not need to be troubled. We are not alone. We are not on our own. We have a choice about whether or not we allow ourselves to be troubled.

In many ways, we are gatekeepers of what we allow and disallow— instructions for going out to war. Deuteronomy 20:3 "And he shall say to them, 'Hear, O Israel: Today you are on the verge of battle with your enemies. Do not let your heart faint, do not be afraid, and do not tremble or be terrified because of them." John 14:1, "Let not your heart be troubled; you believe in God, believe also in Me." John 14:27, "Peace I leave with you, My peace I give to you; not as the world gives do I give to you. Let not your heart be troubled, neither let it be afraid."

---

[31] Read more: https://www.christianquotes.info/quotes-by-author/john-bunyan-quotes/#ixzz4zX5DNm00

Jesus knew he was leaving. He wanted to prepare his disciples and offer them comfort. We have a choice about what we do with the troubles that come to us. We can find ourselves allowing the troubles to overwhelm us, or we can seek help from Jesus, from the scriptures, from prayer and spiritual exercises. When we pass through troubles, they do not need to overwhelm us. Peter walked on water until he started sinking, and Jesus helped him when Peter cried out. Hebrews 12 urges us to look unto Jesus, the author and finisher of our faith. Are we praying from troubled hearts?

Are we praying from confidence in who God is and who God can be in this moment? Are we praying the names of God? The I Am's of Christ? Jesus, You are the Way, the Truth, the Life. The Bread of Life. The Light of the World. The Door. The Good Shepherd. The Alpha and the Omega. The Beginning and the End. The One who came to seek and save that which was lost. The One who came to call sinners to repentance. The One who invited us to receive supernatural peace. Not as the world gives and the One whose words are spirit and life.

Closing Prayer: Oh, Father God, in the name of Jesus, we come to You today and ask You, Lord, to help us with our troubled hearts. Places where we have allowed our hearts to be troubled. Places where we need an infusion of faith to believe Your promises, to believe You. Save us, heal us, deliver us. Come to us. Holy Spirit, come and move in our midst today to call souls to Jesus Christ, who is coming again in power and great glory to receive us to Himself that where he is, there we may also be. Thank You, Lord. In Your name, we pray, Jesus. Amen.

Mary Magdalene (1ˢᵗ Person)
Luke 8:1-2

April 11, 2021

Luke 8:1-2 (NIV) *"After this, Jesus traveled about from one town and village to another, proclaiming the good news of the kingdom of God. The Twelve were with him, and also some women who had been cured of evil spirits and diseases: Mary (called Magdalene) from whom seven demons had come out."*

Good Morning to all of you who are gathered here and to those of you who will be listening later. It is with gratitude and delight that I bring us a message of encouragement this morning.

Let us pray: May the words of my mouth and the meditations of my heart be acceptable in your sight, O Lord, my Strength and my Redeemer. Lord God, You are the One who made us. You are the One who saves us. You are the One who preserves us by Your mighty power. O dear Father, come be in our midst today and honor Your son, Jesus, in our gathering this morning. Holy Spirit, would You come and speak to our hearts? Come and enlighten our minds and embolden our spirits to declare and proclaim the Good News of Jesus today. It is in the wonderful name of Jesus we pray and ask these things, Amen.

Please hear the message as I deliver it today in this first-person rendering.

You may have heard my name. My name is Mary. I am one of the Marys in scripture. There are several Marys— Of course, there is Mary, the mother of Jesus. But there is also Mary of Bethany, the sister of Martha and Lazarus. Then there is Mary, the mother of James and Joseph, and Mary, the wife of Clopas. So that folks do not get confused about which Mary I am, the gospel writers used the town I came from to differentiate my name from our Lord Jesus's mother and the other Marys. My name occurs twelve times in the holy gospels. New Testament Scripture does not mention me by name after the gospels.

And, since that time, since the gospels were written, Church History and cultural mythology have done some imagining about me. Sermons have been preached. Songs have been written. Paintings have been painted. Sculptures have been carved. Books, films, and media have taken GREAT liberties with their imaginations about me. Please, for now, I invite you to suspend what you have heard from popular culture. Clear away any of your ideas and speculations about the 2000 years since I first met Jesus. Since there is not much narrative about me in the gospels, you can understand how imaginations and speculations could have led to fanciful tales and widespread misinformation.

The place I came from is a fishing village by the sea. The village is still there on the Sea of Galilee today. The little town is called Magdala, Migdal, today. They call me Mary of Magdala, Mary the Magdalene, and Mary Magdalene, for short. Some church leaders and authorities have written that I was the woman caught in adultery. Some think I was the sinful woman weeping at the feet of Jesus. Some have even confused me with Mary of Bethany. I am here to tell you today that I am Mary of Magdala, one of the faithful followers of Jesus. I traveled with him from town to town. You can read my name in the first three verses of Chapter 8 of Luke's gospel.

> *After this, Jesus traveled about from one town and village to another, proclaiming the good news of the kingdom of God. The Twelve were with him, and also some women who had been cured of evil spirits and diseases: Mary (called Magdalene) from whom seven demons had come out; Joanna the wife of Chuza, the manager of Herod's household; Susanna; and many others. These women were helping to support them out of their own means.*

You see, my name is there with the notable women who traveled with and supported Jesus and the Twelve. We had our own means of support, and we were on the road with Jesus. Jesus was the rabbi who taught women and men. Usually, rabbis in my time were followed by men. Jesus was a different kind of rabbi. Jesus taught with authority. Jesus had both men and women who followed him and became faithful followers along the way.

Today I would like to take you with me to the tomb of Jesus. That is where we will go early in the morning. Please come along with me as I tell you about what happened to me after the Sabbath, early in the morning, when it was still dark, I had gone to the tomb. It was as early as I could get there after the Sabbath. Before the Sabbath, on the day they crucified my Lord, I was there. I was there with the other women when Jesus looked at us and said, Daughters of Jerusalem, do not weep for me. I saw him dragged away to die. I saw what they did to him. I saw them take him away. I saw him lifted up and crucified on that cross between two criminals. I was there with the other women and John. I watched as my Lord, Jesus, took his last breath and cried out, "It is finished! Father, into your hands, do I commend my spirit." I heard the centurion praise God and say, "Surely this was a righteous man." Luke writes about us (in Chapter 23:49) "But all those [of us] who knew him, including [us] women who had followed him from Galilee, stood at a distance, watching these things." I watched as Joseph of Arimathea and Nicodemus took his body away to the garden tomb. I followed to see the place where they laid my Lord to rest in the tomb. (Luke 23 in verses 55 and 56) [We] women who had come with Jesus from Galilee followed Joseph and saw the tomb and how his body was laid in it. Then [we] went home and prepared spices and perfumes. But [we] rested on the Sabbath in obedience to the commandment. I watched as they rolled the stone in front of the tomb. It was time for the Sabbath. We did not do any work on the Sabbath. We did not leave our homes until the next day, the first day of the week. I was there while it was still dark, just before dawn. I wanted to bring spices and preserve his body for as long as spices work to preserve a body. I wanted to honor his body in death with spices for his body. I wanted to see him one more time. I then asked myself, How? How could this be happening? It was so hard for me to believe that the One who loved me, who loved us, had died such a dreadful death, like a common criminal. So. Much. Evil. The leaders of the synagogue were plotting against him and lying about him. They found false witnesses to accuse him and invent stories to insinuate that Jesus was a threat to the Romans, that Jesus was a threat to the religious leaders, and that Jesus was a threat to the way of life that they had always known. The sign over his head on the cross said, "Jesus of Nazareth, the King of the Jews." The sign was written in Aramaic, Latin, and Greek.

Yes. A king had been born in Bethlehem thirty-something years ago. Shepherds had heard the news that the newborn baby would be wrapped in swaddling clothes and lying in a manger. Magi, wise men from the East, came with their gifts for this king, gold, frankincense, and myrrh. The baby wrapped once in swaddling clothes at his birth was now wrapped in burial clothes, strips of linen, at his death.

I met Jesus after he started his ministry. It was after he grew up in Nazareth after he was baptized by John the Baptist. Jesus traveled around Galilee and ministered in many places. The synagogue in Capernaum is not far from my town of Magdala. In your measurements, Magdala was about 5 miles away from Capernaum. I met him as he was healing the sick, helping the blind to see, causing the deaf to hear, and casting out demons that oppressed folks. I, myself, was one of those who were oppressed by demons. When the gospel writers of Mark and Luke write about me, they say, Mary Magdalene, "out of whom seven demons were cast." Yes. It is true. I am not ashamed of what they write about me.

What is NOT clear is how I got those demons, which demons they were, how long it took for those demons to come out, and how my life changed since the demons went away. I am so glad the demons are gone. I am a living witness that deliverance happens, and oppression can be remedied. You can speculate, you can try to list my demons, you could just imagine. You can try to imagine how bound up in sin I was, but just know this: It is not about where I came from that is important. It is not about which demons I had that are important. It is not about how sinful and caught in sinful ways I was. I tell you that I was completely SET FREE. I was changed. I have been changed. It is like I am a new person since I have been freed from what kept me bound. I am so glad that deliverance is possible. Freedom is possible through Jesus.

I can tell you that if you are bound up in sin and bound up in shame, Jesus can set you free. The good news of the kingdom of God includes deliverance from being captive to the evil one. I gladly became a faithful follower of Jesus.

No matter who you are. No matter what your past has been. No matter how much despair you have suffered. No matter how much fear, how much dread, how much trembling you have endured. In Jesus, there is freedom. There is a release. There is faith, hope, and love.

And now we are going back to that day. As we go to the tomb together EARLY on that first day of the week. There I was at the empty tomb. I saw that the stone had been rolled away. My first thought was that someone had come and had taken my Lord away. I was ready to go and find him. I was weeping and weeping. Matthew, Mark, and Luke record that there were other women with me, and yet the gospel of John focuses on my account at the tomb. And now, let's hear the account from John's Gospel, Chapter 20:

> *Early on the first day of the week, while it was still dark, [I,] Mary Magdalene, went to the tomb and saw that the stone had been removed from the entrance. So [I] came running to Simon Peter and the other disciple, the one Jesus loved, and said, "They have taken the Lord out of the tomb, and we don't know where they have put him!" When all I saw was the empty tomb, I ran to tell the disciples that the tomb was empty. They have taken the Lord away. I told the disciples, "They have taken the Lord out of the tomb, and we don't know where they have put him!"*

You see, an empty space, an empty tomb, was NOT the GOOD NEWS. And just an empty space is just an empty space, especially if they had taken the Lord away.

Then John's gospel records the footrace that Peter and the beloved disciple had that morning. Listen to the account in John (Chapter 20, starting verse 3):

> *So Peter and the other disciple started for the tomb. Both were running, but the other disciple outran Peter and reached the tomb first. He bent over and looked in at the strips of linen lying there but did not go in. Then Simon Peter came along behind him and went straight into the tomb. He saw the strips of linen lying there, as well as the cloth that had been wrapped around Jesus' head. The cloth was still lying in its place, separate from the linen. Finally, the other disciple, who had reached the tomb first, also went inside. He saw and believed. (They still did not understand from Scripture that Jesus had to rise from the dead.) Then the disciples went back to where they were staying.*

I stayed at the tomb when the disciples returned to where they were staying. I had told them with my friends. We had told the disciples that the tomb was empty. The disciples did not believe us. They wanted to see for themselves. Peter and John went running, and John was the first to get there, but Peter was the one who first went into the tomb, and then John followed. What did I see? The empty tomb was empty except for bands of cloth. The cloth wrappings were folded and empty. What did I do? I stayed. I was weeping. And as I was standing outside the tomb, weeping, I bent over to look into the tomb, and I saw two angels in white, seated where Jesus' body had been, one at the head and the other at the foot. (vv. 13-14) They asked me, "Woman, why are you crying?" "They have taken my Lord away," I said, "and I don't know where they have put him." At this, I turned around and saw Jesus standing there, but I did not realize that it was Jesus. I turned, and then I saw Jesus, but I did not recognize him. Here was someone who was at the garden tomb. Could this be the gardener? Then (v. 15) [He] asked [me], "Woman, why are you crying? Who is it you are looking for? "Still Thinking he was the gardener, I said, "Sir, if you have carried him away, tell me where you have put him, and I will get him." I was determined to find my Lord and get him back from wherever they had taken him. (v.16) Jesus said to [me], "Mary." (Mirrium) in Aramaic. [I] turned toward him and cried out in Aramaic, "Rabboni!" (which means "Teacher").

What did I hear? Did you hear it? He said my name, "Mary." It was when Jesus said my name that I recognized him. Up until then, I thought he was the gardener. When I heard him say my name, it was then that I knew. I knew him! Here was Jesus, the One who loved me. Here was Jesus. No one ever cared for me like Jesus. Here was Jesus. Oh, how I love Him. Here was Jesus. JESUS. Risen from the dead.

It was so difficult to comprehend. The stone had been rolled away. The tomb was empty. The burial linens were empty. Here was Jesus. He called me by name. When Jesus calls your name, you know his voice. You know it is him. When you know Jesus, you recognize his voice. We follow Him, the Good Shepherd. The voice of a stranger we do not follow. Knowing the Good Shepherd so well, we know his voice, and he knows us by name. Now listen for Jesus to say *your* name. How does the voice of Jesus sound when he says your name?

If we imagine a harsh voice, a critical voice, an angry voice, we are missing the voice of Jesus. Does it sound like He is angry? If you hear an angry voice calling your name, that voice is NOT Jesus. Harsh, angry, critical voices are the voices of our imagination or voices of our enemy, not the love of our God. Listen again. Listen for the love. Listen for the tender voice. Listen today. He is calling you. He is calling your name. How do you hear his voice? Does it sound like a gentle whisper? Jesus's voice is invitational. Does it sound like the voice of many waters? Jesus has a powerful voice. When Jesus calls your name, how does His voice sound to you? Listen for your name with a voice of tenderness, a voice of welcome, a voice of the One who calls you by your name. Jesus called the disciples by name. Jesus called fishermen by name and asked them to leave their nets and follow Him. Jesus called Zacchaeus by name to come down from the tree. Zacchaeus repented, restored what he had stolen, and decided to follow Jesus. Jesus called Martha by name and told her she was distracted by many tasks. Jesus called Lazarus to come forth from the tomb and be resurrected.

At the garden tomb on that resurrection morning, Jesus called my name, Mary. "Mirrium," in Aramaic. I called him "Rabboni," teacher. We shared a knowing moment together. I was so ready to embrace him, to cling to him, to hold on to him. I thought he was dead and gone, and now here he was, ALIVE. So amazing. When he said my name, I knew it was him. When he said my name, I recognized my Lord. When he said my name, I heard the love. When he said my name, I heard the acceptance. I remembered all of the days of following him. Now he was back from the dead and here with me again. I wanted things to be the way they were before. Now, finally, things could go back to normal. But wait, resurrection life is not like the old normal. Resurrection life is a NEW Normal.

Then, he gave me these instructions (starting in John 20 verse 17) "Jesus said, "Do not hold on to me, for I have not yet ascended to the Father. Go instead to my brothers and tell them, 'I am ascending to my Father and your Father, to my God and your God.'" When Jesus said, "Do not cling to me, for I have not yet ascended to my Father." I wanted to hold on to him and never let him go. But I obeyed his words. (John 20:18) [I], Mary Magdalene went to the disciples with the news: "I have seen the Lord!" And I told them that he had said these things to [me].

And did you hear his instructions, "Go instead to my brothers and tell them, 'I am ascending to my Father and your Father, to my God and your God.'" Brothers! Family. Resurrection has now made the disciples brothers. They are now part of Jesus's family. Part of God's family. Jesus promised us that if he went away, he would not leave us as orphans. Jesus promised that he would come to us. Jesus would send the Comforter, the Holy Spirit, who would be with us and in us.

So, today my brothers and sisters, who are meeting in your time and space and place, listen to me. My voice is 2000 years old. And yet, I am still a credible witness to the resurrection. The disciples wanted to dismiss my message. It was so inconceivable and incredulous that they thought I was telling fables. In your day, and since the day it happened, the message of the resurrection of Jesus continues to be believed and disbelieved. Faithful followers of Jesus have been proclaiming the resurrection of Jesus and the good news for close to 2000 years. Whether you believe me or disbelieve me, I am still a credible witness. I am an eyewitness to the truth and message of the resurrected Lord Jesus. Jesus commissioned me right there at the tomb. In a world where women were looked down upon, Jesus commissioned ME to go tell the disciples. Yes. Jesus sent me, this WOMAN, Mary of Magdala, to tell the Eleven, the brothers, the good news. I was commissioned with the message of the gospel, the good news. And I went and told the good news, "I have seen the Lord!" When I saw him, when I saw Jesus, raised from the dead, my life was forever changed. I was there. I saw him. I saw the Lord. I tell you, He's alive! Jesus has risen. He has risen, indeed! Truly, Jesus is the resurrection and the life, just as He said. And Jesus appeared to me, and he appeared to the disciples in Galilee and many others.

One day, on the Mount of Olives, he gathered us together, and he gave us power and authority to go and tell the Good News, to teach, make disciples, baptize, and proclaim his message to the ends of the earth. And then he ascended into the heavens. He ascended to his Father and our Father. And during the feast of Pentecost, God sent the Holy Spirit to be with us and to be in us to empower us as we continue to proclaim the good news of the gospel of Jesus Christ.

Maybe you have been weeping. Perhaps you feel like you are in a place that is betwixt and between. Maybe you have been calling God's name and not seeing the answers you hoped to see. I can encourage you today that God will see you through. Jesus is worthy to be trusted, to be worshiped, and believed. Maybe you have been telling others and sharing the good news of our risen Savior. Keep sharing the good news of what you have seen and heard, whether or not anyone believes you.

Jesus is calling you. Will you listen? Will you hear Him? Will you tell others what you have seen and heard? His promises are still good. He promised to be with us. He promised never to leave us or forsake us. His promises are still working. Jesus keeps his word. When Jesus calls your name, He is inviting you to come. When Jesus calls your name, He is inviting you to follow Him. When Jesus calls your name, He has an assignment for you. When Jesus calls your name, He has encouragement for you. When Jesus calls your name, He has a purpose for you to fulfill. Jesus is inviting you to a changed life, a new life, a transformed life. A lifelong journey with him. Listen! Now it is YOUR turn. And YOUR turn. And YOUR turn. Jesus is calling you by name. Now, Jesus is calling YOUR name. Amen.

Closing Prayer: Let us Pray. O Lord Jesus, From the very first day we met, we felt Your love and Your invitation to come. We have come here today to say thank You once again. Thank You for the hope that we have in You and in Your power to meet us right where we are with all of our faults and our times of wandering and going astray. Come once again, O Lord, and bring Your salvation and healing grace to places in us that need saving and healing. Thank You, Lord. Amen.

Ministry Time: If anyone would like prayer today after the service, meet us over here, and we will be happy to pray with you and for you.

Benediction: May you know Jesus and the power of his resurrection. May you have eyes to see the Lord and his handiwork. May you have ears to hear the voice of the Lord. May you have a renewed mind to think about those things that are lovely and of a good report. May you have hands to do good May you have feet that are swift to obey the Lord. May You have the heart to love all that the Lord has given you to love. May you go in peace and in the assurance of God's love for you. Amen.

Naaman: Life's Turning Points
2 Kings 5:1

January 22, 2017

2 Kings 5:1 (NASB) *"Now Naaman, captain of the army of the king of Aram, was a great man with his master, and highly respected, because by him the Lord had given victory to Aram. The man was also a valiant warrior, but he was a leper."*

Opening Prayer: Thank You, Lord, for this day that You have made. We will rejoice and be glad in it. We thank You for the times and seasons in which we live, and we thank You for turning points. And we ask that You teach us today from Your word. And we ask for Your Holy Spirit. Holy Spirit, Come and bring Your word to bear on our hearts that we might respond to You and Your invitation to us. In Jesus' name. Amen.

Introduction. In our country, we have recently witnessed elections and the transfer of power from one president to another. It is a process called the peaceful transfer of power. With each peaceful transfer of power, the government shifts with ideas and leaders who need our support and prayer. When there are pivotal moments, hinge moments, and trajectory adjusting moments, we call them turning points. Right now, we are living at a turning point moment in our country. In our world. History is happening. Choices with far-reaching ramifications are being made.

One of my favorite books on church history explains turning point moments in church history. Some of us are studying a class on the Holy Spirit, and on Friday night, we learned about some of these critical turning point moments in church history. In the Bible, we see turning points in the transfer of power and leadership from Moses to Joshua, from Joshua to Judges, from Saul to David, and from David to his son, Solomon. Then we see a divided kingdom in the North under Jeroboam, the son of Nebat, and the kingdom in the south that carries on the Davidic lineage in the land of Judah. We have records of the kings of Israel and Judah in the two books of the Kings and two books of the Chronicles. At the time of the writing of the Books of the Kings, there were many prophets in Israel. There were prophets of Baal, and there were prophets of the true God.

One of the most famous prophets was Elijah. Most of the accounts of Elijah are in 1 Kings. You might remember that he challenged the prophets of Baal on Mount Carmel with dueling sacrifices. The prophets of Baal were to assemble and call on their God, and Elijah would call on his God. And the God who answered by fire would be the true God. After that contest, Elijah ran far away from an angry queen Jezebel who wanted him dead for killing all of the prophets of Baal. And while Elijah was far away, God provided food, spoke to him, and gave him three instructions, one of which was to call Elisha to be his apprentice prophet. Elijah found Elisha plowing in the field with oxen and called him. Elisha burned the plow, cooked the oxen, and went to apprentice with Elijah. The time came for Elijah to be taken away, and Elisha did not want to leave his side. All the schools of the prophets came out and prophesied that this would be the day Elijah would be taken away from Elisha. The peaceful transfer of power came in 2 Kings Chapter 2 when Elijah is about to go to heaven in a whirlwind. If you want to locate 2 Kings 2, I will read from there before we get to the main text in 2 Kings 5 today.

2 Kings 2:6-14 Starting with verse 6:

> *Then, Elijah said to him, "Please stay here, for the Lord has sent me to the Jordan." And he said, "As the Lord lives, and as you yourself live, I will not leave you." So the two of them went on. 7 Now fifty men of the sons of the prophets went and stood opposite them at a distance, while the two of them stood by the Jordan. 8 Elijah took his mantle and folded it together and struck the waters, and they were divided here and there, so that the two of them crossed over on dry ground. 9 When they had crossed over, Elijah said to Elisha, "Ask what I shall do for you before I am taken from you." And Elisha said, "Please, let a double portion of your spirit be upon me." 10 He said, "You have asked a hard thing. Nevertheless, if you see me when I am taken from you, it shall be so for you; but if not, it shall not be so." 11 As they were going along and talking, behold, there appeared a chariot of fire and horses of fire which separated the two of them. And Elijah went up by a whirlwind to heaven. 12 Elisha saw it and cried out, "My father, my father, the chariots of Israel and its horsemen!" And he saw Elijah no more. Then he took hold of his own clothes and tore them in two pieces. 13 He also took up the mantle of Elijah that fell from him and returned and stood by the bank of the Jordan. 14 He took the mantle of Elijah that fell from him and struck the waters and said, "Where is the Lord, the God of Elijah?" And when he also had struck the waters, they were divided here and there; and Elisha crossed over.*

Elisha and Naaman. Today's message is a little farther into the accounts of the prophet Elisha in 2 Kings 5. Locate 2 Kings chapter 5 on your handheld devices or in your printed Bible. In 2 Kings 5, we are going to meet a cast of characters. We will be reading the entire chapter piece by piece and stopping along the way for observations and lessons on turning points. I will start with reading verse 1.

> *Now Naaman, captain of the army of the king of Aram, was a great man with his master, and highly respected, because by him the Lord had given victory to Aram. The man was also a valiant warrior, but he was a leper. 2 Now the Arameans had gone out in bands and had taken captive a little girl from the land of Israel; and she waited on Naaman's wife. 3 She said to her mistress, "I wish that my master were with the prophet who is in Samaria! Then he would cure him of his leprosy." 4 Naaman went in and told his master, saying, "Thus and thus spoke the girl who is from the land of Israel." 5 Then the king of Aram said, "Go now, and I will send a letter to the king of Israel." He departed and took with him ten talents of silver and six thousand shekels of gold and ten changes of clothes.*

Introducing Naaman. NOTICE: Now Naaman, captain of the army of the king of Aram, was a great man with his master and highly respected because by him, the Lord had given victory to Aram. The man was also a valiant warrior, but he was a leper. Notice the description of Naaman. CAPTAIN of the ARMY, Commander of the Army. He is a leader of the army of the King of Aram. King of Syria. The rival to the northeast of Israel. He is highly respected and has great favor with the king. Why does Naaman have favor? Because, by him, the Lord had given victory to Aram. In a time of war with neighbors, the LORD had given the victory to Naaman the Syrian. Naaman of Aram. Naaman was a valiant warrior. Brave, courageous, bold, strong, disciplined, fearless, commanding. But he was a LEPER. He had a skin condition that was disturbing his life and his work. Naaman was miserably afflicted. Life changes when you or your loved one gets a diagnosis of a condition that has no known cure.

Introducing the Unnamed Girl. NOTICE Verse 2 Now, the Arameans had gone out in bands and had taken captive a little girl from the land of Israel, and she waited on Naaman's wife. Here is a little girl who came from Israel. From one of the raids the army made. Taken from her home, her parents, her life. And brought to enemy territory to work as a slave, as a servant in the house of Naaman. Would she be upset about her capture? Would she be faithful to serve in the place where she was taken? Verse 3 She said to her mistress, "I wish that my master were with the prophet who is in Samaria! Then he would cure him of his leprosy." This sounds like she wants things to go well for her master, for her mistress. She could have been silent. She could have served her mistress and never said anything about what she knew. But she had the courage to speak. She had faith that Naaman could be healed, could be cleansed. IF ONLY, IF ONLY. IF ONLY he were with the prophet in Samaria. IF only. Then he would be cured. We do not see her talking to Naaman himself. We see her talking to Naaman's wife.

Introducing the King of Aram. NOTICE 4 Naaman went in and told his master, saying, "Thus and thus spoke the girl who is from the land of Israel."5 Then the king of Aram said, "Go now, and I will send a letter to the king of Israel." He departed and took with him ten talents of silver and six thousand shekels of gold, and ten changes of clothes. Somewhere between verses 3 and 4, the message of THUS and THUS gets to Naaman. His wife tells him, or his wife takes the unnamed girl to tell him, BUT in verse 4, Naaman is having an audience with the king and telling him that the little unnamed girl said THUS AND THUS. And watch it. The king of Aram, the great King of Syria, says GO NOW. At the word of the little girl. The king says. GO. GO NOW. It is a word of hope for healing, for cleansing. It takes faith for Naaman to believe the servant girl, to hope that this is true. To have the confidence to go to the King. And for the king to have faith that THUS and THUS is true. There is healing in Israel. The God of Israel might be more powerful than the God of Aram in eradicating this skin disease. For a price. So. The King does the diplomatic thing and sends a letter to the King of Israel. A letter of introduction with a request for curing leprosy and a payment of 10 talents of silver and six thousand shekels of gold and ten beautiful and elaborate garments. AND Naaman goes to the King of Israel with his entourage.

Introducing the King of Israel vs. 6-7. He brought the letter to the king of Israel, saying, "And now as this letter comes to you, behold, I have sent Naaman my servant to you, that you may cure him of his leprosy." 7 When the king of Israel read the letter, he tore his clothes and said, "Am I God, to kill and to make alive, that this man is sending word to me to cure a man of his leprosy? But consider now, and see how he is seeking a quarrel against me."

NOTICE. The king of Israel does not know what to do with this request from the enemy who has raided his territory and captured goods and slaves. He tears his clothes as a sign that he does not have the power of God and does not want to act in place of God in this request. The king of Israel does not see the hand of God moving in this situation. He sees the surface, and the surface looks like the King of Aram is trying to pick a fight.

SO. We can cause a great deal of upset to ourselves when we misread the signs, and we attribute motives to others that are not there.

Introducing Elisha. vs. 8 It happened when Elisha, the man of God, heard that the king of Israel had torn his clothes, that he sent word to the king, saying, "Why have you torn your clothes? Now let him come to me, and he shall know that there is a prophet in Israel." O King, there is good news. This is not about the king of Aram picking a fight with you. God is alive and well. God sees you, O King, and God sees Naaman, and God sent Naaman to you for him to know that God has good news for Naaman and God has good news for Syria. There is a prophet in Israel. One who can speak for this God that Naaman needs to know. Send him to me. I have every confidence that God will show Naaman that there is a God in Israel. 2 Kings 5:9-12:

> *So Naaman came with his horses and his chariots and stood at the doorway of the house of Elisha. 10 Elisha sent a messenger to him, saying, "Go and wash in the Jordan seven times, and your flesh will be restored to you, and you will be clean." 11 But Naaman was furious and went away and said, "Behold, I thought, 'He will surely come out to me and stand and call on the name of the Lord his God, and wave his hand over the place and cure the leper.' 12 Are not Abanah and Pharpar, the rivers of Damascus, better than all the waters of Israel? Could I not wash in them and be clean?" So he turned and went away in a rage. 13 Then his servants came near and spoke to him and said, "My father, had the prophet told you to do some great thing, would you not have done it? How much more then, when he says to you, 'Wash, and be clean'?" 14 So he went down and dipped himself seven times in the Jordan, according to the word of the man of God; and his flesh was restored like the flesh of a little child and he was clean.*

Naaman goes to Elisha's house. NOTICING. Introducing the messenger in Verse 10. "So Naaman came with his horses and his chariots and stood at the doorway of the house of Elisha. 10 Elisha sent a messenger to him, saying, "Go and wash in the Jordan seven times, and your flesh will be restored to you and you will be clean." NOTICE. Naaman was not expecting to see a messenger. Naaman was expecting to see the prophet. Naaman was not expecting these instructions. Verse 11 But Naaman was furious and went away and said, "Behold, I thought, 'He will surely come out to me and stand and call on the name of the Lord his God, and wave his hand over the place and cure the leper.' 12 Are not Abanah and Pharpar, the rivers of Damascus, better than all the waters of Israel? Could I not wash in them and be clean?" So he turned and went away in a rage.

What was Naaman's Reaction? What did Naaman expect? He expected to be treated as the important person he was. Had not the little girl said that she wished he could meet the prophet in Samaria and be cured? Had not he risked it at her word to go to the king and get the letter of introduction, and had he not brought enough of a reward in silver and gold and fine clothes?

Suppose we put ourselves in Naaman's shoes. How could he be so snubbed by the prophet to send just a messenger? A messenger to greet this one who needs the touch of the prophet? This is infuriating. This is outrageous. This is beyond belief. And the message about the river. The Jordan river. Really? Have we not better rivers in Damascus? Sometimes in our lives, Good ideas can meet Resistance. Things that are the solution to the problem are not well-received. The cure is not accepted. What is our reaction to someone trying to get us to do something that we do not want to do? Naaman's reaction to washing in the Jordan was to immediately reject the idea and make up alternative plans for cleaner rivers in his country.

Think about this. What ideas have we been rejecting lately that we might need to reconsider?

Turning Points In Life Often Meet With Initial Resistance. Introducing Naaman's servants. Verse13 Then his servants came near and spoke to him and said, "My father, had the prophet told you to do some great thing, would you not have done it? How much more then, when he says to you, 'Wash, and be clean'?" *This question is a turning point question moment.* To wash or not to wash. That is the question. Naaman's healing, his cleansing, hangs in the balance here. Naaman has been offended by the prophet. We might remember Proverbs 15:1, "A soft answer turns away wrath." Naaman's servants came near with what I imagine to be a soft approach—entreating as "my father." Pleading with Naaman to consider what Naaman would have been willing to do. They suggested that Naaman would have been willing to do some GREAT thing. And. HOW MUCH MORE, then, when this prophet has sent the message, "Wash, and be clean." Are there things we have been asked to do that we think are beneath us? We wanted to have something GREAT to do, and we were given instructions that we did not expect. Who do we have in our lives to ask the turning point questions?

Good Leaders Are Willing To Take Advice. Maybe you feel like you have no power or influence in a situation. Think of the servant girl. She had no physical power working as a slave. But she had influence because she shared the hope that what she knew could help her master. Good leaders are willing to take advice. Good leaders listen. Notice: If you are a leader today, If I am a leader today, we need to be aware that some of the best advice might come from unlikely sources. Someone we might not have previously considered just might hold a key turning point place in our lives.

Naaman Obeys. Notice what happens in verse 14, "So he went down and dipped himself seven times in the Jordan, according to the word of the man of God; and his flesh was restored like the flesh of a little child and he was clean." Imagine Naaman the first time. Second. Third. Fourth. Fifth. Sixth. And what if he stopped? Was there any hesitation? Was there any doubt? But he did not stop. He dipped the seventh time, and then, at the seventh time, his flesh was restored as the flesh of a little child. Where else have we seen seven times? Gen 33:3 Jacob bows before Esau seven times, Joshua 6 seven times around the city of Jericho. 1 Kings 18 Elijah sent the servant seven times to look for rain. Cleansing a leper. The priest was to dip in the blood seven times and sprinkle it seven times for cleansing. For further study, the laws of cleansing a leper are in Leviticus 14 and involve sacrifices and sprinkling seven times.

What If There Had Been Incomplete Obedience? What if Naaman had dipped in the Jordan 6 times? We would not have the healing ending to this episode. Here are questions that come to mind in this lesson. How many stories are not told? How many victories are not won? How many chapters are not written because humans did not completely obey? Where is there incomplete obedience in my life? 2 Kings 5:15-16:

> *When he returned to the man of God with all his company, and came and stood before him, he said, "Behold now, I know that there is no God in all the earth, but in Israel; so please take a present from your servant now." 16 But he said, "As the Lord lives, before whom I stand, I will take nothing." And he urged him to take it, but he refused.*

Elisha takes nothing. The ten talents of silver could have weighed 750 pounds. The 600 shekels of gold could have weighed 150 pounds. The ten changes of clothing were returning. All of it was going back in peace to Syria. Israel's God did not need these gifts as favors to buy the cleansing of the leper. God's cleansing and healing grace was freely given and freely received. 2 Kings 5:17-19:

> *Naaman said, "If not, please let your servant at least be given two mules' load of earth; for your servant will no longer offer burnt offering nor will he sacrifice to other gods, but to the Lord. 18 In this matter may the Lord pardon your servant: when my master goes into the house of Rimmon to worship there, and he leans on my hand and I bow myself in the house of Rimmon, when I bow myself in the house of Rimmon, the Lord pardon your servant in this matter." 19 He said to him, "Go in peace." So he departed from him some distance."*

NOTICE v 17. Here is the one who despised the waters of the Jordan in comparison to his rivers in Damascus, who now wants to take back mule loads of dirt from Israel to worship the true God Naaman asks for forgiveness in the line of duty as he accompanies his master. The Lord sees Naaman's heart. Sometimes we are called to go and do things that we do because we have a job to do. They are not illegal or immoral, but they could look like a compromise to some outsiders. The Lord knows Naaman's heart. Naaman truly has seen the hand of the true God in his life and he has been changed. VERSE 19. blessing from Elisha. GO in peace. 2 Kings 5:20-24:

> *But Gehazi, the servant of Elisha the man of God, thought, "Behold, my master has spared this Naaman the Aramean, by not receiving from his hands what he brought. As the Lord lives, I will run after him and take something from him." 21 So Gehazi pursued Naaman. When Naaman saw one running after him, he came down from the chariot to meet him and said, "Is all well?" 22 He said, "All is well. My master has sent me, saying, 'Behold, just now two young men of the sons of the prophets have come to me from the hill country of Ephraim. Please give them a talent of silver and two changes of clothes.'" 23 Naaman said, "Be pleased to take two talents." And he urged him, and bound two talents of silver in two bags with two changes of clothes and gave them to two of his servants; and they carried them before him. 24 When he came to the hill, he took them from their hand and deposited them in the house, and he sent the men away, and they departed.*

Gehazi's Greed. Gehazi was not content to see this offer of wealth go away. He wanted something. Gehazi blames Elisha for not taking what was offered. Notice that in verse 10, the messenger who came out to greet Naaman does not have a name. We cannot be certain whether or not it was Gehazi. So. Here is Naaman getting away with all of this wealth, and Gehazi hatches a plan to get some. He lies in the name of his master, Elisha. His covetousness leads to deviousness. He hid his treasures, much like Achan did after the battle of Jericho. 2 Kings 5:25-26:

> *But he went in and stood before his master. And Elisha said to him, "Where have you been, Gehazi?" And he said, "Your servant went nowhere." 26 Then he said to him, "Did not my heart go with you, when the man turned from his chariot to meet you? Is it a time to receive money and to receive clothes and olive groves and vineyards and sheep and oxen and male and female servants? 27 Therefore, the leprosy of Naaman shall cling to you and to your descendants forever." So he went out from his presence a leper as white as snow.*

Elisha knew. We cannot lie to God. Elisha blessed Naaman and cursed Gehazi. The power to bless and to curse is in our tongue. We are capable of using our words to bring life and death. Elisha knew that Gehazi had lied and could have set up a stumbling block for this new believer in Israel's God. Gehazi had broken the trust of Elisha. And we do not see Gehazi being repentant here. He lost his health and his position and brought harm to his family forever. Sin has consequences. We cannot lie and expect God to bless us. What we say matters. The little girl spoke the truth, and her influence led to the cleansing and renewal of Naaman's body and soul. Gehazi spoke a lie, and his influence led to a curse for him and for his household for generations.

Case of Missed Opportunities. What opportunities are we missing because we do not speak? When we have an idea. Maybe even a prompting from the Holy Spirit that we quench or quell or suppress. What opportunities are we missing because we do not listen when someone proposes something we consider to be outrageous or preposterous? What opportunities do we need to miss because they would be sinful? What if Gehazi had not seized the opportunity for personal gain at the expense of the truth? Missed opportunities can be turning points as much as opportunities taken. We need discernment to know which opportunities to take and which to reject.

What Can We Celebrate? In the turning points in the account of Naaman: Naaman believes an unlikely and unnamed servant girl who had the courage to speak. Naaman's resistance to the instructions and his offense at the prophet who did not come out to meet him personally were overcome by the soft answer and the reasonable questions of Naaman's servants who helped him see the light. Naaman did obey the instructions to wash in the Jordan seven times. Naaman's life was forever changed, and he wanted to take the dirt of the land from the God of Israel, who had cleansed and healed him back home with him. Naaman went home to Syria with a blessing. The prophet had said, Go in peace. The God of Israel had shined light and kindness on an enemy of Israel.

The account of Naaman is a significant chapter in life's turning points. Lest we think that is the last we hear of Naaman. Naaman is not isolated in the Book of 2 Kings. No. Turn with me to Luke 4. Jesus has stood up in the synagogue and read from the Prophet Isaiah and declared that favorable year of the Lord and then see what it says next in Luke 4: 24-27:

And He said, "Truly I say to you, no prophet is welcome in his hometown. 25 But I say to you in truth, there were many widows in Israel in the days of Elijah, when the sky was shut up for three years and six months, when a great famine came over all the land; 26 and yet Elijah was sent to none of them, but only to

Zarephath, in the land of Sidon, to a woman who was a widow. 27 And there were many lepers in Israel in the time of Elisha the prophet; and none of them was cleansed, but only Naaman the Syrian."

We have hope. We see Jesus, in Luke 4, announcing his mission in the synagogue from Isaiah 61:18-19, "The Spirit of the Lord is upon Me, Because He anointed Me to preach the gospel to the poor. He has sent Me to proclaim release to the captives, And recovery of sight to the blind, To set free those who are oppressed, To proclaim the favorable year of the Lord." Jesus has entrusted us with that mission. We are still called to preach the gospel to the poor, to proclaim release to the captives, to proclaim recovery of sight to the blind, to set free those who are oppressed, and to proclaim the favorable year of the Lord. Today is the day of salvation. Today is the day of cleansing. Today is the day to open our hearts to God's love and mercy. Jesus wants to save us and set us free. Will we hear Him calling us today?

Closing Prayer: O Lord, Gracious God, God of All of the Nations of the Earth. We thank You for seeing us and knowing us, for positioning us in places of influence. We believe You have us right where You want us, and we submit our hearts and lives to You. Grant us the courage to speak when we sense Your holy nudges to speak and the courage to act when we respond to Your invitation for action. For those who are suffering today with physical illnesses that need healing, Holy Spirit, come and heal. For those whose hearts need healing today, we invite You, O God, to work in our hearts. Grant us repentance. Grant us grace. Cleanse us and heal us. Forgive us for not speaking, not acting, and avoiding occasions for influence. We pray for our country in this transition of power in our government. We pray for Your kingdom to come and Your will to be done. O God, we cry out to You. Forgive our nation's sins, O God, and heal our land. In Jesus' mighty and matchless name, we pray, Amen.

Ministry Time. Does anyone need healing today in their body or soul? Has there been an opportunity for you to act or speak with influence this week: That you felt you obeyed God's prompting to act or speak? Did you think you failed to follow God's prompting to act or speak? How might we pray for you?

Nic at Night
John 3:1

April 12, 2015

John 3:1 (NASB) *"Now there was a man of the Pharisees, named Nicodemus, a ruler of the Jews; this man came to Jesus by night."*

Introduction: How many of us stay up late at night? How many of us get up early in the morning? I used to be more awake at "night." In the past few years, I have become an early morning person. When I was in my 20s, one summer at L'Abri in Switzerland, my friends and I would stay up late discussing theology. Since then, my husband, Allen, and I have attended some conferences, and we have stayed up later with prayer and discussions. The best times in the last few years of staying up late to discuss theological themes have been when we have participated in Movie Nights For Thinkers And Seekers at the Sculleys' home.[32] We watch movies together and discuss what we noticed about the characters, the plot, the themes, and the theological implications. Today, we will consider a portion of the Gospel of John, Chapter 3. This is an account of a man named Nicodemus and his theological conversation with Jesus.

Today's message is near the beginning of the book of John in the New Testament. It is the 4th gospel account. Turn past Matthew, Mark, and Luke to arrive at John. We could spend years just studying the book of John. It is simple enough for children to understand and deep enough for adults to study for a lifetime. The Gospel of John opens in Chapter 1 with Jesus as the Word who was in the beginning with God, who is God, who chose to come to earth as the Light, and who gives power to become children of God to as many as believe and receive him.

We see the forerunner, John, baptizing in the wilderness. We hear the message, "Behold the Lamb of God." We see early followers of Jesus, Andrew, Simon, and Nathaniel. Chapter 2 starts with the wedding at Cana, in which Jesus turns water into wine. At the end of Chapter 2, we have a record of signs and wonders. The end of Chapter 2 says, "Now when He was in Jerusalem at the Passover, during the feast, many believed in His name,

---

[32] Movie Nights for Thinkers and Seekers, http://movienightsforthinkersandseekers.com/.

observing His signs which He was doing. 24 But Jesus, on His part, was not entrusting Himself to them, for He knew all men, 25 and because He did not need anyone to testify concerning man, for He Himself knew what was in man."

Now we come to Chapter 3. "Now there was a man of the Pharisees, named Nicodemus, a ruler of the Jews; 2 this man came to Jesus by night and said to Him, "Rabbi, we know that You have come from God as a teacher; for no one can do these signs that You do unless God is with him." Let's stop there and look at the Pharisees. Nicodemus was a Pharisee. Who were the Pharisees? Where did they come from? What did they believe? The Pharisees were considered the "separated ones." In history, after the exile and before the advent of Christ, there was a group of Jews called the Hasidim, or God's loyal ones. We have records as early as 135 B.C. of them being known as the Pharisees.

Here are some characteristics: They prided themselves in being keepers of the law of Moses. They were looking for a messiah in the line of David, who would be an earthly king who would free them from the oppressive Roman rule. Not looking for God to come in the form of humanity. In the *New Bible Dictionary*, H. L. Ellison says, "Basic to the Pharisees conception of religion was the belief that the Babylonian Exile was caused by Israel's failure to keep the Torah (The Mosaic law), and that its keeping was an individual as well as a national duty."

They added hedges, customs, and traditions around the law so that the actual laws would not be broken. They kept themselves clean and free from contact with sinners and Gentiles so that they would avoid being defiled. In his book, *New Testament Survey*, M. C. Tenney says, "They were separatists, or Puritans of Judaism, who withdrew from all evil associations and sought to give complete obedience to every precept of the oral and written law."

The Pharisees were bound to have a clash with Jesus because they outwardly tried to keep the written and oral laws and temple worship. This led to clashes with Jesus because Jesus challenged their customs, traditions, and their hearts. Some of the clashes with Jesus came over the law and the Sabbath, eating with tax collectors and sinners and healing the sick on the Sabbath, picking grain on the Sabbath, eating with ceremonially unclean hands, and forgiving sins, which the Pharisees considered to be blasphemy. Jesus criticized the Pharisees for their self-righteousness, for burdening the people with legal precepts they invented. Jesus denounced the Pharisees publicly for their hypocrisy and spiritual blindness. He said that they were outwardly clean but full of greed and wickedness inside. Jesus was a threat to their leadership and popularity. Many persons followed Jesus. The Pharisees set traps for Jesus and tried to trick him with questions about inheriting eternal life, the greatest commandments, and the laws of divorce. They eventually plotted to kill him by handing him over to the Roman Governor. Not all of the Pharisees were aloof to Jesus. We see Nicodemus, the Pharisee, coming to Jesus at night.

Nicodemus Came at Night. Verse 1, This man came to Jesus by night. He comes to Jesus at night. Night speaks of darkness, no light. Things happen at night. These were days before Edison and the electric lights, candles, and fires. Here are some other verses that refer to "night" in the Gospel of John: John 9:4 (NASB), "We must work the works of Him who sent Me as long as it is day; night is coming when no one can work." John 11:10 (NASB), "But if anyone walks in the night, he stumbles, because the light is not in him." John 21:3 (NASB), after the crucifixion, Simon Peter said to them, "I am going fishing." They said to him, "We will also come with you." They went out and got into the boat, and that night they caught nothing.

Nicodemus watched, observed, and concluded that Jesus must be a person sent from God because Rabbi, we know that You have come from God as a teacher; for no one can do these signs that You do unless God is with him." Nicodemus calls Jesus, Rabbi, Teacher. Nicodemus was a teacher, and he addressed Jesus as Rabbi. He also says "WE know," the plural for the Pharisees, not just as one individual who has observed, but as a representative of the WE. So, they had seen the signs. They had noticed Jesus was getting a following, and Nicodemus believed God was with Jesus.

John 1 tells us that in the beginning, the Word was with God, and the Word WAS God. We then see how the WORD became flesh and dwelt among us and how for those who believed God gave the power to become children of God to those who believe in his name.

Let's read starting in Chapter 1:9-13 about Jesus,

> *There was the true Light which, coming into the world, enlightens every man. 10 He was in the world, and the world was made through Him, and the world did not know Him. 11 He came to His own, and those who were His own did not receive Him. 12 But as many as received Him, to them He gave the right to become children of God, even to those who believe in His name,13 who were born, not of blood nor of the will of the flesh nor of the will of man, but of God.*

So, after Nicodemus noticed that no one could do the signs Jesus did UNLESS God was with him, One might expect that Jesus would say, "Yes,

Nicodemus. Not only is God with ME, but I AM." There are several places in John Jesus says I AM. Who can think of some of the "I AM" statements of Jesus in the Book of John? I will read some of them. If you have one, raise your hand.

John 6:35 Jesus said to them, "I am the bread of life; he who comes to Me will not hunger, and he who believes in Me will never thirst." John 8:12, Then Jesus again spoke to them, saying, "I am the Light of the world; he who follows Me will not walk in the darkness, but will have the Light of life." John 10:7, "So Jesus said to them again, "Truly, truly, I say to you, I am the door of the sheep." John 10:11, "I am the good shepherd; the good shepherd lays down His life for the sheep." John 11:25, Jesus said to her, "I am the resurrection and the life; he who believes in Me will live even if he dies." John 15:5, "I am the vine, you are the branches; he who abides in Me and I in him, he bears much fruit, for apart from Me you can do nothing."

But, No! Jesus does NOT offer any "I AM" verses to Nicodemus. Jesus says something quite unexpected after Nicodemus has just talked about signs that Jesus has done. 3 Jesus answered and said to him, "Truly, truly, I say to you, unless one is born again, he cannot see the kingdom of God." "BORN AGAIN," Born from above. Now Nicodemus seems really confused. 4 Nicodemus said to Him, "How can a man be born when he is old? He cannot enter a second time into his mother's womb and be born, can he?"

Let's talk about birth. We are born—babies are carried and born—birth pains come, contractions come, and we know the baby is coming, or a C-Section is scheduled, and we know the baby is coming. When a baby is born, the amniotic fluid sac releases the fluid. The water breaks, and then the bloody parts happen as the mother heals. So is everyone who is born of the flesh. The cord has to be tied off and severed, or the baby will bleed. The mom needs to deliver the placenta and heal from the process. So is everyone who is born of the flesh. We have flesh and blood, and we are nurtured in a watery place in our mother's womb.

(Read the Henri Nouwen quote here with the twins talking):

> This was originally intended for helping patients understand death, but it can also help understand new birth. from Henri Nouwen's book on *Dying and Caring*. It is a story about a conversation between twins in their Mother's womb. The sister said to the brother, "I believe there is life after birth." Her brother protested vehemently, "No, no, this is all there is. This is a dark and cozy place, and we

155

have nothing else to do but cling to the cord that feeds us." The little girl insisted, "There must be something more than this dark place. There must be something else, a place with light where there is freedom to move." Still, she could not convince her twin brother. After some silence, the sister said hesitantly, I have something else to say, and I'm afraid you won't believe that, either, but I think there is a mother. Her brother became furious, "A mother!" he shouted. What are you talking about? I have never seen a mother, and neither have you. Who put that idea in your head? As I told you, this place is all we have. Don't you feel these squeezes every once in a while? They're quite unpleasant and sometimes even painful. I think that these squeezes are there to get us ready for another place, much more beautiful than this, where we will see our mother face--to--face. Don't you think that's exciting?

Just like the twins were getting ready for life after the womb, we have the opportunity for a new birth spiritually, being born from above, being born again.

Jesus goes on. John 3:5-7:

> *Jesus answered, "Truly, truly, I say to you, unless one is born of water and the Spirit he cannot enter into the kingdom of God. 6 That which is born of the flesh is flesh, and that which is born of the Spirit is spirit. 7 Do not be amazed that I said to you, 'You must be born again.'*

In John 1, John the Baptist is baptizing. Let's turn back to Chapter 1:29-34:

> *The next day he saw Jesus coming to him and said, "Behold, the Lamb of God who takes away the sin of the world! 30 This is He on behalf of whom I said, 'After me comes a Man who has a higher rank than I for He existed before me.' 31 I did not recognize Him, but so that He might be manifested to Israel, I came baptizing in water." 32 John testified saying, "I have seen the Spirit descending as a dove out of heaven, and He remained upon Him. 33 I did not recognize Him, but He who sent me to baptize in water said to me, 'He upon whom you see the Spirit descending and remaining upon Him, this is the One who baptizes in the Holy Spirit.' 34 I myself have seen and have testified that this is the Son of God."*

Now go back to Chapter 3. We have just heard Jesus saying to Nicodemus that You must be born again, born from above, born of the Spirit. Now Jesus starts talking about the wind, verse 8, "The wind blows where it wishes and you hear the sound of it, but do not know where it comes from and where it is going; so is everyone who is born of the Spirit." The wind blows. We see the effects of the wind, and we conclude that the wind is blowing. Flags unfurl, laundry fluffs, trees bend. The wind is blowing. Jesus takes being born of the flesh and shifts to being born of the Spirit. Being born of the Spirit is like the wind. We can be free to blow and move. And there will be effects. In a sermon in Athens, the Apostle Paul preaches that it is in Him we live and move and have our being (Acts 17). Paul writes in Galatians that the fruit of the spirit is love, joy, peace, patience, gentleness, goodness, kindness, and self-control. Against such, there is no law, yet there are effects.

We like to be with persons who truly love, have joy, walk in peace, have patience, demonstrate goodness and kindness, and are faithful, gentle, and self-controlled. Not only do we like to be with those persons who love and exhibit the fruit of the Spirit. We also pray that we would be so full of the Holy Spirit that we become those persons. We want the wind of the Holy Spirit to blow through us. No one has seen the wind. No one has seen the wind, yet we see the sailboats on the lake. We feel our clothes blowing. We walk on the beach and catch the ocean breeze. We feel the Spirit.

As I lead praise and worship times at the healthcare facility, one of the favorite songs is Every Time I Feel the Spirit moving in my heart, I will pray, sing, shout, and dance. What about a verse that says, "Every time I feel the Spirit moving in my heart I will love, forgive, lay hands on the sick, set captives free, open the eyes of the blind, be generous with all with which I have been so graciously entrusted?" What about US?

What happens when we feel the wind? Here is Nicodemus coming to Jesus at night with observations. No one can do what you do UNLESS God is with him. And Jesus changes the subject. No one can see the kingdom of God UNLESS they are born from above. UNLESS they are born anew. UNLESS they are born again. UNLESS they are born of water and of the Spirit.

Nicodemus, there is another dimension you do not know about. There is the realm of the Spirit. There is the Kingdom of God. The letter of the law kills, but the Spirit gives life and peace. You, Nic, have known the law. You, Nic, are a Pharisee, a teacher, a leader, and a ruler in Israel. You are a leader of the people. You sit in judgment of right and wrong according to the laws and standards. BUT, There is another dimension that does not fit in your box, Nic. It is the dimension of the Kingdom of God, of the Spirit, the Holy Spirit. This Holy Spirit is none other than the Spirit of the Living God. And the Father who loved the world so much that He GAVE his only begotten Son. Even as Moses lifted up the serpent in the wilderness, Nic, so the Son of Man must be lifted up that whoever believes in him may have eternal life. John 12:32 "And I, if I am lifted up from the earth, will draw all men to Myself."

God, the Spirit, gives life and breath. God the Spirit empowers us to be able to blow intentionally with purpose. God's purposes. Persons born of the wind receive God's love, God's son, God's plans and purposes, and God's kingdom. Persons born of the wind live and move and have our being in Him. Persons born of the wind are borne by, carried by the wind, And the conversation continues starting in verse 9.

> *Nicodemus said to Him, "How can these things be?" 10 Jesus answered and said to him, "Are you the teacher of Israel and do not understand these things? 11 Truly, truly, I say to you, we speak of what we know and testify of what we have seen, and you do not accept our testimony. 12 If I told you earthly things and you do not believe, how will you believe if I tell you heavenly things? 13 No one has ascended into heaven, but He who descended from heaven: the Son of Man. 14 As Moses lifted up the serpent in the wilderness, even so must the Son of Man be lifted up; 15 so that whoever believes will in Him have eternal life. 16 "For God so loved the world, that He gave His only begotten Son, that whoever believes in Him shall not perish, but have eternal life. 17 For God did not send the Son into the world to judge the world, but that the world might be saved through Him. 18 He who believes in Him is not judged; he who does not believe has been judged already, because he has not believed in the name of the only begotten Son of God. 19 This is the judgment, that the Light has come into the world, and men loved the darkness rather than the Light, for their deeds were evil. 20 For everyone who does evil hates the Light and does not come to the Light for fear that his deeds will be exposed. 21 But he who practices the truth comes to the Light, so that his deeds may be manifested as having been wrought in God.*

Was that the end of the story of Jesus and Nicodemus? NO! Nicodemus appears two more times in the Gospel of John. Turn to Chapter 7:40-53:

> *Some of the people therefore, when they heard these words, were saying, "This certainly is the Prophet." 41 Others were saying, "This is the Christ." Still others were saying, "Surely the Christ is not going to come from Galilee, is He? 42 Has not the Scripture said that the Christ comes from the descendants of David, and from Bethlehem, the village where David was?" 43 So a division occurred in the crowd because of Him. 44 Some of them wanted to seize Him, but no one laid hands on Him. 45 The officers then came to the chief priests and Pharisees, and they said to them, "Why did you not bring Him?" 46 The officers answered, "Never has a man spoken the way this man speaks." 47 The Pharisees then answered them, "You have not also been led astray, have you? 48 No one of the rulers or Pharisees has believed in Him, has he? 49 But this crowd*

which does not know the Law is accursed." 50 Nicodemus (he who came to Him before, being one of them) said to them, 51 "Our Law does not judge a man unless it first hears from him and knows what he is doing, does it?" 52 They answered him, "You are not also from Galilee, are you? Search, and see that no prophet arises out of Galilee." 53 Everyone went to his home.

What happened to Nic? In John 7, a question from Nic changes things for Jesus. The last place we see Nicodemus is later in John. Let's go to John 19, starting in verse 38, and read about Joseph of Arimathea.

After these things Joseph of Arimathea, being a disciple of Jesus, but a secret one for fear of the Jews, asked Pilate that he might take away the body of Jesus; and Pilate granted permission. So he came and took away His body. 39 Nicodemus, who had first come to Him by night, also came, bringing a mixture of myrrh and aloes, about a hundred pounds weight. 40 So they took the body of Jesus and bound it in linen wrappings with the spices, as is the burial custom of the Jews. 41 Now in the place where He was crucified there was a garden, and in the garden a new tomb in which no one had yet been laid. 42 Therefore because of the Jewish day of preparation, since the tomb was nearby, they laid Jesus there.

Nic. The one who came at night. John 19:39, "Nicodemus, who had first come to Him by night, also came, bringing a mixture of myrrh and aloes, about a hundred pounds *weight*." Here is Nic, serving without words, faithfully following and serving, bringing 75 or 100 pounds of spices. Look at a spice jar in your house and note the weight. What about us?

Are we walking in the night or in the light? If we are walking in the night, Jesus said there were persons who loved darkness rather than light because their deeds were evil. We are not called to walk in darkness. We are called to walk in the light as he is in the light. Walking in the light involves transparency, shining, honesty, and truthfulness. Romans 13:11-14 invites us to put on the Armor of Light.

Do this, knowing the time, that it is already the hour for you to awaken from sleep; for now salvation is nearer to us than when we believed. 12 The night is almost gone, and the day is near. Therefore let us lay aside the deeds of darkness and put on the armor of light. 13 Let us behave properly as in the day, not in carousing and drunkenness, not in sexual promiscuity and sensuality, not in strife and jealousy. 14 But put on the Lord Jesus Christ, and make no provision for the flesh in regard to its lusts.

Here we are. We all have an opportunity to receive Jesus as Lord today. We can Be born again. We can invite Jesus to take us out of darkness into his marvelous light. We can be empowered to live by the indwelling Holy Spirit. We can Be ready to move by the promptings of the Holy Spirit. We do not need to live as secret Christians here in our town. In some parts of the world believers are meeting in underground churches. They are persecuted, tortured, and martyred.

How much will it cost us to follow Jesus? How much are we willing to serve Him? Are we willing to speak a kind word to someone, notice someone that might be lonely? Maybe today, we know we have been trying to keep the ten commandments. Maybe we are trying to live a good life, to be respectable and be respected. Today we know there is more. We need the wind of God's Spirit. Maybe there is someone we need to think differently about. We have been watching their life, and we have noticed things about them that we have perhaps jumped to conclusions about and about them. Maybe we have concluded that this person is just this way BECAUSE, and then fill in the blank. Today, are we willing to surrender our judgments and conclusions about them and the reasons we think they act that way? Because, whatever reason we have been thinking, WE might want to pray and ask God to forgive US for judging them _____ fill in the blank, and ask God to help us become loving and forgiving.

Ministry Time. We can ask the Lord to help us today and this week to be filled with the wind of the Holy Spirit. Maybe there is someone here who has been sick in your soul or your body, and you need a healing touch today. We will invite the wind of God to come and blow on us. There are people who will pray with you today. Let this be a day of new beginnings for us in some area of our lives. Come and receive from the Spirit of God today.

Closing Prayer: Lord, we want to come to You in the Daytime, in the Light. We want to walk in the light as You are in the light. In You, there is no darkness at all. We receive Your light. We want to be those persons who shine Your light. We want to live and move and have our being in You. We want to walk by the Spirit and be empowered by the Spirit. We want to walk in love. O, Lord, hear our cry. Help us to be born again, born anew persons to bring You honor and glory, for Jesus' sake, Amen.

Persistence in Prayer
Luke 18:1

August 8, 2021

Luke 18:1 (NRSV), *"Then Jesus told them a parable about their need to pray always and not to lose heart."*

Opening Prayer: Lord God, our Father in Heaven, we would see Jesus today and hear Your word. Encourage our hearts today with truth from Your holy scriptures and Your Holy Spirit who inspired them. In the name of the one who loved us and gave himself for us, our Lord Jesus Christ, the Messiah, Amen.

Introduction: Perhaps we have heard the phrase, persistence pays off. Persistence is an attribute of our character that helps us to keep going. It is an inner resolve that motivates us to keep going, keep working, keep practicing, keep on keeping on, and steadily continue. When people give up, they stop pursuing a goal. They stop pressing through the pain. They stop moving towards their original intention. Some of the synonyms for persistence are perseverance, indefatigability, tenacity, and endurance. Perseverance applies to lots of areas in life. Persevering with an ill spouse, in sickness, and in health, seeking medical help for illness with prayers and physicians. Persevering with seeking healthy resolutions for relationships, for marriages, for areas of conflict and misunderstanding. Persevering through economic downturns and praying for provision and next steps. Persevering through the various places and stages of grief. Persistence and perseverance in what we have been called to finish and to finish well.

God perseveres with us. God is not willing that any should perish but that all should come to repentance. God is not slow concerning his promise as some count slowness.

Olympics Illustration: We watched some of the 2020 Olympics in Tokyo in 2021. Some persistence and perseverance were involved in putting together the games this year amid a pandemic. The persistence of the athletes was evident. We see the games, the competition, the medals. We do not see all the practices, the many hours of swimming, running, jumping, cycling, and gymnastic practices. We hear the commentators with the human-interest stories of overcoming odds and opposition to either win medals or try to win medals.

Hiking Illustration: Allen and I have gone hiking on occasion in National Parks and State Parks. If we know, there is a reward for getting to the end of the hike, a beautiful vista, a waterfall, a reason to keep climbing. We persevere, we persist, we put one foot in front of the other, breathe, hydrate, and keep going. There are a few memorable hikes that involved persistence and wisdom and encouragers on the way. I can truly say that on several occasions, I would have given up if it were not for encouragers along the way.

On Tuesday this week, I was hiking at Brasstown Bald and asked some folks who had been to the top of the mountain if it was worth it. How much farther? It looked like the climb was straight up. It took several encouragers to tell me that I was halfway, more than halfway, just around the bend and another turn after that. It took persistence and the help of encouragers to continue the climb. This week, we were also visiting Anna Ruby Falls, and when we were on our way downhill, we saw some folks on a bench. I asked, "are you going up, or are you heading back down?".I met some folks who had gone just so far and were sitting on a bench, deciding that it was not worth the journey uphill for various reasons. We encouraged the bench sitters to continue the journey to the top. The top was worth seeing. We explained the route and the places to rest along the way.

Connection to Prayer: Persistence is something that we are encouraged to have as a part of our armor in prayer.

In Ephesians 6:18 (NRSV), "Pray in the Spirit at all times in every prayer and supplication. To that end keep alert and always persevere in supplication for all the saints." And this verse from Romans 12:12 (NRSV), "Rejoice in hope, be patient in suffering, persevere in prayer. And now today's main sermon text comes from the gospel of Luke.

We may remember that Luke's gospel offers us glimpses into the prayer life of Jesus, how Jesus taught the disciples to pray, and encouragement to keep praying. The Sermon title today is "Persistence in Prayer."

Our text today is from the gospel of Luke, Chapter 18. One of the parables Jesus taught about prayer is found in Luke 18:1-8. The definition of a parable from *Encountering the New Testament* glossary is: (not precisely quoted): "Story used by ancient teachers and prophets to convey a profound spiritual truth. A parable usually has points of contact with everyday life. Parables frequently require some significant decision on the hearer's part. In Jesus' ministry, parables served to change lives, not just to entertain or provide information."

Turn with me to Luke 18:1-8. The titles in our Bibles for this text may vary. Some call it The Parable of the Persistent Widow. Others call it The Parable of the Widow and the Unjust Judge. Listen as I read the first eight verses of Luke 18, and then we will notice some things together.

> *Then Jesus told them a parable about their need to pray always and not to lose heart. 2 He said, "In a certain city there was a judge who neither feared God nor had respect for people. 3 In that city there was a widow who kept coming to him and saying, 'Grant me justice against my opponent.' 4 For a while he refused; but later he said to himself, 'Though I have no fear of God and no respect for anyone, 5 yet because this widow keeps bothering me, I will grant her justice, so that she may not wear me out by continually coming.'" 6 And the Lord said, "Listen to what the unjust judge says. 7 And will not God grant justice to his chosen ones who cry to him day and night? Will he delay long in helping them? 8 I tell you, he will quickly grant justice to them. And yet, when the Son of Man comes, will he find faith on earth?"*

Let's notice some things together now. The purpose of the parable is in verse 1 that we always ought to pray and not lose heart. And so, the scene is set for a case of injustice. The law enforcement judge in a certain city is described as a person who does not fear God or respect people. If we focus on the judge, we see that this person does not weigh the scales fairly. He decides cases according to what he wants to do, according to his own understanding, according to the way he feels, and may not judge according to the law. He does not fear God in anything he does. He does not see the need to reverence the Lord. It could be that there is no one this judge is afraid of, and he answers to himself. This judge has come to power and does not think he is accountable to God or to the persons who come to his court. He can choose to rule in their favor, or he can choose to rule against them. This judge has a reputation for being unjust, for being capricious, for being unfair, and for disregarding God and people.

A litigant in his court cannot appeal for the sake of God because the judge does not fear God. A litigant in his court cannot appeal for the sake of people because he does not care about what anyone thinks of him. The community cannot shame the judge into doing the right thing in an honor/shame culture. The judge would be impervious to any shaming. The judge did not see the need to please God or to judge the cases fairly.

The text does not say this. History tells us that this judge could have been one of the judges in Jesus' day who took bribes to hear cases, and if the litigants did not pay, he would not hear their cases. And we know that throughout history, there have been unjust judges, and there are unjust judges today in courts around the world. There are persons making cases day by day, and judges rule in their favor or against them. There was corruption in the legal system in Judea in the time of Jesus. And there were and are unjust judges in courts all over the world.

For contrast's sake, the opposite of this unjust judge would be a just judge who knows they are accountable to God to rule with justice and make the best decisions. They take oaths to serve justly and add the words, "So help me God," to their vows to serve as judges. They fear God and take the ruling of cases very seriously. They also know that they serve the people of their town, city, and jurisdiction well while upholding the law and doing what is good, fair, and just for their court cases.

Here, Jesus wants the listeners to notice this unjust judge. Perhaps Jesus' listeners could relate to the unfairness of the legal system in their day. The nation of Israel was occupied by the Romans. The unjust judge could have been appointed by Rome to hear cases. We are not told of the judge's nationality. This parable is not about the occupying force in the courtroom. It is this judge's failure to judge rightly that has earned him the dubious distinction of being called an unjust judge.

Now that the listeners understand how unfair this judge is, they can imagine bringing a case to this court. The idea that the listeners would have is that no matter what their case is, no matter how unfairly they had been treated, in order to even take a case to court, this judge had such a reputation that they might give up before they even presented their case. Jesus has set up the story with a scoundrel, an unscrupulous person, and an unfair person in power. His listeners would probably not need to go very far in their imaginations to imagine such a courtroom scene.

Jesus now has the attention and imagination of his listeners. Enter the persistent widow. We do not have her name. What do we know about her? We know that she is a woman. She is a woman who was once married, and now her husband has died. She is likely dressed in such a way to signify her widowhood. In Jesus' day, widows often wore mourning clothes. Women would get married as early as age thirteen, so she may not have been an old woman.

She is alone unless she has children who are caring for her. If this widow had a son, he would most likely be the one to care for his mother and go to court for her to try to get justice for her case. We do not see her son in court. We do not see her father, her uncle, her brother, or any male relative. We see this widow, this solitary woman, this bereaved woman. And why does the woman come to court? This widow had an adversary, an opponent. The adversary was troubling her to the point that the only place she could go was to the local court to make her case. She needed justice.

Back to Verse 3, "Now there was a widow in that city; and she came to him, saying, 'Get justice for me from my adversary." (or 'Grant me justice against my opponent.') She made her case. She asked the unjust judge to get justice for her from her adversary, her opponent.

She requested justice. The Greek word there means "to vindicate one's right, to do one justice, to protect, defend one person from another. And we see that she asked for vindication more than once. And the judge heard her case eventually.

Now let's look at Verses 4-5 (NKJV), "And he would not for a while; but afterward he said within himself, 'Though I do not fear God nor regard man, 5 yet because this widow troubles me I will avenge her, lest by her continual coming she weary me.'"

The judge said this about himself, "I do not fear God nor regard man." What changed the judge? Verse 5 Yet! Yet, because this widow troubles me, I will avenge her. I will grant her justice because this widow troubles me. First, something in the persistence of this widow troubled the judge. Second, "lest by her continual coming she weary me." She will wear me out by continually coming. Her persistence was causing the judge to be wearied. His resolve was waning. The judge had a conversation with himself. He thought to himself, if I avenge this widow, she will leave me alone. It is better for me to avenge this widow even though I do not fear God or regard humans just because she troubles me.

We notice that this widow was powerless in her society. Her only recourse against the injustice of her adversary was to go to this court and face this unjust judge and make her case. She went alone, a widow with a case of injustice from her adversary to a broken court system with an unjust judge.

So, one thing we see is that God can use an unjust judge to bring about justice. God can work in the midst of the corrupt systems of the world. God can change hearts and minds and inspire persons to do the right thing who do not even fear God. We see that persistence in this widow was the key to her influence on the unjust judge. He ruled in her favor and avenged her against her adversary so that she would leave him alone, even though he admittedly did not fear God or regard mortals.

What will we learn about God when we see this parable? Look at the next verse, verse 7. "And will not God grant justice to his chosen ones who cry to him day and night? Will he delay long in helping them?" We are to learn that God is not unjust. God is contrasted with the unjust judge. Jesus sets up this unjust judge to be the antithesis of what God's rule and reign look like in the kingdom. God is not unjust in the ways God acts. God's justice is higher than we can think or imagine. Psalm 33:5 (NRSV), "He loves righteousness and justice; the earth is full of the steadfast love of the Lord." Psalm 89:14 (NRSV), "Righteousness and justice are the foundation of your throne; steadfast love and faithfulness go before you."

God is merciful and just. One day the books will be opened, and the judge of the universe will rule with righteousness and justice on all cases that need to be judged. In the meantime, Jesus wants his listeners to pray and not give up. We are not powerless when we are praying. We do not need to try to "wear God down" by our continual coming to the throne in prayer. God is not a parent who will be worn down with our nagging and pestering.

If we are asking according to God's will, God hears us, and we will have our petition. Sometimes parents say no to children. And sometimes, we ask for things from God, and the answer is no. We do not need to nag God like a child pestering a parent until the parent is so frustrated that they say, okay. The apostle James says sometimes we ask amiss. We are asking for things that are not for our own ultimate good. What are we asking from God? His kingdom to come and His will to be done on earth as it is in heaven. We are asking for God's righteousness and justice to prevail.

The books are not balanced here, on this side of eternity. This is very freeing to know that one day, one day, one day. The will of the Lord will always be done on earth as it is in heaven. We still pray for the will of God to be done here because we, as God's children, have a part in inviting what is already happening in heaven, where God's will is always done to be done here on earth.

On earth, where battles rage and injustices happen

On earth, where there are wars and rumors of wars

On earth, where there are earthquakes and fires and floods

On earth, where families are in turmoil and various addictions are prevalent

On earth, where a pandemic has blanketed the earth,

On earth, where persons are displaced by violence and terror

On earth where persons are trafficked by oppressors

On earth, where persons who need oxygen to breathe do not have access to it

On earth where persons who need food go hungry

How long? O Lord, we pray. We cry out with lament, verse 7, "And will not God grant justice to his chosen ones who cry to him day and night? Will he delay long in helping them?" God will grant justice to his chosen ones who cry out to him day and night. God will not delay long in helping them. Notice. Long is a relative term. Will God delay long? How long is long? As long as it takes. God listens to the cries of the righteous ones. God listens to the cries of God's children.

In Revelation 6, God listened to the cries of the martyrs from under the throne who cried out. "How long, O Lord, will it be before you avenge us?" Rev 6:9-11:

> *When he opened the fifth seal, I saw under the altar the souls of those who had been slaughtered for the word of God and for the testimony they had given; 10 they cried out with a loud voice, "Sovereign Lord, holy and true, how long will it be before you judge and avenge our blood on the inhabitants of the earth?" 11 They were each given a white robe and told to rest a little longer, until the number would be complete both of their fellow servants and of their brothers and sisters, who were soon to be killed as they themselves had been killed.*

Back in Luke 18, Jesus told the listeners this parable in verse 1, "Then He spoke a parable to them, that we always ought to pray and not lose heart" (not lose heart, not give up, not become discouraged, not stop praying and seeking, asking, knocking). And now look at verse 8. "I tell you, he will quickly grant justice to them. And yet, when the Son of Man comes, will he find faith on earth?"

Two parts to verse 8. Jesus tells us that those who cry out to God, day and night, will be heard and avenged speedily, quickly. The second part of verse 8 is a question, And yet when the Son of Man comes, will he find faith on the earth? Jesus leaves his listeners with a question about what happens between the time of the telling of the parable and the day that the Son of Man comes to rule and reign on earth. What will happen? Will hearts be turned toward God? Will people pray with faith and not give up? Will Jesus find faith on the earth? If God hears our cries, If God listens to our complaints, our laments, about injustice, if God cares about justice in our lives, in our communities, in our world, how much more inspired can we be with this parable of the persistent widow whose case was heard with an imperfect judge, an unjust judge, a judge who did not fear God or mankind? Even the unjust judge ruled in her favor and avenged her of her enemy.

This parable sets up an argument from the lesser to the greater. If an unjust judge with power and position can rule in the widow's favor, how much more will God, the Just Judge, hear our prayers and petitions as we cry out night and day? How much more will God hear us as we cry out to the Judge of All the Earth? Remember Abraham petitioned on behalf of the righteous persons in Sodom when God was going to destroy Sodom and Gomorrah in Gen 18.22-25:

> *So the men turned from there, and went toward Sodom, while Abraham remained standing before the Lord. 23 Then Abraham came near and said, "Will you indeed sweep away the righteous with the wicked? 24 Suppose there are fifty righteous within the city; will you then sweep away the place and not forgive it for the fifty righteous who are in it? 25 Far be it from you to do such a thing, to slay the righteous with the wicked, so that the righteous fare as the wicked! Far be that from you! Shall not the Judge of all the earth do what is just?"*

Another example of perseverance and persistence is in Luke 11:5-8, starting in verse 5. The chapter starts with the disciples asking Jesus to teach them to pray.

> *And he said to them, "Suppose one of you has a friend, and you go to him at midnight and say to him, 'Friend, lend me three loaves of bread; 6 for a friend of mine has arrived, and I have nothing to set before him.' 7 And he answers from within, 'Do not bother me; the door has already been locked, and my children are with me in bed; I cannot get up and give you anything.' 8 I tell you, even though he will not get up and give him anything because he is his friend, at least because of his persistence he will get up and give him whatever he needs.*

In the Middle East, in Jesus' day, the houses were often one room. When it was time for bed, all the children lined up on the floor, and the parents were all in the same room. So, here the children are "in bed," all lined up on the floor on their mats. This is very inconvenient for the dad to hear a knock on the locked door. Jesus says, because it is his friend, and this friend is persistent, the dad will get up and give the friend the bread and whatever he needs. Continue reading Luke 11:9-13:

> *So, I say to you, Ask, and it will be given you; search, and you will find; knock, and the door will be opened for you. 10 For everyone who asks receives, and everyone who searches finds, and for everyone who knocks, the door will be opened. 11 Is there anyone among you who, if your child asks for a fish, will give a snake instead of a fish? 12 Or if the child asks for an egg, will give a scorpion? 13 If you then, who are evil, know how to give good gifts to your children, how much more will the heavenly Father give the Holy Spirit to those who ask him!"*

Here is another "How much more" explanation from Jesus. If we who are evil know how to give good gifts to our children, how much more will the Heavenly Father give the Holy Spirit to those who ask? So, how do we proceed when we see injustice in the world and do not see what we consider good outcomes? The unjust judge ruled in favor of the poor and powerless widow. And how much more do we need to work for justice for the poor and vulnerable of this world?

We might think that we are powerless to act. And yet we can learn from the scriptures that we can do some things. We can pray and put feet and hands to our prayers. How much more will the Father give the Holy Spirit to those who ask? How much more should we partner with the Lord in what the Lord is doing here in the already-but-not yet kingdom? The injustices of the world are all around us. We can pray to the Judge of All the Earth as Abraham did, "Will not the judge of the earth do right?"

How much more are we called to do the works of the kingdom, proclaim the good news to the poor, heal the sick, open blind eyes and set at liberty those who are oppressed? Where are we doing the stuff? Where are we advocating for the poor and powerless? Maybe we are called to work in the legal system to make laws that would have outcomes that line up with godly principles. Maybe we are called to be mediators in cases of injustice where two parties are at odds, and we work out reconciliation plans with them? Maybe we are called to be fair in the ways we interact with our friends and neighbors.

We are called to notice injustice and not to turn a blind eye to injustice. We are called to pray, to give, to act, to challenge injustice in whatever sphere of influence the Lord has given us. James 1:25 NRSV "But those who look into the perfect law, the law of liberty, and persevere, being not hearers who forget but doers who act—they will be blessed in their doing." Micah 6:8 (NRSV) "He has told you, O mortal, what is good; and what does the LORD require of you but to do justice, and to love kindness, and to walk humbly with your God?

Our hope is not for an unjust judge to pronounce justice for us against our adversary. No. By no means! We are not relying on the courts of this world for ultimate justice. Our God is a God of justice, and God will justify us through the blood of Jesus, who died as a propitiation for our sins. God will sanctify us as we work out our salvation with fear and trembling because it is God who works in us to will and to do God's good pleasure. If we are asking rightly and according to God's will, God hears us, and we shall receive what we have petitioned, maybe not immediately, but eventually.

Philippians 4:6, "Do not worry about anything, but in everything by prayer and supplication with thanksgiving let your requests be made known to God." Colossians 4:2 "Devote yourselves to prayer, keeping alert in it with thanksgiving." When we pray for justice in world situations, we are not coming to an unjust judge. Jesus fought injustice by coming here in the fullness of time to redeem us from our sin and the sinful patterns of oppression and injustice.

We have a high priest, Jesus, who "ever lives to make intercession for us." (Hebrews 7:25). Jesus is familiar with the injustices of this world. And, in the end, we know Matthew 24:14 "And this good news of the kingdom will be proclaimed throughout the world, as a testimony to all the nations; and then the end will come.

The Hallelujah Chorus from Handel that in the Revelation of Jesus Christ. Revelation 11:15, "Then the seventh angel blew his trumpet, and there were loud voices in heaven, saying, "The kingdom of the world has become the kingdom of our Lord and of his Messiah, and he will reign forever and ever."

Closing Prayer: God, You are the "Judge of All the Earth," as Abraham called You. You are holy, righteous, just, and true. Help us in our prayers, Lord God, as we appeal to You for the injustices that we see all around the world. Help the persons and groups who fight injustice. Hear their cries for justice and answer, O God, as Your children cry out to You day and night. We come into Your courts with praise and thanksgiving for who You are and how You hear and answer us when we cry out to You. In the name of Jesus, the One who taught us to pray, Our Father in Heaven, hallowed be Thy name, Thy kingdom come, Thy will be done, on earth, as it is in heaven. Give us this day our daily bread and forgive us our debts as we forgive our debtors. And lead us not into temptation but deliver us from evil, for Thine is the kingdom and the power and the glory forever. Amen.

Ministry Time. For those who want to respond to the message and have prayer and ministry time, a few of us will be here up to the front on your right side to pray with you.

Benediction: Go in peace to love and serve the Lord and our neighbors. May we do justly, love mercy, and walk humbly with our God. Amen.

Pondering Mary
Luke 2:19

Mother's Day May 14, 2017

Luke 2:19 (NASB), *"But Mary treasured all these words and pondered them in her heart."*

Opening Prayer. O Lord, our God, how excellent is Your name in all the earth. Thank You for our mothers. Thank You for Mother's Day. Thank You for all the ways that You shower love and affection on us and through us. And we ask that You would be with us today as we consider Your Word and lessons that You might teach us from it. In Jesus' name. Amen.

Introduction. Some of our mothers are with us. Some women here today are mothers, but their children are not with them. Some of our mothers live elsewhere. Some of us have been bereaved of our mothers, and we still miss them. If you are sitting near a mother today, even if she is not your mother, greet her and say Happy Mother's Day. All of us here are not mothers, but all of us have had a mother. Some pregnant women have realized they could not take care of a child and have chosen to let another family raise the child through the adoption process. Some of us have been blessed with mothers who have adopted us. Physically and spiritually. Not every woman who gives birth knows how to be a mother. All of us have had mothers who are less than perfect. And we need to be able to forgive our mothers for some or many things that we might still be blaming them for doing or not doing. And so.

Mother's Day is a day of many emotions. Some mothers have suffered the incredible pain of losing a child or children. Working as a chaplain in trauma in hospitals, especially in the nursing facility where I work, I have spent time with mothers wailing when they hear news of their child's death. Many women wanted to have children but could not have children. For various reasons, Mother's Day is a day to be sad, grieve the missed opportunity, and feel many emotions. BUT Mother's Day is more than a sad day. While we want to come alongside and walk with those who are sad and grieving on this day, Mother's Day is also a day to rejoice. A day to be thankful for our mothers. We would not be where we are today if we had not been born if we did not have mothers. Mothers receive cards and gifts. And appreciation. Some receive phone calls; others receive text messages or emails or social media messages. Mother's Day is a profitable day for restaurants and flower shops. I am in the stage of life of having a living mother, being a mother, and watching and appreciating my daughters-in-law as they mother their children, our grandchildren. Aren't grandchildren the BEST? So, as I was praying and pondering about how to preach today, and what to preach today, I looked at mothers in the Bible. Which mother would hold keys to the Word of the Lord for us today? I thought of several mothers in Scripture. And in my praying and pondering, I pondered a mother who pondered.

Pondering Mary. So, today, I am inviting us to ponder Mary. Mary, the mother of Jesus. The sermon title today is Pondering Mary. We will ponder a woman who pondered. Turn with me in your Bibles or select on your devices the Third book in the New Testament, the Gospel of Luke. Chapter 2. We will spend time in the gospels today with Mary and see what lessons we can learn from her motherhood. Mary, the mother of Jesus, is present. On our way to Luke, we see Mary only in Matthew and Luke in the infancy narratives, the accounts of Jesus's birth. Mark and John do not tell us early stories of Jesus. In Matthew, she is named and described but has no voice. For instance, in Matthew 1:18, "Now the birth of Jesus the Messiah took place in this way. When his mother Mary had been engaged to Joseph, but before they lived together, she was found to be with child from the Holy Spirit." Mary is present by name in Matt, Mark, Luke, and Acts. Her voice is heard in both Luke and in John.

In the Gospel of Luke, Mary is named, visited, has a voice, and we hear more about her life in Luke than anywhere else in the gospels. And it is in Luke that we hear about Mary pondering and treasuring things in her heart in three places. Our key verse, Luke 2:19, today comes from the visit of the shepherds after the birth of Jesus. They had seen an angelic host praising God and saying Glory to God in the Highest and on earth peace. Luke 2:15-20:

> *When the angels had left them and gone into heaven, the shepherds said to one another, "Let us go now to Bethlehem and see this thing that has taken place, which the Lord has made known to us." 16 So they went with haste and found Mary and Joseph, and the child lying in the manger. 17 When they saw this, they made known what had been told them about this child; 18 and all who heard it were amazed at what the shepherds told them. 19 But Mary treasured all these words and pondered them in her heart. 20 The shepherds returned, glorifying and praising God for all they had heard and seen, as it had been told them.*

Key Verse Luke 2:19. Pondered. to combine, i.e. (in speaking) to converse, consult, dispute, (mentally) to consider, (by implication) to aid, (personally) to join, attack:—confer, encounter, help, make, meet with, ponder. The story on the way to the key verse. A lot happens on the way to the angel appearing to the shepherds and Mary pondering these things. Let's go back to Luke chapter 1 for the visit of Gabriel to Mary in her hometown of Nazareth. Luke 1:26-29, "In the sixth month the angel Gabriel was sent by God to a town in Galilee called Nazareth, 27 to a virgin engaged to a man whose name was Joseph, of the house of David. The virgin's name was Mary. 28 And he came to her and said, "Greetings, favored one! The Lord is with you." 29 But she was much perplexed by his words and pondered what sort of greeting this might be."

Luke 1:30, 34-35:

> *The angel said to her, "Do not be afraid, Mary, for you have found favor with God. Mary said to the angel, "How can this be, since I am a virgin?" 35 The angel said to her, "The Holy Spirit will come upon you, and the power of the Most High will overshadow you; therefore the child to be born will be holy; he will be called Son of God.*

How can this Be? STOP! WAIT! Mary was hearing this wonderful news. This child will be the promised Messiah. From the throne of David. The Lord God is fulfilling his promise. This is the child, the son, the messiah whose kingdom will never end. He will reign over the house of Jacob forever. This is the promised Son of GOD. Do not be afraid. You have found favor with God. Promises fulfilled. Isaiah 7:14, "Therefore the Lord Himself will give you a sign: Behold, a virgin will be with child and bear a son, and she will call His name Immanuel." And Isaiah 9:6-7:

> *For a child will be born to us, a son will be given to us; And the government will rest on His shoulders; And His name will be called Wonderful Counselor, Mighty God, Eternal Father, Prince of Peace. 7 There will be no end to the increase of His government or of peace, On the throne of David and over his kingdom, To establish it and to uphold it with justice and righteousness From then on and forevermore. The zeal of the Lord of hosts will accomplish this.*

And there is more good news. Another sign from God. Verses 36-37, "And now, your relative Elizabeth in her old age has also conceived a son; and this is the sixth month for her who was said to be barren. 37 For nothing will be impossible with God." Here is something to ponder. Nothing will be impossible with God. We can take that to our prayer closets. We can believe

God to do what God has promised even if it looks impossible. Nothing will be impossible with God.

Nazareth and Judean Culture. A woman's greatest achievement was to give birth, preferably to a boy baby. And then it was a great achievement to raise a child. A child who believed and trusted in God. A child who respected tradition and a child who lived a morally upright life. The angel told Mary about Elizabeth and Elizabeth's good news. Wonderful news in that culture. But what about Mary? And now we see in Mary her willingness to hear and believe the good news the angel had delivered to her. Mary said Let it be unto me.

Back to Luke 1:38, "Then Mary said, "Here am I, the servant of the Lord; let it be with me according to your word." Then the angel departed from her. Mary is the servant of the Lord. This young woman, this virgin, this one knows the stories of the Messiah. She knows about the promises. She is a servant OF THE LORD. And she submits to be of service TO THE LORD.

She willingly agrees. Not in the let it be of the "Que sera sera," whatever will be will be or of the "Let it Be" of the Beatles' famous hit with "When I find myself in times of trouble Mother Mary comes to me speaking words of wisdom let it be."[33] Not in the Frozen song Let it Go. But in a most holy acceptance and surrender. Let IT BE DONE unto me according to your Word. 2 Chron 16:9 For the eyes of the Lord range throughout the entire earth, to strengthen those whose heart is true to him. And God found Mary. And she said, Here am I. Let it be done unto me according to your word. God is still looking for mothers, for persons who will say, Here I am, let it be done unto me, according to your word.

In those days, there were no abortion clinics and no going back. A woman cannot be a little bit pregnant. When a woman is pregnant, the child grows, and the mother's body changes, indicating that life is growing inside—being pregnant before marriage was a sign of shame in that culture. In Matthew, we read that Joseph had to be told in a dream not to be afraid to take Mary as his wife, that this was indeed from the Lord. Mary had a willingness to bear reproach and shame. Mark Lowrey's song, Mary Did You Know? "Mary did you know that your baby boy will some day walk on water? Mary did you know that your baby boy will save our sons and daughters? Did you know

---

[33] Songwriters: Lennon, John / McCartney, Paul Let It Be Lyrics © Sony/ATV Music Publishing LLC.

that your baby boy is heaven's perfect Lamb? This sleeping child you're holding is the great I Am."[34] Mary had a willingness to be pregnant with the Word. Be it done unto me according to your word. Elizabeth's greeting: Luke 1:41-45:

> *When Elizabeth heard Mary's greeting, the child leaped in her womb. And Elizabeth was filled with the Holy Spirit 42 and exclaimed with a loud cry, "Blessed are you among women, and blessed is the fruit of your womb. 43 And why has this happened to me, that the mother of my Lord comes to me? 44 For as soon as I heard the sound of your greeting, the child in my womb leaped for joy. 45 And blessed is she who believed that there would be a fulfillment of what was spoken to her by the Lord."*

Mother of my Lord. Elizabeth recognizes Mary as "the mother of my Lord," and John leaps in Elizabeth's womb. Elizabeth says Mary is blessed because Mary believed the angel to fulfill the promise. And then, we see Mary's response to what she had been pondering. Her pondering and her receptivity have led to praise. Mary praises God in Luke 1:46-56:

> *And Mary said, "My soul magnifies the Lord, 47 and my spirit rejoices in God my Savior, 48 for he has looked with favor on the lowliness of his servant. Surely, from now on all generations will call me blessed; 49 for the Mighty One has done great things for me, and holy is his name. 50 His mercy is for those who fear him from generation to generation. 51 He has shown strength with his arm; he has scattered the proud in the thoughts of their hearts. 52 He has brought down the powerful from their thrones, and lifted up the lowly; 53 he has filled the hungry with good things, and sent the rich away empty. 54 He has helped his servant Israel, in remembrance of his mercy, 55 according to the promise he made to our ancestors, to Abraham and to his descendants forever." 56 And Mary remained with her about three months and then returned to her home.*

This song of praise is similar to Hannah's song in 1 Samuel 2. Mary had to have been taught the scriptures for this song of praise to burst forth from her heart.

Mary in Matthew's Gospel, Chapter 1:16-25:

> *And Jacob the father of Joseph the husband of Mary, of whom Jesus was born, who is called the Messiah. 17 So all the generations from Abraham to David*

---

[34] Mark Lowry – Mary Did You Know Lyrics.

are fourteen generations; and from David to the deportation to Babylon, fourteen generations; and from the deportation to Babylon to the Messiah, fourteen generations.18 Now the birth of Jesus the Messiah took place in this way. When his mother Mary had been engaged to Joseph, but before they lived together, she was found to be with child from the Holy Spirit. 19 Her husband Joseph, being a righteous man and unwilling to expose her to public disgrace, planned to dismiss her quietly. 20 But just when he had resolved to do this, an angel of the Lord appeared to him in a dream and said, "Joseph, son of David, do not be afraid to take Mary as your wife, for the child conceived in her is from the Holy Spirit. 21 She will bear a son, and you are to name him Jesus, for he will save his people from their sins." 22 All this took place to fulfill what had been spoken by the Lord through the prophet: 23 "Look, the virgin shall conceive and bear a son, and they shall name him Emmanuel," which means, "God is with us." 24 When Joseph awoke from sleep, he did as the angel of the Lord commanded him; he took her as his wife, 25 but had no marital relations with her until she had borne a son; and he named him Jesus.

Living with Jesus. In Luke 2, Joseph and Mary take Jesus to the Temple for dedication, where they meet Simeon and Anna. In Matthew 2, the Magi visit, and then Joseph takes the family to Egypt to escape the wrath of Herod. Matthew 2:19-23 (The Return from Egypt):

When Herod died, an angel of the Lord suddenly appeared in a dream to Joseph in Egypt and said, 20 "Get up, take the child and his mother, and go to the land of Israel, for those who were seeking the child's life are dead." 21 Then Joseph got up, took the child and his mother, and went to the land of Israel. 22 But when he heard that Archelaus was ruling over Judea in place of his father Herod, he was afraid to go there. And after being warned in a dream, he went away to the district of Galilee. 23 There he made his home in a town called Nazareth, so that what had been spoken through the prophets might be fulfilled, "He will be called a Nazorean."

This is where the Matthew account fits with the Magi and the flight to Egypt, and the return to Nazareth. The Return to Nazareth Luke 2:39-40, "When they had finished everything required by the law of the Lord, they returned to Galilee, to their own town of Nazareth. 40 The child grew and became strong, filled with wisdom; and the favor of God was upon him."

Grew and Became Strong. We usually see Jesus as a baby or as a man. But here, the scriptures say that Jesus grew and grew and became strong, filled with wisdom; and the favor of God was upon him. So what might it have been like for Mary to feed Jesus? To bathe him or to wash his dirty feet. Wash his clothes. To teach him how to talk? To watch him learn to walk. Learn to play? What foods to eat? To teach him about his relatives? The culture. The traditions. The scriptures? What did Mary teach? The Bible says that Jesus learned and grew.

Mary learned the ways of God from her family. Mary had a mother and father who taught her how to love God, how to be a follower of God, how to be receptive to God...how to wait for God and for God's promise. What would biblical mothers teach? These are some of the same things that mothers teach today. Psalm 71:6, "Upon you I have leaned from my birth; it was you who took me from my mother's womb. My praise is continually of you." Psalm 131:2, "But I have calmed and quieted my soul, like a weaned child with its mother; my soul is like the weaned child that is with me." Psalm 139:13, "For it was you who formed my inward parts; you knit me together in my mother's womb." Proverbs 1:8, "Hear, my child, your father's instruction, and do not reject your mother's teaching;" Proverbs 6:20, "My child, keep your father's commandment, and do not forsake your mother's teaching."

What did Mary Teach? Stories of how loved children are. Where they came from, hometown stories, parents growing up stories. Children love to hear stories. I can imagine Mary telling Jesus stories. Can you imagine telling Jesus stories.? Tell me again. Tell me again—stories to tell. But only Mary could tell Jesus the stories of the angel appearing to her, stories of the shepherds coming to visit him at his birth, stories of the Magi traveling from far away, stories of his relatives, especially her visit with Elizabeth and the baby John. Mary had a front-row seat in watching Jesus interact with other children and family members. Mary had a special place in teaching Jesus about God and about who he was. Until one day, it changed. They took a trip to Jerusalem.

Losing Jesus and finding him at the Temple. Luke 2:41-51:

> *Now every year his parents went to Jerusalem for the festival of the Passover. 42 And when he was twelve years old, they went up as usual for the festival. 43 When the festival was ended and they started to return, the boy Jesus stayed behind in Jerusalem, but his parents did not know it. 44 Assuming that he was in the group of travelers, they went a day's journey. Then they started to look for him among their relatives and friends. 45 When they did not find him, they returned to Jerusalem to search for him. 46 After three days they found him in the temple, sitting among the teachers, listening to them and asking them questions. 47 And all who heard him were amazed at his understanding and his answers. 48 When his parents saw him they were astonished; and his mother said to him, "Child, why have you treated us like this? Look, your father and I have been searching for you in great anxiety." 49 He said to them, "Why were*

you searching for me? Did you not know that I must be in my Father's house?"
50 But they did not understand what he said to them. 51 Then he went down
with them and came to Nazareth, and was obedient to them.

His mother treasured all these things in her heart. (Mary treasured the greatest treasure). Mary gave her heart, her soul, her mind, her strength, and her body to fulfill God's word to her through the angel. She treasured all of these promises and things. Verse 52, "And Jesus increased in wisdom and in years, and in divine and human favor."

Let us look briefly at John's gospel. The one after Luke in the New Testament scriptures. Mary is not named; she is referred to as the mother of Jesus. She is referred to as "Woman" in John 2 and John 19. She is obliquely and derogatorily referred to as the mother of an illegitimate child, Jesus, in John 8. We only see Mary, specifically, twice in John's gospel. The first time is in Chapter 2 (the other time is at the cross in Chapter 19.) Mary invites Jesus to help the host who ran out of wine. John 2:1-5:

> *On the third day there was a wedding in Cana of Galilee, and the mother of*
> *Jesus was there. 2 Jesus and his disciples had also been invited to the wedding. 3*
> *When the wine gave out, the mother of Jesus said to him, "They have no wine."*
> *4 And Jesus said to her, "Woman, what concern is that to you and to me? My*
> *hour has not yet come." 5 His mother said to the servants, "Do whatever he tells*
> *you."*

John 2:12, "After this he went down to Capernaum with his mother, his brothers, and his disciples; and they remained there a few days." Children grow up. There comes a time in a child's life when they grow up and launch into adulthood. Jesus left home, was baptized, tempted in the desert, and called his disciples. And so, After the wedding in Cana, We do not see Mary exercising control or influence over Jesus in John's gospel. We do see her coming to him during his ministry in the other three gospels. Scenes where Mary tries to see him. Matt 12. Mark 3, Luke 8, and Matt 12. Here is the one from Luke 8:19-21:

> *Then his mother and his brothers came to him, but they could not reach him*
> *because of the crowd. 20 And he was told, "Your mother and your brothers are*
> *standing outside, wanting to see you." 21 But he said to them, "My mother and*
> *my brothers are those who hear the word of God and do it.*

SO, WE SEE THAT Jesus opens up the family of God to those who hear the word of God and do it.

Jesus Came to Show us the Father. I must be about my Father's business. If you have seen me, you have seen my Father. Hebrews 1 "exact representation of the Father." He honored his mother, but Jesus came to be the way back to the Father. Through the power of the Spirit. John 1:12, "As many as received him to them he gave the power to be the children of God." The sons of God. The daughters of God. At the Cross, we see the women in Matthew 27:55-56, Mark 15:40-41, and Luke 22:48-49. We will look at the account in John's gospel.

John 19:25-27, "Meanwhile, standing near the cross of Jesus were his mother, and his mother's sister, Mary the wife of Clopas, and Mary Magdalene. 26 When Jesus saw his mother and the disciple whom he loved standing beside her, he said to his mother, "Woman, here is your son." 27 Then he said to the disciple, "Here is your mother." And from that hour the disciple took her into his own home."

Responsibility for Mother. Jesus provided for his mother's care even as he was dying. Behold thy son. Behold thy mother. Jesus honored his father and his mother. Pondering Mary Suffered and Rejoiced. Mary suffered when Jesus was rejected and despised and when Jesus was falsely accused. When Jesus was flogged and crucified. Simeon had said that a sword would pierce her heart. But Mary also rejoiced to see Jesus, her savior and Lord, raised from the dead. Mary believed in Jesus and the resurrection enough to be with the disciples waiting for the promise. And the last time we see Mary in the scriptures waiting for the promise in Acts 1:3-5:

> *After his suffering he presented himself alive to them by many convincing proofs, appearing to them during forty days and speaking about the kingdom of God. 4 While staying with them, he ordered them not to leave Jerusalem, but to wait there for the promise of the Father. "This," he said, "is what you have heard from me; 5 for John baptized with water, but you will be baptized with the Holy Spirit not many days from now.*

Then, After The Ascension, Acts 1:12-14:

> *Then they returned to Jerusalem from the mount called Olivet, which is near Jerusalem, a sabbath day's journey away. 13 When they had entered the city, they went to the room upstairs where they were staying, Peter, and John, and James, and Andrew, Philip and Thomas, Bartholomew and Matthew, James son of Alphaeus, and Simon the Zealot, and Judas son of James. 14 All these were constantly devoting themselves to prayer, together with certain women, including Mary the mother of Jesus, as well as his brothers.*

Lessons from Pondering Mary. Her willingness to yield her will to God's will. Her willingness to both rejoice and suffer. Her willingness to bear the reproach of others. Her willingness to raise a child who was called to save his people from their sins, to be God with us, to be God among us, to show us the Father's heart of God. Her willingness to suffer the death of her own child. Willingness to be cared for by the beloved disciple in Jesus' dying assignment. Willingness to wait for the Holy Spirit with the disciples.

What are we called to do? As we consider Mary, as we ponder Mary. We are invited to receive God's Word made flesh in Jesus. We, who have accepted Jesus into our hearts, carry Jesus with us wherever we go. We cannot be a little bit pregnant. Or a little bit a Christian. The seed that was planted in us is an incorruptible seed. It is a seed of the Kingdom. It is the life of Christ. It is going to bear fruit. The seed of the Kingdom, the life of Christ in us, will grow in compassion and love. We have a relationship with the Holy One, the Righteous One, the Prince of Peace, the King of Kings, the Lord of Lords, the one who wanted to gather Jerusalem under his wings as a hen gathers her chicks, but they would not. If we know Jesus, we want to know Jesus more. We have a spiritual hunger. And we are growing spiritually. We spend time pondering and praying.

Ministry Time. We can learn a lot about Jesus by pondering Mary. Mary came to know Jesus as the Way, the Truth, and the Life. Mary was there with the disciples and received the empowerment of the Holy Spirit on the Day of Pentecost. If you want to receive Jesus today, to be born anew, to have the life of Jesus, the company of Jesus, the fellowship of the sufferings of Jesus, the love of God in your heart, you can receive Jesus today. You can join us in prayer as we close and invite Jesus into our hearts. If you are listening online and need prayer. Contact us. For those who are here today, we are here to pray with you.

Prayer. O Lord God, we come to You today. Some of us have already invited You to come into our hearts, to be Lord of our lives. We pray that You will strengthen us with Your power and help us to be rooted and grounded in Your love that we might love You with the love You deserve to be loved with. Some of us desire to have a real and personal relationship with You. We pray with those who are even now feeling Your Spirit's invitation to join the family, confessing their sins and receiving Your forgiveness. We know that we have all sinned and need a savior. Jesus save us, cleanse us from our sins, and heal our brokenness. Help us to walk with You all of our days. Amen.

Prayers for the New Year
Hosea 14:2

December 30, 2018

Hosea 14:2 (NASB) *"Take words and return to the Lord."*

Opening Prayer. O God, teach us from Your word today. Teach us from Your heart. Teach us as we prepare for the New Year. We love You, Lord. We adore you, Christ, the Lord. We want to grow in grace and in the knowledge of our Lord and Savior, Jesus Christ, in whose name we pray, Amen.

Introduction. Today we want to look at Prayers for the New Year. This is the last Sunday of the year, and New Year's Day happens this week. In my lifetime, I have heard people speak about resolutions for the New Year. You might have some. Read more. Exercise more. Change eating habits. What about prayers? What prayers shall we pray in the New Year?

Allen and I plan to travel more this year. We plan to see some National Parks. As I prepare to travel, I have certain suitcases I pack if we go by car. I have others I pack if we are taking a flight to our destination. What I take with me matters with the way I am traveling. The amount of room I have in my suitcase depends on how I travel. The things I pack to take with me when flying cannot weigh too much. So I am learning to travel with the essentials and not too much baggage.

The prayers I take with me. When it comes to prayer, I look back on prayers I have prayed, prayer books I have read, and prayer lessons I have learned and taught. And I have some thoughts to share with us today. Hosea 14:2, "Take words and return to the Lord."

If I stand on the edge of the New Year and look back, I have wonderful memories of prayer classes, prayer retreats, prayer summits, prayer partners, many ways to pray, and glorious answers to prayers. And I am challenged to think that the best prayers are still to be prayed. The past is wonderful and difficult and challenging and full of joy.

But the New Year offers new invitations. The best prayers are yet to be prayed. The journey with Jesus continues. Day by day. So, I set out to ask people what life-changing prayers they had prayed, and I received several answers I plan to share with you. If I am gathering prayers to take with me, life-changing prayers that have helped others may also help us. Life-changing prayers might be helpful to keep or pray again as we travel through this next year. Here are some of the results of what people regard as life-changing prayers.

The Lord's Prayer. (Recite) Praying for the kingdom to come on earth as it is in heaven. One of the residents in the nursing facility Prayed Psalm 23, Psalm 34, and Psalm 37 every day. Others have Psalm 91, 103, and other favorite Psalms. Perhaps you have favorite Psalms you recite or pray on a regular basis.

As we meditate on Scripture, Scripture becomes a part of us. The word is hidden in our hearts. And we find ourselves tapping into the Scripture we have memorized and praying Scripture and God's promises to us. What are some of the promises we will take with us into this New Year? Promises "I will never leave you or forsake you." "Jesus ever lives to make intercession." "Come boldly unto the throne of grace to receive mercy and grace in our time of need." "God has given us great and precious promises so that we have everything we need for life and godliness in Christ Jesus."

Serenity Prayer. "Lord, help me to accept the things I cannot change, the courage to change the things I can, and the wisdom to know the difference." This prayer continues to be life changing. It was written by theologian Reinhold Niebuhr in the early 1930s, and it has gained widespread recognition through recovery programs such as Alcoholic Anonymous.

One of the prayers I have thought of is the simple prayer written more than 765 years ago. It was reprised in the 1970 musical Godspell, based on the book of Mark. The song lyrics see thee more clearly, love thee more dearly, follow thee more nearly. Day by day. That goes something like this. To know thee more clearly. Love thee more dearly. Follow thee more nearly. Thanks be to thee, my Lord Jesus Christ, for all the benefits which thou hast given me, for all the pains and insults which thou hast borne for me. O most merciful Redeemer, Friend and Brother, may I know thee more clearly, love thee more dearly, and follow thee more nearly. Amen. Richard, Bishop of Chichester. 1197-1253.

Jesus, in Colossians 1, is Lord of All, generally, globally. But what about personally? How did Jesus become Lord of your life? Think about the time, if there was a time, that you asked Jesus to be your savior and Lord. For some of us, this prayer happened recently; for some of us, it happened years ago.

For some of us listening, today could be the day you decide to ask Jesus to come into your heart and life and make necessary changes.

Some Important Prayers. Lord Jesus, save me and be Lord of my life. Fill me with Your Holy Spirit. Help me to know you and love you. Let me hear your voice. Teach me to pray.

Life is a Process. All of us are on a journey of life. None of our lives are identical. We are all uniquely made and shaped by our families, our friends, our environments, and our social locations. My journey to Jesus started generations ago. Somewhere in my history, at least one of my ancestors prayed for me. And I have prayed for my children and my children's children and the generations that follow me. And that may be your story, too.

Prayed by Others. Some of the prayers that have changed my life and the lives of those I know and love were prayed by others. Grandmothers, grandfathers, mothers, fathers, family members, and friends. Some of us are here today or listening online because others have prayed for us. We are still praying for others, and one day our prayers will be answered. If God has given us the prayers to pray, God will answer them.

Jesus and Holy Spirit pray. Scripture tells us that Jesus prays for us and the Holy Spirit prays for us. Jesus. Hebrews 7:25, John 17 Holy Spirit. Romans 8:26,36. And Sometimes I sit with the Lord and ask, dear Jesus, what are you praying for me today? What are you praying about this situation in the world today? Please give me your heart for this person or place or circumstance. One of the great prayers In Scripture is in our text today from Ephesians the 1st chapter. We will start reading in verse 15. Ephesians is located on our devices after Galatians. It is the 10th book in the New Testament after the four gospels, Acts, Romans, 1st and 2nd Corinthians, and Galatians. If you get to Philippians, turn back one book. The apostle Paul planted many churches and prayed for those believers he had met as well as the ones he had only heard about. Ephesians starts with greetings and some theological offerings before Paul writes this wonderful prayer. This is a highly recommended prayer that has stood the test of time, with many intercessors praying it along the centuries. Here we go.

Look at Ephesians 1. We will start in verses 15-19:

> *For this reason I too, having heard of the faith in the Lord Jesus which exists among you and your love for all the saints, do not cease giving thanks for you, while making mention of you in my prayers; that the God of our Lord Jesus Christ, the Father of glory, may give to you a spirit of wisdom and of revelation*

in the knowledge of Him. I pray that the eyes of your heart may be enlightened, so that you will know what is the hope of His calling, what are the riches of the glory of His inheritance in the saints, and what is the surpassing greatness of His power toward us who believe.

Praying Prayers in Scripture. As we learn to pray, one of the best ways is to see the Bible as a starting point, a launching pad, and a way to get in tune with the Holy Spirit. If the writers of the scriptures were inspired by the Holy Spirit, if the Holy Spirit lives in me, if I am filled with the Holy Spirit, then sitting with Scripture and pondering Scripture will birth prayers in my heart. Writing to a Blank Page One of the lessons I have learned in writing is to write to a theme or an idea and not to stare at a blank page. So as I open a document, I place an idea on the page, and then I write about it. Prayer is like that. If we start by staring into space, words may or may not come. But if we start with Scripture, we have words we can pray that will lead to other prayers.

Ephesians 1, "wisdom and revelation in the knowledge of him." Paul asks that the God of our Lord Jesus Christ, the Father of Glory, will give to us the Spirit of wisdom and revelation in the knowledge of Him. Phrase by phrase. As we ponder this phrase, who comes to mind that needs the Spirit of wisdom and revelation? Wisdom. To live life and make decisions. Revelation to understand what we see when it is revealed to us. Secrets. Mysteries. Things that have been hidden from us, but now God is revealing to us with wisdom. In the knowledge of Him. Who needs to know Jesus more deeply? More clearly.? Who needs that prayer today? I pray that the eyes of your heart may be enlightened. Who needs to have light in our souls that will offer us greater insight? Who shall we pray for with this phrase? Lord, I pray for _____that they would have the eyes of their hearts enlightened with understanding. With wisdom and revelation.

Next phrase. "So that you will know what is the hope of His calling," What is the hope of our calling in Him and His calling for us? For this, let's look at Philippians 3:14, "I press on toward the goal for the prize of the upward call of God in Christ Jesus."

Now let's back up in Philippians. Chapter 3:7-14:

But whatever things were gain to me, those things I have counted as loss for the sake of Christ. More than that, I count all things to be loss in view of the surpassing value of knowing Christ Jesus my Lord, for whom I have suffered the loss of all things, and count them but rubbish so that I may gain Christ, and may be found in Him, not having a righteousness of my own derived from the

Law, but that which is through faith in Christ, the righteousness which comes from God on the basis of faith, that I may know Him and the power of His resurrection and the fellowship of His sufferings, being conformed to His death; in order that I may attain to the resurrection from the dead. Not that I have already obtained it or have already become perfect, but I press on so that I may lay hold of that for which also I was laid hold of by Christ Jesus. Brethren, I do not regard myself as having laid hold of it yet; but one thing I do: forgetting what lies behind and reaching forward to what lies ahead, I press on toward the goal for the prize of the upward call of God in Christ Jesus.

"Forgetting what is behind, I press on." That word "forgetting" is not about forgetting the scriptures or about forgetting our testimony of what the Lord has done for us. It is about not dwelling on the past or counting on what we have done in the past as if we have done enough to get by. And now we can coast. No.it is an onward and upward call in Christ Jesus. To know Him, love Him, and serve Him. Because He is worthy.

Who needs that prayer today? To know Jesus. To follow Him onward and upward?

Lord, I want THAT for which you have laid hold of me Philippians 3. Look at verse 12. Here is a life-changing prayer. Like the hope of His calling in Ephesians 1. My spiritual director asked how this prayer had changed my life. Allen and I started to see circumstances and situations change once we started faithfully praying the "that" prayer. It has to do with purpose, destiny, alignment, discernment, wisdom, guidance, direction, protection, provision, and pathways. THAT for which Christ Jesus laid hold of us. Just knowing we were laid hold of. We were wanted, we were valued, and we were created specifically for THAT. We had the confidence to move forward. To press on. To forget/let go of what lies behind and press forward for the mark of the high calling of God in Christ Jesus.

Back to Ephesians 1. "What are the riches of the glory of His inheritance in the saints?" We are his inheritance, and he is our inheritance, and there are riches of the glory in this inheritance that we have yet to know or understand. How God so LOVED the world that he GAVE his only son. And now we are recipients of that great love and that great gift of salvation. And that glorious inheritance. All of the saints for all of the years for all of the centuries, for as many as received Him, he gave them the power to become the children of God. Adopted in the beloved. Earlier in Ephesians 1. Ephesians 1:10-14:

In Him also we have obtained an inheritance, having been predestined according to His purpose who works all things after the counsel of His will, to the end that we who were the first to hope in Christ would be to the praise of His glory. In Him, you also, after listening to the message of truth, the gospel of your salvation—having also believed, you were sealed in Him with the Holy Spirit of promise, who is given as a pledge of our inheritance, with a view to the redemption of God's own possession, to the praise of His glory.

A Glorious inheritance. The riches of his glorious inheritance in his saints. Truly this is a glorious inheritance. Who needs this prayer? Who needs to know that the Lord loves them and has an inheritance for them? Who needs to know that they are the inheritance of the Lord? That with His blood, He valued them enough to pay for their transgressions? Who needs that prayer? Lord, I pray right now for _____ that the riches of your glorious inheritance may be made known to them that they would know that they have been sealed by the Holy Spirit as a pledge of our inheritance. And that they would know you and love you more, Lord Jesus.

Great power. The next phrase in Ephesians 1 is verse 19, "and what is the surpassing greatness of His power toward us who believe." And so. What is the surpassing greatness of His power? First, let's look at 2 Corinthians 4, and then we will come back to Ephesians 1. Incomparably great power. For us who believe. Also, see the surpassing greatness of his power in 2 Cor 4:6-9:

For God, who said, "Let light shine out of darkness" made his light shine in our hearts to give us the light of the knowledge of God's glory displayed in the face of Christ. But we have this treasure in jars of clay to show that this all-surpassing power is from God and not from us. We are hard pressed on every side, but not crushed; perplexed, but not in despair; persecuted, but not abandoned; struck down, but not destroyed.

This all-surpassing power can be our prayer for us or someone we love.

Power. So many kinds of power are available to us through the Holy Spirit. We have the power to become the children of God. We have the power to overcome the evil one. We have the power to be more than overcomers through Him who loved us. We have the power to live, to love, to serve. This is *dunamis*, dynamite power. We are not powerless, dear friends. God has given us power. Great and mighty power. Continuing in Ephesians 1:19-23,

These are in accordance with the working of the strength of His might which He brought about in Christ, when He raised Him from the dead and seated Him at His right hand in the heavenly places, far above all rule and authority and power and dominion, and every name that is named, not only in this age but also in the one to come. And He put all things in subjection under His feet, and gave Him as head over all things to the church, which is His body, the fullness of Him who fills all in all.

We can have the Spirit of wisdom and revelation to be wise, to see clearly. We can have the knowledge of Him to understand and know Christ. We HAVE a glorious inheritance even as we ARE Christ's inheritance. Christ has purchased us and has invested in us. And has built us. And has formed us. And the Holy Spirit is conforming us and transforming us. We can have incomparably great power, the *dunamis*, dynamite, power for life, and godliness in Christ Jesus.

Who needs this prayer? I do. We do. Let's take this prayer with us into the New Year. As we grow in the spiritual life, we can look back and see that perhaps we are not as angry this year as we were last year. Perhaps we are not as fearful this year as we were last year. What fruit of the Spirit has grown in our lives this year? Are we more loving, joyful, peaceful, and patient? As we are conformed to the image of Christ and transformed by the renewing of our minds, the Holy Spirit will grow fruit in us. Our character will change. This is more than behavior modification. This is transformation. One of the social media messages yesterday was a call for testimonies from pastors and members as we have seen the Holy Spirit at work this past year. Or as we see incredible things in this next year. They are gathering testimonies for the National Conference next summer to encourage our faith. That the Holy Spirit comes and brings glory to Jesus through answers to our cries. Our desperate prayers. Our faith-filled prayers.

So, as we face the New Year, my encouragement to us is to take prayers with us that have been life-changing prayers. Take Ephesians 1. Sit with it. Pray it. Pray it for yourself. Pray it for others. Memorize it. Carry it around in your heart. Find it flowing out of you as you pray for others. So many wonderful prayers. Maybe you will take your favorite Psalms, your favorite hymns, and your favorite worship songs. I plan to pack the verses I have memorized. And I also plan to memorize more verses this next year. I plan to pack the worship songs and hymns that are prayers. And learn more this next year. Here are some suggestions. Take Ephesians 1. Take "Lord, teach me to pray." Jesus taught His disciples this prayer pattern. Start with Our Father in heaven, adore Him and hallow His name. Ask for God's rule and reign to come to earth as it is in heaven. Request provision for today. Daily bread. Ask for forgiveness in the same way we offer forgiveness to those who owe us debts or who have trespassed against us. Let us not be tempted with evil. Deliver us from evil's grasp, because Father, because Lord, Yours is the kingdom. Yours is the power. Yours is the glory. For how long? Forever!

Chichester reprise. See thee more clearly. Love thee more dearly. Follow thee more nearly. Day by day. Lord, I want to hear Your voice. John 10 says My sheep listen to my voice. My sheep hear my voice. I am one of your sheep. I want to hear Your voice; I want to listen to your voice. Before I prayed the "sheep" prayer, I spent a lot of my prayer life talking at God. Saying words to a faraway God in the sky somewhere way far away. And hoping I would be heard. Now, I am still learning to listen to the whispers of God, the divine nudges, to recognize the call to obedience in certain circumstances.

Not my will, but Thine be done. Prayer of relinquishment, a prayer of surrender. I remember a Jack Deere teaching tape from the 1990s in which I heard him teach this prayer "Lord Jesus, I want to love you with the love you deserve to be loved with. Father give me Your heart for Your son, Jesus, that I may love Him with that kind of Love." Worship songs. Dwell in the midst of us. Come and dwell in this place. Dwell in the midst of us. You can have Your way. Not our will, but Yours be done."[35] "Jesus, be the center, be my source, be my life, Jesus."[36]

Hymns. Example: Be Thou my Vision, O Lord of my heart Naught be all else to me, save that Thou art Thou my best Thought, by day or by night Waking or sleeping, Thy presence my light Be Thou my Wisdom, and Thou my true Word I ever with Thee and Thou with me, Lord Thou my great Father, I Thy true son Thou in me dwelling, and I with Thee one Riches I heed not, nor man's empty praise Thou mine Inheritance, now and always Thou and Thou only, first in my heart High King of Heaven, my Treasure Thou art High King of Heaven, my victory won May I reach Heaven's joys, O bright Heav'n's Sun Heart of my own heart, whate'er befall Still be my Vision, O Ruler of all.[37]

---

[35] "Dwell," https://www.allthelyrics.com/lyrics/vineyard/dwell-lyrics-1120989.html.

[36] "Jesus, be the Centre," https://www.allthelyrics.com/lyrics/vineyard/be_the_centre-lyrics-1120988.html.

[37] "Be Thou My Vision," https://hymnary.org/text/be_thou_my_vision_o_lord_of_my_heart, Translator: Mary E. Byrne, Mary Elizabeth Byrne, M.A. (July 2, 1880 – January 19,

Get alone with Jesus and pray. Ask what specific prayer assignments you have for the next year. And if there is a particular passage of Scripture to pray, learn, and meditate upon. We all have different prayer assignments. Prayer is more than requesting something from God. We have focused on one aspect of life-changing prayers, requests. Concentric circles Start with us. Our family, Our friends, Our church, Our community, state, country, and world. Lord, teach us to pray. Lord, birth/plant/supply prayers in us that You want to answer. Teach us to pray Scripture. Give us Your heart for those around us. Those You have entrusted us to pray for. Lord, what are our prayer assignments/investments from You for this next year?

Closing Prayer: O, dear Lord, we thank You for Your presence with us today. We thank You for the privileges of knowing You and loving You as Your precious children. We thank You for the Spirit of wisdom and revelation, for the eyes of our understanding being enlightened for the hope of our calling, for the glorious inheritance, for the surpassing greatness of Your mighty power at work in us. Fill us afresh and anew with Your Holy Spirit for Jesus's sake, Amen. Even so, Come, Holy Spirit.

1931) was born in Ireland. She translated the Old Irish Hymn, "Bí Thusa 'mo Shúile," into English as "Be Thou My Vision" in Ériu (the journal of the School of Irish Learning), in 1905.

Priscilla, Aquila, and Apollos
Acts 18:26

October 17, 2021

Acts 18:26 (NRSV), *"He (Apollos) began to speak boldly in the synagogue; but when Priscilla and Aquila heard him, they took him aside and explained the Way of God to him more accurately."*

Let us pray: O Lord, this morning, we come to You, to Your throne of grace, to receive mercy and grace in our time of need. We need to hear from You today, Lord. As we open Your holy scriptures, we ask that you speak to us from their pages and that Your Holy Spirit, who inspired the scriptures, will speak to our hearts with what we need for life, faith, and edification and encouragement today, In Jesus' name, Amen.

Introduction. Does anyone like to look at maps? I know that maps help me understand where I have been and where I am going. When we plug in a destination into our GPS, it takes the address and connects to a satellite in the sky, and comes back with a plan to get us from here to there. So, today, we are going along with Paul and his friends from city to city, and it might help us to know where these cities are in relationship to one another and where they are so we can visualize these travels. Some of us have maps in the back of our Bibles. Others of us can locate these places on our devices along the way.

Let's begin with Corinth. This morning we are looking at the scripture starting in Acts 18. We will read a bit and then notice some things.

> *After this Paul left Athens and went to Corinth. 2 There he found a Jew named Aquila, a native of Pontus, who had recently come from Italy with his wife Priscilla, because Claudius had ordered all Jews to leave Rome. Paul went to see them, 3 and, because he was of the same trade, he stayed with them, and they worked together—by trade they were tentmakers. 4 Every sabbath he would argue in the synagogue and would try to convince Jews and Greeks.*

Verse 1. After Paul left Athens on his second missionary journey, he went to Corinth. Do you see Corinth on the map? Today we are going to Corinth and Ephesus. Find Corinth and Ephesus. Okay. Corinth is about 50 miles west of Athens in Achaia. From west to east, we have Spain, Italy, Achaia (modern-day Greece), and Asia Minor, and then following down the coast, we come to Caesarea and the way to Jerusalem.

Corinth had a famous history, including in the early fine art of painting.[38] Corinth had led the Aegean confederacy in the Hellenistic period; after Rome fought that confederacy, Lucius Mummius destroyed the Greek city in 146 B.C.E. Julius Caesar restored it, however, as a Roman colony (Laus Iulia Corinthus) a century later in 44 B.C.E. In 27 B.C.E., Augustus made it the capital of Achaia, and by now, it had become a multicultural metropolis. In Corinth, Paul found a Jewish married couple, Priscilla and Aquila. They had left Rome to come to Corinth when Claudius had ordered all of the Jews to leave Rome. The year in history is CE 49. We know that Pricilla and Aquila were tentmakers. They had the same trade as Paul did. Whenever Paul went to a city, he went to the synagogue to reason with the people attending the synagogue and set up his business of tentmaking. Verse 4 says that every Sabbath, Paul would argue in the synagogue and try to convince the Jews and the Greeks. Paul carried the good news of the gospel that Jesus Christ is the Messiah, the Lord, the Savior, and that the promised One had come in Jesus the Christ. Paul stayed with Priscilla and Aquila. They had fellowship together in knowing the Lord Jesus and working in the same trade. Let's continue reading verses 5-8:

> *When Silas and Timothy arrived from Macedonia, Paul was occupied with proclaiming the word, testifying to the Jews that the Messiah was Jesus. 6 When they opposed and reviled him, in protest he shook the dust from his clothes and said to them, "Your blood be on your own heads! I am innocent. From now on I will go to the Gentiles." 7 Then he left the synagogue and went to the house of a man named Titius Justus, a worshiper of God; his house was next door to the synagogue. 8 Crispus, the official of the synagogue, became a believer in the Lord, together with all his household; and many of the Corinthians who heard Paul became believers and were baptized.*

So, we see that opposition arose, and Paul said that from now on, he would go to the Gentiles, and he went next door to the synagogue to the house of Titius Justus, who was a worshiper of God. And we read about Crispus, the official of the synagogue who became a believer in the Lord. Crispus and his household were baptized, and many of the Corinthians who heard Paul became believers and were baptized. In verse 11, it says that Paul stayed there in Corinth for a year and six months, teaching the word of God among the

---

[38] Keener, Craig S. *Acts: an Exegetical Commentary: Volume 3 : 15:1-23:35*, Baker Academic, 2014.

people. It was during this time he wrote 1 and 2 Thessalonians. Then, in verse 18, we see him leaving to go to Antioch in Syria and on to Ephesus. He took Priscilla and Aquila with him, and they set sail. It is about 250 miles to sail across the sea to Antioch in Syria and Ephesus. Paul's Return to Antioch in verses 18-23:

> *After staying there for a considerable time, Paul said farewell to the believers and sailed for Syria, accompanied by Priscilla and Aquila. At Cenchreae he had his hair cut, for he was under a vow. 19 When they reached Ephesus, he left them (Pricilla and Aquila) there, but first, he himself went into the synagogue and had a discussion with the Jews. 20 When they asked him to stay longer, he declined; 21 but on taking leave of them, he said, "I will return to you, if God wills." Then he (Paul) set sail from Ephesus. 22 When he had landed at Caesarea, he went up to Jerusalem and greeted the church, and then went down to Antioch. 23 After spending some time there he departed and went from place to place through the region of Galatia and Phrygia, strengthening all the disciples.*

We see that Paul left Priscilla and Aquila in Ephesus in verse 19 and continued on his missionary journeys, and so now we come to verse 24. Let's read on. (Ministry of Apollos). "Now there came to Ephesus a Jew named Apollos, a native of Alexandria. He was an eloquent man, well-versed in the scriptures. 25 He had been instructed in the Way of the Lord; and he spoke with burning enthusiasm and taught accurately the things concerning Jesus, though he knew only the baptism of John." Let's notice here this man, Apollos, who was a native of Alexandria in Egypt. Alexandria was well known for its learning opportunities for those with sufficient resources. The famous library of Alexandria, though it was possibly no longer standing, had been huge (Strabo 2.1.5). At least by the second century, Alexandria's university was more prestigious than the ancient schools of Athens. [39] (Talk about Alexandria and the Jewish community there.) Apollos was an orator, and it says in verse 24 that he was an eloquent man. He was well-versed in the scriptures, and he had been instructed in the way of the Lord. He spoke with burning enthusiasm, and he taught the things of Jesus accurately even though he only knew the baptism of John.

Apollos had been baptized with the baptism of John. The baptism of repentance. He had not yet been baptized with the baptism of Jesus, the baptism of the Holy Spirit and fire. John the Baptist occupied a vital ministry in preparing the way of the Lord. Apollos knew about Jesus and proclaimed

---

[39] Keener, Craig S. *Acts: an Exegetical Commentary: Volume 3: 15:1-23:35*, Baker Academic, 2014.

the good news about Jesus, but he only had part of the story. Apollos needed more. Apollos apparently knew the basic story of Jesus but not much about the church and its ministry. Probably not familiar with the Jesus movement— that is, the church. Unlike what is usually argued for John's disciples in 19:4, Apollos already believed in Jesus. He seems to have been a follower of the message about Jesus yet not part of and (cf. Luke 9:49– 50).[40] Acts 18:26 "He began to speak boldly in the synagogue; but when Priscilla and Aquila heard him, they took him aside and explained the Way of God to him more accurately."

Priscilla and Aquila could listen to the speakers in the synagogue and discern what they had heard. They called Apollos and took him aside to explain what he needed to know. Verse 26 says they explained the Way of God to him more accurately. It is important to have the gift of discernment, to hear something, and to know what is missing.

Priscilla teaches privately, even if she takes the lead, and the public/private dichotomy was the primary cultural objection to women teaching publicly. Even in public, exceptions could be respected in the case of exceptional women, provided the conventional societal order was normally maintained. Paul's letters praise women for spreading the gospel (Rom 16:1– 7; Phil 4:2– 3) even as his letters also follow social conventions of the day in restricting some speech (1 Cor 14:34– 35). Even though his setting is private, Apollos's willingness to learn from her alongside her husband might imply that, for him, Priscilla was such an exceptional woman. She was noteworthy enough to merit the later praise of John Chrysostom for both her artisan work and her preaching. [41]

Now, in verses 27-28 of Acts 18. "And when he (Apollos) wished to cross over to Achaia, the believers encouraged him and wrote to the disciples to welcome him. On his arrival, he greatly helped those who through grace had become believers, 28 for he powerfully refuted the Jews in public, showing by the scriptures that the Messiah is Jesus." So that is when Apollos went to Corinth in Achaia and had a ministry there, powerfully refuting the Jews in public with his rhetorical prowess and showing by the scriptures that the Messiah is Jesus. Eloquence was a mark of education and respectability. Meanwhile, Paul continues his missionary journey and comes back to Ephesus. While Apollos was in Corinth, Paul passed through the interior regions and came to Ephesus, where he found some disciples. Acts 19:2-7:

---

[40] Keener, Craig S. *Acts: an Exegetical Commentary: Volume 3: 15:1-23:35*, Baker Academic, 2014.

[41] Craig S. Keener. 1-2 Corinthians. Cambridge University Press, 2005.

He said to them, "Did you receive the Holy Spirit when you became believers?" They replied, "No, we have not even heard that there is a Holy Spirit." 3 Then he said, "Into what then were you baptized?" They answered, "Into John's baptism." 4 Paul said, "John baptized with the baptism of repentance, telling the people to believe in the one who was to come after him, that is, in Jesus." 5 On hearing this, they were baptized in the name of the Lord Jesus. 6 When Paul had laid his hands on them, the Holy Spirit came upon them, and they spoke in tongues and prophesied—7 altogether there were about twelve of them.

So, we see that Paul also had met disciples along the way who had been baptized with the baptism of John, and they needed to know about being baptized in the name of Jesus and receiving the Holy Spirit with the laying on of hands. And now, let's turn to 1 Corinthians. This letter was written by Paul when he was in Ephesus in about AD 55 and carried by Timothy as mentioned in 1 Cor 4:17. To the Corinthians to address some of the things Paul had heard about what was going on in Corinth. And here we find divisions in the church.

Look at 1 Corinthians, Chapter 1. After the lovely salutation in verses 1-9, we come to verses 10-17.

Now I appeal to you, brothers and sisters, by the name of our Lord Jesus Christ, that all of you be in agreement and that there be no divisions among you, but that you be united in the same mind and the same purpose. 11 For it has been reported to me by Chloe's people that there are quarrels among you, my brothers and sisters. 12 What I mean is that each of you says, "I belong to Paul," or "I belong to Apollos," or "I belong to Cephas," or "I belong to Christ." 13 Has Christ been divided? Was Paul crucified for you? Or were you baptized in the name of Paul? 14 I thank God that I baptized none of you except Crispus and Gaius, 15 so that no one can say that you were baptized in my name. 16 (I did baptize also the household of Stephanas; beyond that, I do not know whether I baptized anyone else.) 17 For Christ did not send me to baptize but to proclaim the gospel, and not with eloquent wisdom, so that the cross of Christ might not be emptied of its power.

So, Paul is addressing the divisions in the church. By this time, some of the believers were starting to say that they followed Cephas (Peter) and some followed Apollos, and some followed Paul. Paul is challenging the believers here to follow Jesus and not to look at their favorite teachers to follow the teachers, but to follow Christ. When Paul says in verse 17 that Christ sent him to proclaim the gospel, we know that Paul did not consider himself to be eloquent. Apollos was eloquent. Paul had his own ways of proclaiming

Jesus and telling of Paul's testimony of how Jesus met him and sent him to bring the good news to proclaim the gospel. (Christ the Power and Wisdom of God) Continuing 1 Cor 1:18-25:

> *For the message about the cross is foolishness to those who are perishing, but to us who are being saved it is the power of God. 19 For it is written, "I will destroy the wisdom of the wise, and the discernment of the discerning I will thwart." 20 Where is the one who is wise? Where is the scribe? Where is the debater of this age? Has not God made foolish the wisdom of the world? 21 For since, in the wisdom of God, the world did not know God through wisdom, God decided, through the foolishness of our proclamation, to save those who believe. 22 For Jews demand signs and Greeks desire wisdom, 23 but we proclaim Christ crucified, a stumbling block to Jews and foolishness to Gentiles, 24 but to those who are the called, both Jews and Greeks, Christ the power of God and the wisdom of God. 25 For God's foolishness is wiser than human wisdom, and God's weakness is stronger than human strength.*

And so, Paul contends for the gospel in the way the Lord has called him to contend for the gospel. Verse 23. We proclaim Christ crucified, a stumbling block to the Jews and foolishness to Gentiles, but to those who are the called, both Jews and Greeks, Christ, the power of God, and the wisdom of God.

That is good news! Good news for Jews and Greeks. Good news for us. Jesus Christ is the power (*dunamis*) of God and the wisdom (Sophia) of God. Dunamis strength, power, ability. Sophia: supreme intelligence. The wisdom of God is evinced in forming and executing counsels in the formation and government of the world and the scriptures.

As Paul continues to encourage and admonish the believers in Corinth, he writes in Chapter 3 about the divisions among them being of the flesh and not of the Spirit. In Chapter 3 of 1 Corinthians, we read in verses 1-9:

> *And so, brothers and sisters, I could not speak to you as spiritual people, but rather as people of the flesh, as infants in Christ. 2 I fed you with milk, not solid food, for you were not ready for solid food. Even now you are still not ready, 3 for you are still of the flesh. For as long as there is jealousy and quarreling among you, are you not of the flesh, and behaving according to human inclinations? 4 For when one says, "I belong to Paul," and another, "I belong to Apollos," are you not merely human? 5 What then is Apollos? What is Paul? Servants through whom you came to believe, as the Lord assigned to each. 6 I planted, Apollos watered, but God gave the growth. 7 So neither the one who plants nor the one who waters is anything, but only God who gives the growth. 8 The one who plants and the one who waters have a common purpose, and each will receive*

wages according to the labor of each. 9 For we are God's servants, working together; you are God's field, God's building.

Here, Paul is encouraging and admonishing the Corinthians that each one has their part. I planted. Apollos watered. Only God gives the growth.

When we were at Lilburn Daze on Saturday, October 9th, we had a booth called Everyone Gets to Play. Some called to the people walking by, Come and play. Some cheered on the people who were playing, and some gave prizes. In all of it, we saw lots of participation, and each of us used our gifts to plant, water, and give glory to God.

Paul did not discount the work of Apollos. Paul honored the work of Apollos but saw it as different than the work the Lord had called him, Paul, to do. I planted. Apollos watered. God gave the increase. Some of us plant, some of us water, and God is able to get the glory in all of the work that is done for the kingdom of God. At the end of 1 Corinthians 3:18-23:

> *Do not deceive yourselves. If you think that you are wise in this age, you should become fools so that you may become wise. 19 For the wisdom of this world is foolishness with God. For it is written, "He catches the wise in their craftiness," 20 and again, "The Lord knows the thoughts of the wise, that they are futile." 21 So let no one boast about human leaders. For all things are yours, 22 whether Paul or Apollos or Cephas or the world or life or death or the present or the future—all belong to you, 23 and you belong to Christ, and Christ belongs to God.*

Again. Paul, Apollos, and Peter are human leaders who belong to Christ. So, let's see what happens to Priscilla and Aquila. Priscilla and Aquila are mentioned again in three places. In 1 Corinthians 16:19. At the end of this letter to Corinthians, Paul sends greetings from Aquila and Priscilla, who have a church in their house. The churches of Asia send greetings. Aquila and Prisca, together with the church in their house, greet you warmly in the Lord.

When Paul writes the letter to the Romans in 56-58AD in his 3rd missionary journey when he was in Corinth for three months (Acts 20:2-3). In Chapter 16:3-5, he is sending greetings to Prisca and Aquila (Prisca is the name. Priscilla is the diminutive of that name.) "Greet Prisca and Aquila, who work with me in Christ Jesus, 4 and who risked their necks for my life, to whom not only I give thanks, but also all the churches of the Gentiles. 5 Greet also the church in their house." Paul says that Priscilla and Aquila risked their necks for Paul's life. They have now returned to Rome. By the time Paul writes Romans, Prisca and Aquila are hosting a church in their home.

2 Timothy 4:19. When Paul writes to Timothy, he asks Timothy to greet Priscilla and Aquila. Final Greetings and Benediction "Greet Prisca and Aquila, and the household of Onesiphorus."

So, let's see what happens to Apollos. 1 Corinthians 16:12, "Now concerning our brother Apollos, I strongly urged him to visit you with the other brothers, but he was not at all willing to come now. He will come when he has the opportunity." Here Paul calls Apollos, our brother, and it is apparent in Paul's writing to the Corinthians that Paul strongly urged Apollos to visit them, and yet Apollos was not willing to come now. So, Paul writes to the Corinthians that Apollos will come when he has the opportunity. (Paul was not in charge of Apollos).

Titus 3:13 "Make every effort to send Zenas, the lawyer, and Apollos on their way and see that they lack nothing." Paul is still watching over the church and asking that Titus send Zenas and Apollos be sent on their way and lack nothing, provide for them and their journey.

So, let's see what happens to us. If we have been baptized as followers of Christ, it is a baptism to follow Jesus wherever he leads us. If Jesus has baptized us with the Holy Spirit and fire, we have asked Jesus to send the Holy Spirit to come and baptize us with the power and wisdom of God, and we have evidence in our lives of the fruit of the Spirit growing. We are growing in the fruit of the Spirit. We are to take up our crosses daily and follow Jesus. We are to abide in the Vine. We are to love one another. We are to produce fruit in keeping with repentance. We are to work together as ambassadors for Christ inviting people to be reconciled to God. Divisions happen in nations, cultures, and the ways we understand what is happening. In our nation, we can pray for God to heal divisions.

Paul spoke specifically to the divisions in the church at Corinth. Some were following him, and some were following Apollos. We do not need to be divided over teachers or various ways in our world that would seek to divide us. We need the wisdom from God and the mind of Christ.

Listen to 1 Corinthians 2:6-16:

> *Yet among the mature we do speak wisdom, though it is not a wisdom of this age or of the rulers of this age, who are doomed to perish. 7 But we speak God's wisdom, secret and hidden, which God decreed before the ages for our glory. 8*

None of the rulers of this age understood this; for if they had, they would not have crucified the Lord of glory. 9 But, as it is written, "What no eye has seen, nor ear heard, nor the human heart conceived, what God has prepared for those who love him"10 these things God has revealed to us through the Spirit; for the Spirit searches everything, even the depths of God. 11 For what human being knows what is truly human except the human spirit that is within? So also no one comprehends what is truly God's except the Spirit of God. 12 Now we have received not the spirit of the world, but the Spirit that is from God, so that we may understand the gifts bestowed on us by God. 13 And we speak of these things in words not taught by human wisdom but taught by the Spirit, interpreting spiritual things to those who are spiritual. 14 Those who are unspiritual do not receive the gifts of God's Spirit, for they are foolishness to them, and they are unable to understand them because they are spiritually discerned. 15 Those who are spiritual discern all things, and they are themselves subject to no one else's scrutiny. 16 "For who has known the mind of the Lord so as to instruct him?" But we have the mind of Christ.

Listen to Ephesians 2:19-22 (The Message)

That's plain enough, isn't it? You're no longer wandering exiles. This kingdom of faith is now your home country. You're no longer strangers or outsiders. You belong here, with as much right to the name Christian as anyone. God is building a home. He's using us all—irrespective of how we got here—in what he is building. He used the apostles and prophets for the foundation. Now he's using you, fitting you in brick by brick, stone by stone, with Christ Jesus as the cornerstone that holds all the parts together. We see it taking shape day after day—a holy temple built by God, all of us built into it, a temple in which God is quite at home.

Ministry Time. We are going to have a ministry time now in the service where the music is going to play softly, and we are going to wait for the Holy Spirit to touch us. After the music for a while, I will offer the benediction and dismiss us to go in grace and peace to love and serve the Lord. Now, as the music plays, I would like to encourage us to sit quietly for a bit and invite the Holy Spirit to move in our hearts. Some of us will pour out love to God as the worship music is offered to the Lord. Some of us will feel the Holy Spirit prompting us to go and ask a brother or sister for forgiveness. Some of us may want to come forward and kneel at the altar. Some of us may just feel the Holy Spirit inviting us to pray for those the Holy Spirit is touching today. When the Holy Spirit comes with manifestations of power and presence, some will weep. Some will experience joy. Some will have other expressions. Some will receive physical healing in their bodies. We will spend time listening and if you want someone near you to pray with you, go to them. If you want someone on the ministry team to pray with you, come and stand up here to my left. If you just want to come to the altar, come to the altar.

Closing Prayer. Come, Holy Spirit. Meet us here with Your manifest presence. Help us to love Jesus more. Fill us with Your presence. Fill us with Your power. Invite us to forgive those we need to forgive. Heal our hearts. Heal our bodies. Restore to us the joy of our salvation. Renew a right spirit within us. We love You, Lord Jesus, and welcome You, Holy Spirit, the gift that Jesus promised to those who would wait in Jerusalem until they received power from on high. And so, we wait.

Hear the benediction: from 2 Corinthians 14:11-13: Finally, brothers and sisters, farewell. Put things in order, listen to my appeal, agree with one another, live in peace; and the God of love and peace will be with you. 12 Greet one another with a holy kiss. All the saints greet you. 13 The grace of the Lord Jesus Christ, the love of God, and the communion of the Holy Spirit be with all of you.

Queen of Sheba
1 Kings 10:1-3

July 23, 2017

1 Kings 10:1-3 (ESV) *Now when the queen of Sheba heard of the fame of Solomon concerning the name of the Lord, she came to test him with hard questions. 2 She came to Jerusalem with a very great retinue, with camels bearing spices and very much gold and precious stones. And when she came to Solomon, she told him all that was on her mind. 3 And Solomon answered all her questions; there was nothing hidden from the king that he could not explain to her.*

Introduction: When I was a little girl in Sunday School, we re-enacted Bible Stories. We had the dress-up clothes to assist us in our re-enactment. I might have been 6 or 7 years of age when I was selected to play the Queen of Sheba. So excited. I wore a long flowing cape, a tiara, long gloves, and had a couple of lines. I think my lines were something like, "O, King Solomon, I have heard about your wisdom and splendor. The half has not been told." I also think I had to bow to the king, and I have had a place in my heart for her ever since.

Lifestyles of the Rich and Famous have fascinated people for as long as there has been a history of people. We have heard of many rich and famous people through the years. Some build monuments to themselves. Some are known for their benevolent acts and deeds. Their philanthropy. There was a series on television in the 80s and 90s by that name, Lifestyles of the Rich and Famous. Yachts, mansions, cars, investments, and persons to care for them, their possessions, and their investments. Who are the rich and famous people you think of today? Someone may be writing stories about them or making art depicting them, or making films and documentaries about them.

In the Bible, we can read of the wealth of Abraham with his many flocks and herds. The vastness of the land the Lord provided for him in the book of Genesis. We can read of Job. in the book by his name. and his great prosperity that was here and then gone. Taken away. Swiftly. Until God restored his health, his family, and his wealth. And then there was Solomon. Solomon was known for his wealth, his lifestyle, and his wisdom. Solomon in Scripture. Where can we find Solomon in scripture? Solomon's life is depicted in 1 Kings, and 2 Chronicles. Writings attributed to Solomon can be found in the wisdom literature of the Bible. Examples. Proverbs, Ecclesiastes, and Song of Solomon.

To cast an overview. Solomon lived and ruled in the Ancient Near East about a thousand years before Christ. In the 970-931 BCE range. He was in succession in the united monarchy of Israel. Saul, David, Solomon. His father was King David, and his mother was Bathsheba. David was a man of war, and Solomon had peace in his time. His kingdom stretched from the Euphrates River to the land of the Philistines and the border of Egypt. When Solomon was rich and famous, he received a visit from the first queen mentioned in scripture, the Queen of Sheba. Kings had wives, but they were not referred to with the ruling word. Malkah, the feminine noun for Melek, King. Ruler. The Queen of Sheba occupies part of the account of King Solomon's reign in 1 Kings 10 and 2 Chronicles 9. We will be opening our Bibles to 1 Kings 10 or selecting 1 Kings 10 on our devices shortly to read this account.

Before we do, I think we need to know that the story of the Queen of Sheba lives on in legends, folktales, drama, art, and history. If you search for her story on the internet or in the library, you could find movies made about her and many chapters of her life that are not recorded for us in the sacred text. European artists in the Renaissance tended to depict her as blonde-haired and blue-eyed. She probably had dark skin, dark hair, and dark eyes. Movie makers tended to find a way to make her visit to Solomon into a love story. Some legends suggest that she was the beloved in the Song of Solomon. Some of the history and legends of Ethiopia call her by the name Makeda and name her son Menelik. Some claim and believe that Solomon fathered her son Menelik I. They trace her reign and the Solomonic dynasty to the emperor, Haile Selassie, in the 20th century, who was forced out of power in 1974. The 1 Kings 10 and 2 Chronicles 9 accounts do not mention a love story. That is in the realm of possibility but not in the Bible. Other claims are made that she was from the south of the Arabian peninsula, in what we know today as Yemen. The history of Yemen claims her, too. Jesus refers to the queen of Sheba as the queen of the South.

Here is a map of North Africa and the Arabian peninsula. For those listening online, you can search for it to see what I am describing. Describe Map. Here is Jerusalem. Here is the Arabian peninsula. Here is Yemen in the south of the Arabian peninsula. Here is Ethiopia. Here is the Red Sea. Here is the Indian Ocean. The way to the Orient for spices and the spice trade and maybe, possibly, the way to Ophir for gold. Here is the Gulf of Aqaba. The queen of Sheba would have traveled from the south of Arabia here, where Yemen is today, or from just across the Red Sea here in Ethiopia all of the way to Jerusalem by land or by sea to as far as one could go by sea and then by land. Distance between the gulf of Aqaba and Jerusalem. 345 km. (214 miles). From Yemen to Jerusalem as the bird flies is 2249 km. (1397) miles. From Ethiopia is 2564 km. (1593 miles) as the bird flies.

The Queen of Sheba. Let's look at the text in 1 Kings 10:1-7 (ESV)

> *Now when the queen of Sheba heard about the fame of Solomon concerning the name of the Lord, she came to test him with difficult questions. So she came to Jerusalem with a very large retinue, with camels carrying spices and very much gold and precious stones. When she came to Solomon, she spoke with him about all that was in her heart. Solomon answered all her questions; nothing was hidden from the king which he did not explain to her. When the queen of Sheba perceived all the wisdom of Solomon, the house that he had built, the food of his table, the seating of his servants, the attendance of his waiters and their attire, his cupbearers, and his stairway by which he went up to the house of the Lord, there was no more spirit in her. Then she said to the king, "It was a true report which I heard in my own land about your words and your wisdom. Nevertheless I did not believe the reports, until I came and my eyes had seen it. And behold, the half was not told me. You exceed in wisdom and prosperity the report which I heard.*

Let's stop there for now. What have we seen? She, the queen of Sheba, probably lived around 1200 miles away, at the tip of the Arabian peninsula or just across the Red Sea from there. She heard about the fame of Solomon. this was likely on a shipping route or a caravan route or a trade route. She heard about the fame of Solomon concerning the name of the Lord. What name of the lord would impress you 1200 miles away? Could it be the all-wise God? All powerful god? Majestic in splendor, God? She heard about the fame of Solomon concerning the name of the Lord, and she came seeking. What did she find?

Difficult questions. So, she came to test him with difficult questions. Enigmas. Riddles? [Story of the two women and one live baby 1 Kings 3:16-28] How many questions can a woman ask? Who, what, when, where, how, why? How many questions are in the heart of a powerful, regal woman? How many questions would we ask if we had the opportunity to sit down with the wisest person in the world who knew God? What kinds of questions would we ask?

Remember when God asked Solomon a question about what Solomon wanted? Let's go back a couple of pages to Chapter 3 Solomon's request 1 Kings 3:7-9:

Now, O Lord my God, You have made Your servant king in place of my father David, yet I am but a little child; I do not know how to go out or come in. Your servant is in the midst of Your people which You have chosen, a great people who are too many to be numbered or counted. So give Your servant an understanding heart to judge Your people to discern between good and evil. For who is able to judge this great people of Yours?

And then we read God's Answer. 1 Kings 3:10-15:

It was pleasing in the sight of the Lord that Solomon had asked this thing. God said to him, "Because you have asked this thing and have not asked for yourself long life, nor have asked riches for yourself, nor have you asked for the life of your enemies, but have asked for yourself discernment to understand justice, behold, I have done according to your words. Behold, I have given you a wise and discerning heart, so that there has been no one like you before you, nor shall one like you arise after you. I have also given you what you have not asked, both riches and honor, so that there will not be any among the kings like you all your days. If you walk in My ways, keeping My statutes and commandments, as your father David walked, then I will prolong your days." Then Solomon awoke, and behold, it was a dream. And he came to Jerusalem and stood before the ark of the covenant of the Lord, and offered burnt offerings and made peace offerings, and made a feast for all his servants.

Request for wisdom Solomon asked, "Give Your servant an understanding heart to judge Your people to discern between good and evil" God said, "You have asked for yourself discernment to understand justice, behold, I have done according to your words. Behold, I have given you a wise and discerning heart, so that there has been no one like you before you, nor shall one like you arise after you. I have also given you what you have not asked, both riches and honor, so that there will not be any among the kings like you all your days."

Back to the Queen of Sheba in 1 Kings 10:2, "So she came to Jerusalem with a very large retinue, with camels carrying spices and very much gold and precious stones." It is likely this journey took quite a while. The camels would need to eat and rest. The travelers and attendants would need to eat and rest. She was traveling for miles across the desert. They could have taken ships as far as ships could go. But this was in the days before the Suez canal. She did not arrive empty-handed. She came bearing gifts and tributes.

Continuing verses 2 and 3, "When she came to Solomon, she spoke with him about all that was in her heart. Solomon answered all her questions; nothing was hidden from the king which he did not explain to her." Solomon took time for her. Solomon listened to her. Solomon was able to answer ALL of her questions. ALL of her questions. Nothing was hidden from the king that he did not explain to her. No question was so difficult that Solomon had to say, "I don't know." Listening. If you have ever had someone to listen to you truly, you know what a gift that is. Someone who could say. Is there anything else? Is there anything else? Counselors, spiritual directors, and coaches are trained to listen genuinely. But there was none like Solomon. We do not know how long this visit lasted. We just know that the queen of Sheba had time to speak with Solomon about all that was in her heart.

Continuing verses 4-5. "When the queen of Sheba perceived all the wisdom of Solomon, the house that he had built, the food of his table, the seating of his servants, the attendance of his waiters and their attire, his cupbearers, and his stairway by which he went up to the house of the Lord, there was no more spirit in her." LOOK at this list. The queen of Sheba perceived all the wisdom of Solomon. The queen of Sheba saw the house that he built—magnificently adorned with gold and cedar. And skilled craftsmanship. The House of the Forest of Lebanon. Reference in Chapter 7:2ff. The food on his table. How much food would it take to feed all of the people who sat at his table? The seating of his servants, the attendance of his waiters, and their attire. Dressed to match? And his cupbearers. They had to taste the wine in case the wine was poisoned or not good enough. And his stairway that he had built to go up to the house of the Lord. There was no more spirit in her. It Took Her Breath Away. And she saw that it was better than she had imagined. (To read further about Solomon's wealth and wisdom, look at Chapter 4 starting at verse 20.)

Back to Chapter 10 and verses 6-7, "Then she said to the king, "It was a true report which I heard in my own land about your words and your wisdom. Nevertheless, I did not believe the reports, until I came and my eyes had seen it. And behold, the half was not told me. You exceed in wisdom and prosperity the report which I heard.""

She finally believed the report she had heard. We have heard the saying that Seeing is believing. She had to see it to believe it. It was a true report. But the half was not told. The half was not told. You exceed in wisdom. You exceed in prosperity. You are better in person than the report I heard. Now let's read the remainder of the account of the queen of Sheba in 1 Kings 10, verses 8-13:

> *How blessed are your men, how blessed are these your servants who stand before you continually and hear your wisdom. Blessed be the Lord your God who*

delighted in you to set you on the throne of Israel; because the Lord loved Israel forever, therefore He made you king, to do justice and righteousness." She gave the king a hundred and twenty talents of gold, and a very great amount of spices and precious stones. Never again did such abundance of spices come in as that which the queen of Sheba gave King Solomon. Also the ships of Hiram, which brought gold from Ophir, brought in from Ophir a very great number of almug trees and precious stones. The king made of the almug trees supports for the house of the Lord and for the king's house, also lyres and harps for the singers; such almug trees have not come in again nor have they been seen to this day. King Solomon gave to the queen of Sheba all her desire which she requested, besides what he gave her according to his royal bounty. Then she turned and went to her own land together with her servants.

Notice this in verses 8-9. The queen of Sheba recognizes how blessed and happy the servants are to stand before Solomon and hear his wisdom. I wonder this morning. Are we happy and blessed serving the One true God as the servants of Solomon were serving in a time of peace and prosperity? She blesses the Lord God who delighted in Solomon. She recognizes that God set Solomon on the throne of Israel because the Lord loved Israel and made Solomon king to do justice and righteousness. v. 10 She brought him millions of dollars of gold at today's prices. Suppose you have traveled to the Middle East and have gone to the spice markets. The half has not been told of the aromas and scents and colors and consistency of the barrels of spices and the mixture of aromas in front, to the side, and behind you. Truly an amazing experience of abundance.

Continuing verses 11-12. These ships also arrived with gold, almug trees, and precious stones for King Solomon. Hiram was known for the shipbuilding, and these sailors would sail all the way to Ophir and back. It took years to sail around to Ophir (somewhere in the Orient) and back. This special wood from the almug trees was used for musical instruments and for the king's house and the house of the Lord. More about almug trees. Smith's Bible Dictionary, "It is probable that this tree is the red sandalwood, which is a native of India and Ceylon [Sri Lanka]. The wood is very heavy, hard and fine-grained, and of beautiful garnet color." The end of the Story of the queen of Sheba.

1 Kings 10:13, "King Solomon gave to the queen of Sheba all her desire which she requested, besides what he gave her according to his royal bounty. Then she turned and went to her own land together with her servants." This is the end of the account in 1Kings. What did she ask for? King Solomon gave to the queen of Sheba ALL HER DESIRE which she requested. Besides what he gave her according to his royal bounty. We have heard of some of

Solomon's royal bounty. We can imagine that he sent food and provisions for the journey and gifts of State for her treasury. And she returned home to her own land with her servants.

This would have been the end of the story except that Jesus recognized the queen of Sheba as the queen of the South in Matt 12:42 and Luke 11:31. Luke 11. Context words. Lord, teach us to pray. Ask, and it will be given to you. Seek, and you shall find. Knock, and the door shall be opened. Let's turn to Luke 11:31, "The queen of the South will rise up with the men of this generation at the judgment and condemn them because she came from the ends of the earth to hear the wisdom of Solomon, and, behold, something greater than Solomon is here."

One greater than Solomon. As wise as Solomon was. As powerful as Solomon was. As rich as Solomon was. Jesus is greater than Solomon. We must "seek first the Kingdom of God and his righteousness, and all these things shall be added unto you." We are to seek wisdom to seek Jesus. Jesus is greater than Solomon. Christ is the Wisdom of God in 1 Cor 1:30. If Solomon's wisdom was known all over the known world in the time of Jesus, how much more does Jesus, the wisdom of God, need to be known all over the world now?

Luke 11: 11-13, "How much MORE will your heavenly Father give the Holy Spirit to those who ask Him?" Luke 12: 27-28, "Consider the lilies, how they grow: they neither toil nor spin; but I tell you, not even Solomon in all his glory clothed himself like one of these. But if God so clothes the grass in the field, which is alive today and tomorrow is thrown into the furnace, how much more will He clothe you? You of little faith."

We need an infusion of faith. Faith that does not need to see with our eyes to believe. Faith that God will provide. Faith that God is good. Faith that God is wise. Faith that God loves us. Faith that believes that nothing can separate us from God's love. If the queen of Sheba could say that the half had not been told of Solomon's wisdom, we can say that the half has not been told of how far God came to save us and love us.

Someone here today, or listening online, has heard of this Jesus, this One who astounded the religious leaders of His day. The One who has continued to astound generations since He walked the face of the earth. This same Jesus the Christ, the Son of the Living God, is alive and well and listening, watching, noticing, and loving. Jesus told His disciples that He was going to prepare a place for them. When John saw the visions and recorded them for us in the book of Revelation, John described an amazing new Jerusalem. More wonderful than anything Solomon had built. The amazing thing is that we can know this Jesus. We can be in a relationship with this Jesus. This same Jesus wants us to seek Him and know Him. The Father will give the Holy Spirit to those who ask. Let us ask. Pray with me.

Closing Prayer: Father, You love us. Lord Jesus, You love us. Holy Spirit, You love us. We love You because You first loved us. For all those listening who want to know You better, draw us to Your heart of love for us. Thank You, Jesus, for coming to earth and living among us. Thank You for Your willingness to leave the glories of heaven to come and ransom us, to deliver us from the kingdom of darkness into Your marvelous light. All wise God, save us today. Heal us today. Forgive us today. Deliver us today as we seek You, Jesus, the Source of Wisdom. Fill us with Your Holy Spirit. For YOUR Great Name's sake. Amen.

Practical Exercise. The half has not been told. I have a folder for each of the tables. In each folder, you will find papers cut in half. This is an exercise in Wisdom. We are going to pray together for one another. On each paper is half of a proverb. We are going to use the tables over here to put the Proverbs together. When the proverbs are together, we will use them for our prayer time. Assemble four proverbs at each table. Use the four proverbs to pray for one another. After using the proverbs to pray for one another, if anyone needs special prayer, we will be here. Amen.

Redeeming Martha
Luke 10:38

July 24, 2022

Luke 10:38 (NRSV) *"Now as they went on their way, he entered a certain village where a woman named Martha welcomed him."*

Prayer: O Lord God, Thank You for Your great salvation and redemption. Teach us today. We pray in Jesus' name, Amen.

Introduction. Maybe some of us have siblings, and we are not alike. I have a sister, and I am not like her. Maybe you have sisters and brothers, and you are not like them. We are all gifted differently. Today we are going to open our Bibles to the Gospel of Luke, Chapter 10. Luke, Chapter 10, starting in verse 38. And we are going to meet two sisters.

Luke 10:38-42 (NRSV):

> *Now as they went on their way, he entered a certain village where a woman named Martha welcomed him. 39 She had a sister named Mary, who sat at Jesus's feet and listened to what he was saying. 40 But Martha was distracted by her many tasks, so she came to him and asked, "Lord, do you not care that my sister has left me to do all the work by myself? Tell her, then, to help me." 41 But the Lord answered her, "Martha, Martha, you are worried and distracted by many things, 42 but few things are needed—indeed only one. Mary has chosen the better part, which will not be taken away from her.*

Let's look at the text and see if we can glean some hope here. The message this morning is entitled, Redeeming Martha. Here we have the account of two sisters, Martha and Mary. Jesus loves both of them dearly. Martha invited Jesus. A woman named Martha welcomed him into her home. Martha's home. Martha is the host in her home. Think about inviting Jesus to your home. If Jesus came to dinner at our homes, we would probably want to plan the meal, put out the best dishes and eating utensils, think about what to purchase at the grocery store, and have everything all prepared. In Bible times, there were no supermarkets with already prepared foods. One could not just go shopping and buy dinner already prepared. There were no fast-food drive-throughs and no food delivery services.

We remember back in Genesis 18 when the angels visited Abraham, and he ran to tell his wife and his servants to prepare the food. He made sure that the visitors had water for their feet and freshly baked bread and freshly slaughtered meat. In the story we read today, we do not hear about servants. We do not hear about animals to be slaughtered or a garden to be picked. We know that Jesus was not alone. If Martha had baked bread that morning, there might have been enough to share with one person. What kind of meal would be fit to serve Jesus? Fish and bread? She may have to go to the fish market to get the fish.

We have several accounts of Table fellowship in the gospel of Luke. Here are two places in the gospel of Luke where Jesus is invited to dinner. Luke 5:29 (NIV) "Then Levi held a great banquet for Jesus at his house, and a large crowd of tax collectors and others were eating with them." Luke 7:36 (NIV) "When one of the Pharisees invited Jesus to have dinner with him, he went to the Pharisee's house and reclined at the table." (Remember, This Pharisee did not provide water for washing his feet, hands, or face.)

Jesus gave instructions to the disciples he sent out on ministry trips. Jesus sends the twelve. Luke 9:4 "Whatever house you enter, stay there until you leave that town." Earlier in this chapter, Jesus sends the 72. Luke 10:5 and 7 "When you enter a house, first say, 'Peace to this house.' Stay there, eating and drinking whatever they give you, for the worker deserves his wages. Do not move around from house to house."

Here, in Luke 10:38-42, Martha was the host. She is the one who opened her home. She is the one who cleaned the space, gathered the provisions, set out the provisions, and could have wanted to keep her reputation for being an excellent host, having a welcoming home, caring for her guests, and providing well for anyone who came under her roof. Making space for the disciples and making sure everyone is comfortable.

Think about Martha's hands as she makes preparations for the food and hosting. I think of Martha's hands with flour, kneading bread, cutting fish with a knife, and preparing to serve the food to the guests. She may have had a broom to sweep the floor before inviting the guests into her home. She might have drawn water at the well to provide basins for foot-washing. She may have washed the towels to dry the feet, and she may have pressed the olives for oil to fry the fish and bake in the bread.

Jesus enters a household with Martha and Mary. Jesus is present in the house with them. It is likely that Jesus has other disciples with him. We meet Mary in verse 39, "She had a sister named Mary, who sat at Jesus's feet and listened to what he was saying." When Mary sits at Jesus's feet, the implication is that Mary is taking her place as a disciple of the Lord, learning from Jesus's rabbinical teaching. (Paul sat at the feet of Gamaliel. Acts 22:3)

One of the good things about Jesus was that he did not limit his followers to men. Luke 8 mentions several notable women who followed him. In Luke 10, Mary sat at his feet as a disciple, and Jesus commended her for learning from him. Now, Amid hosting Jesus, something happens internally in Martha. Her fairness meter starts up. This fairness meter can start up in us when we work on a team.

Have you ever had a job where you feel like you have done your part and someone does not do their fair share? And then the fairness meter starts measuring. And little thoughts start. That is not fair. They are not doing their fair share of the work. I have done more than my fair share—comparing what we have done and what others do.

When Martha starts becoming offended at the lack of help from her sister, Martha asks, "Lord, don't you care?" Remember, this is not the only Lord, don't you care question. Remember when Jesus was asleep in the boat with the disciples and the storm came up? What did the disciples ask Jesus? Mark 4:38 (NIV), "Jesus was in the stern, sleeping on a cushion. The disciples woke him and said to him, "Teacher, don't you care if we drown?" Jesus gets up and brings peace to the storm by telling the storm to be still.

Let's notice that Martha does not speak directly to Mary. Martha complains to Jesus. As much as we want Jesus to be the judge of fairness and to take our side, Jesus may not be dragged into a family dispute. We cannot count on Jesus to take our side of what we think is fair. And fairness continues to be a big deal in church folks, workplaces, and family lives. Our ways of measuring fairness are not God's ways of measuring fairness.

In the responsibility of hosting Jesus, Martha felt abandoned to do the work by herself. In this Lukan account, Mary seems to get the credit for being a star pupil. In her provisions, Martha became distracted by many things, encumbered by many things, and weighed down by many things. Jesus is not comparing the character of Martha with the character of Mary. Martha has a fairness meter that starts measuring herself and what she is doing against what Mary is NOT doing. This seed of comparison grows.

Martha does not take her sister aside and say, "Mary. I know it is important to learn from Jesus, and you are sitting at his feet, taking the position of a disciple that Jesus encourages women to take. How awesome for you. I am so happy that you are sitting there and eating every word that is proceeding from the mouth of God. Jesus has bread to feed you that is heavenly food, and you are able to sit there and experience the stories of Jesus and the parables and ask Jesus what these things mean. Mary, you keep learning, and then come and share what you are learning with me."

No. Martha's voice of comparison says, "It is not fair. What I am doing is more important than what she is doing. Just look at all the work I have to do and I have so much work to do, and NO ONE is helping me. I just cannot get all of this work done. When I invited Jesus to my home, I took on the hosting responsibilities. A good host makes sure there is water for feet to be washed. A good host ensures the floor is swept and the mats are ready to sit on. A good host provides water for thirsty travelers and food for the hungry ones." Martha had an internal checklist of things that needed to be done and were not getting done without help. Martha asks Jesus for help. She was not asking Jesus to get up and help her. She was asking Jesus to command Mary to get up and help Martha so that Martha could finish the preparations.

Jesus is not going to grant Martha's request. Jesus is not going to get into the middle of this sister situation and decide for Martha against Mary to take Martha's side. In the "It's not fair, Jesus" argument and appeal, Martha asks Jesus, Don't you CARE that my sister has left me alone? Martha doubts that Jesus cares how hard Martha has been working. Martha has been waiting for Mary to realize that Mary has abandoned Martha to work alone while Mary **just sits** there, not helping. Martha feels like it is unfair and that Jesus does not care. Jesus is letting Mary sit there and learn when there is so much work. Jesus, don't you care that my sister has left me to do all of this alone? Tell her to come and help me.

Jesus often does the unexpected. When Jesus says, "Martha, Martha," we need to hear his voice as an invitation. For years I imagined and attached a condemnatory tone to those words, *"Martha, Martha."* That was not the voice of Jesus. Suppose you hear "Martha, Martha" in your spirit with the pointing of the finger tone of voice that is the accusation of the enemy. Jesus talks with an invitation, not an accusation.

Martha Martha, you are anxious, worried, disturbed, and troubled in your spirit. I imagine Jesus saying something like this, "Serving with your heart at peace is welcomed. Being anxious, worried, disturbed, and troubled about serving is not serving me." "Martha, Martha, what you think might be serving me may not be the way of serving me at this moment. You are distracted, dear Martha." That is my imagination.

Now, if Martha came to you for advice, what would you tell her? If Martha came to me for advice, I think I would offer this to Martha, "Martha, You have gifts. Your sister has gifts. Be faithful to the gifts you have been given. You can trust Jesus even though what you perceive is not what you expected."

We can notice that Jesus kept his relationship with Martha and Mary healthy by not getting involved in settling sister disputes. When Martha asked, Don't you care? I wonder what was happening in Martha that she would think that Jesus did not care?.And, I wonder what goes on in us when we think Jesus does not care? When the disciples thought they were drowning in the boat while Jesus was asleep, they asked him, "Teacher, don't you care?" It is human sometimes to wonder if God has forsaken us. But the disciples had an opportunity to see that Jesus did care. They had opportunities to love and serve Jesus beyond the storm in the boat.

One of the pitfalls readers fall into here is taking sides in a way that Mary wins and Martha loses. Martha was invited to hear what Jesus was sharing with the disciples. Jesus did not want Martha to miss out on what was better at the moment. Jesus had food that was spiritual food. He said Mary had chosen the "better part," and scholars have argued about what that "better part" means. Some theories are that serving dinner is temporal while sitting at the feet of Jesus has eternal rewards. Jesus did not explain what he meant by the better part.

It is a pitfall to say Mary is better than Martha. Spirituality teachers use Mary as a model of the contemplative path of spirituality. It is being present with Jesus and sitting at Jesus's feet.

It is also a pitfall to say Martha is better than Mary. Martha gets things done while Mary sits and learns from Jesus. Martha is more mature in her faith because she knows how to serve and not just sit there. Or the types of disciples who serve are better than those who just sit still.

Unfortunately, these sisters have been compared with one another in history, with Martha representing Active Spirituality and Mary representing Contemplative Spirituality and choosing which one we are likelier to be. This active or contemplative is a false choice—a false dichotomy. Just to show you how this continues to be a thing of comparison in our culture, there are spirituality quizzes that ask women, Are you a Mary or a Martha?[42] And then, these quizzes proceed to ask questions with the idea that being a Martha is bad and being a Mary is good.

That is why Martha needs to be redeemed. Lest we neglect the physical food, there is a story that comes from the time of the church after the book of Acts and before 500 CE. In those days, some Christ-followers went out to the desert and lived alone or lived in small communities together. We call these Christ followers the desert fathers and mothers of the church.

This story is a desert wisdom story about a brother who comes to visit Abba Silvanus at Mount Sinai. When he sees the brothers at work, he says to the old man: "Do not work for the food that perishes. For Mary has chosen the good part." The older man calls a disciple to give this brother a book and an empty cell. At the end of the day, the visitor is very hungry and wonders why no one has called him to eat. Abba Silvanus explains that he himself and the others are not so spiritual as to be able to go without earthly food and so must work for it, but since he, the visitor, has chosen the good part, they didn't think he wanted to eat earthly food. "When the brother heard this, he repented and said: Mary needs Martha, and it is really by Martha's help that Mary is praised."[43]

There are plenty of disciples, Christ-followers, through the ages and today that are stuck in feeling like they have been looked down upon in their efforts to serve Jesus. This is not just about women disciples and followers serving Jesus. Jesus often turns things upside down. For example, Just before we meet Martha and Mary, a lawyer asks Jesus. Who is my neighbor? Jesus tells the story of the good Samaritan. There was faith in action with the way the good Samaritan cared for the wounded person on the side of the road. And then Jesus asks the lawyer, "Who proved to be a neighbor?"

Some of us have expectations of Jesus that Jesus does not seem to be answering in the way we want the answers to come, the timing of the answers, and the manifestation of the miracles we want to happen. Some of us have expectations that have been seemingly unanswered for a long time, for years. We might be asking the question Martha asked, Jesus, don't you care that fill-in-the-blank has left me to do all this work alone? Tell them to help me. I need help here. Jesus, do something.

---

[42] Reference https://charlesstone.com/are-you-a-mary-or-a-martha-leader-take-this-quiz-to-find-out/ .

[43] Saying #5 in.https://www.johnsanidopoulos.com/2018/01/life-and-sayings-of-holy-abba-silvanus.html.

Jesus answered Martha. You are "distracted by many things." Was Jesus saying to Martha, "You are trying to do too much? More than you need to do?" What about all the good works for the kingdom of God, the folks doing the "I was hungry, and you fed me," the stuff of the kingdom? Jesus praises them, too. The ones who feed the hungry, clothe the naked, visit the sick and imprisoned. What then is the good path, the good way of spirituality?

This "aha" thought came to me this week, "It is possible to ignore the very presence of God while trying to do something for Jesus, trying to do something for God." We can distract ourselves instead of meeting with God. God can be right there, and we can be off doing something we think will please God. We need to discern at the moment when we are avoiding paying attention to Jesus. Jesus, who is present with us.

Could it be that the better part is being with Jesus when we are sitting and actively serving? We can do both. This is not an either/or spirituality. The body of Christ needs those who contemplatively sit AND those who actively serve.

We have so many examples of practicing the presence of Jesus throughout church history. Frank Laubach, the missionary to the Moros people in the Philippines, comes to mind today with his game of minutes learning to pay attention to the presence of God one second per minute and one minute per hour and then increasing the noticing. Frank Laubach was responsible for the "each one teach one" method of language learning in the Philippines among the people. If you have time later, look up Frank Laubach and read about the good works he did while paying attention to Jesus and practicing the presence of God.

The point is being with Jesus in the times we are attentively sitting and the times we are actively serving. We practice being with Jesus in our ordinary lives. Times to sit and focus. Times to act and do the good things Jesus invites us to do to share the good news, heal the sick, to feed the hungry. Take the presence of God with us where we go. Serving Jesus is part of discipleship, part of following Jesus.

We must redeem Martha from being stuck in the "Martha, Martha" verse. Let's look at two cases of serving. When Jesus heals Peter's mother-in-law (Matthew 8:14-15), "When Jesus entered Peter's house, he saw his mother-in-law lying in bed with a fever; he touched her hand, and the fever left her, and she got up and began to serve him." Notice that she got up and began to serve him. And in Luke 22:27, "When a dispute arose among the disciples about which of them was the greatest, Jesus turned it on its head when he said, "I am among you as one who serves."

Jesus is among us as one who serves. It was not out of place for Martha to serve. Martha was the one who invited Jesus. It was the heart of Martha that wondered if Jesus cared, that compared all the work she had to do with the lack of help she was getting to do it. Martha's worry was not needed.

And Martha does not stay stuck in these few verses in Luke 10. I wonder, how many times do we freeze a person or a situation in a particular memory or pain, and we do not allow that person to grow beyond that place, to have new mercy? I know some persons who have frozen me in a time ten years ago, twenty years ago, or thirty years ago in their last experience of me without allowing me room to grow, learn and be forgiven. We need to allow persons we have frozen the opportunity to thaw, to grow.

Let's look at a time later, in the Gospel of John, closer to the time of Jesus's death. We learn in John 11 that Martha and Mary had a brother, Lazarus, who died. The sisters sent word to Jesus and asked Jesus to come because their brother was very ill. Jesus delayed two more days before returning to Bethany to see about Lazarus. Both sisters have the same line of complaint, "If you had been here, my brother would not have died." (Verses 21 and 32.)

In the John account, Martha is the one who confesses that Jesus is the Messiah. Jesus reveals to Martha the truth. "I am the resurrection and the life." Martha believes. John 11:23-27:

> *Jesus said to her, "Your brother will rise again." Martha said to him, "I know that he will rise again in the resurrection on the last day." Jesus said to her, "I am the resurrection and the life. Those who believe in me, even though they die, will live, and everyone who lives and believes in me will never die. Do you believe this?" She said to him, "Yes, Lord, I believe that you are the Messiah, the Son of God, the one coming into the world.*

Martha has confessed with her mouth and believed in her heart that Jesus is the Messiah of God, the one coming into the world to bring salvation to God's people. Martha has moved from distraction to active devotion. Martha has become the proclaimer of faith. Lord, I believe you are the Messiah, the Son of God, the one coming into the world. Remember Jesus asking the disciples, "Who do you say that I am and hearing Peter's confession, "You are the Christ, the Son of the Living God." Jesus commends Peter. Here, Martha makes a similar confession. After the resurrection, Thomas sees the resurrected Jesus with nail prints and a sword-scar on his side. Thomas says, My Lord, and My God and confesses his belief.

After Martha makes this confession, then Martha sends for Mary. Mary had been sitting in the house while Martha went out to meet Jesus. Mary repeats the "If you had been here, my brother would not have died" expectation. Jesus asks where Lazarus is, and they say, "Come and see," Jesus. Jesus weeps. Jesus asks for the stone to be rolled away and calls, "Lazarus, come forth." Lazarus is raised from the dead and needs to be unwrapped from the grave clothes.

Now, let's look at one last place, John 12, verses 1-3:

> *Six days before the Passover Jesus came to Bethany, the home of Lazarus, whom he had raised from the dead. There they gave a dinner for him. Martha served, and Lazarus was one of those reclining with him. Mary took a pound of costly perfume made of pure nard, anointed Jesus's feet, and wiped them with her hair. The house was filled with the fragrance of the perfume.*

In John 12, we see growth in Martha. Martha is serving at the table, and Lazarus is present as one of those reclining with Jesus. We see no complaining here, no asking Jesus to intervene and tell Mary to help Martha. Martha is doing what she is gifted to do, serve the Lord with table fellowship. Mary is doing what she is gifted to do, serve the Lord by anointing his feet.

What about us? Maybe we find ourselves encumbered about, weighed down, and distracted with many things. Maybe we find ourselves disappointed in the delays of Jesus in answering our prayers. Maybe we find ourselves asking Jesus, "Don't you care?" Maybe we have some residual resentment in our hearts. Maybe *we* want to grow in our walk with Jesus and to stop being stuck in a stereotype, like the Martha stereotype from Luke 10. This is a day of redemption. Today is a day of salvation.

Ministry Time. This time to respond to the message is for you. We are going to invite the musicians to come and play softly. Please respond to the message and meet with God while God's presence is here today. Opportunity to respond to the message. Today we are going to do something different. I am not going to invite you to come up here for prayer. We have lots of folks who will pray with you. Raise your hand where you are, or stand up where you are. Maybe you feel like you are distracted, encumbered about, and weighed down by many things. Maybe you feel like Jesus is delaying in answering your prayers. Raise your hand where you are, or stand up where you are. Or maybe this is you: Today, Jesus, I want to be the disciple you would have me to be. I want to serve you with gladness. I want to follow you faithfully.

If that is you, please raise your hand or stand up right where you are. For the rest of us, If you see someone raising their hand near you, take someone with you and go to them and ask them if they would like you to pray with them. If you see someone standing near you, take someone with you and go to them and ask them if they would like you to pray with them. Ask them, "What do you want Jesus to do for you today?"

This is where everyone gets to play. Everyone gets to pray. Offer a prayer or receive prayer. If you are new with us today, we invite you to watch and see what the Lord is doing in our midst. Feel free to watch people pray for one another and join in as observers or participants. If you want prayer, do not leave without meeting with Jesus here.

Closing Prayer: Come, Lord Jesus. Holy Spirit, come. Meet us here. Come with Your presence. Come with Your power. Come with Your kindness. Change us. Renew our minds. Help us to hear Your invitation to us to be with You where You are. To notice where You are working and to join You on Your mission. Amen.

Rejoice and Weep
Romans 12:15

October 2, 2020

Romans 12:15, *"Rejoice with those who rejoice and weep with those who weep."*

Opening Prayer. Thank You, O Lord, for this time to open Your holy scriptures, learn from You, and hear Your words in our hearts. Teach us Your ways, dear Jesus. Amen.

Introduction. Each week at LVC, we have a Continuing the Conversation segment of our service before the sermon in which we share our praises and prayer requests. We share our joys and challenges. And then we pray for one another. The university where I teach adjunct classes has a university email. There I receive emails from the Dean of the Chapel entitled Celebration or Sympathy. The celebration emails usually start with "We are delighted to celebrate with," and then the details of a newborn baby with the parents, brothers, and sisters are announced. The sympathy emails usually start with "We wish to extend our heartfelt sympathy to," and then it goes on with the details of the losses and arrangements.

Some Reasons for gatherings. For rejoicing. Celebrations like baby showers, wedding showers, graduation, and retirement. Sadness. Cancer diagnoses, hospitalizations, surgeries. Loss of jobs, businesses, fires, floods, storms. Loss of pets. Other calamities. And then there are Funerals with visitation, wake, service, graveside, and memorial services. In our communities, we celebrate with those who are celebrating and share in the sorrows of those who have experienced losses.

This season, we are studying a series of "Words to Live By" in Romans 12. This is in the context of letting our love be genuine from verse 9. Today we are considering verse 15 "Rejoice with those who rejoice and weep with those who weep." We will look at examples in scripture of rejoicing and examples in scripture of weeping or mourning. Let's look first at Ecclesiastes 3. This chapter is about a time and season for every purpose under heaven. Ecclesiastes 3:4 reads, "a time to weep, and a time to laugh; a time to mourn, and a time to dance."

In the ministry of Jesus, he went about doing good, healing the sick, casting out demons, and these were signs that the kingdom of God had come. In Luke 10, Jesus sends out the Seventy-Two and gives them the power to heal, set people free, and they return with rejoicing. Luke 10:17-20:

> "The seventy-two returned with joy, saying, "Lord, even the demons are subject to us in your name!" And he said to them, "I saw Satan fall like lightning from heaven. Behold, I have given you authority to tread on serpents and scorpions, and over all the power of the enemy, and nothing shall hurt you. Nevertheless, do not rejoice in this, that the spirits are subject to you, but rejoice that your names are written in heaven."

Then we read that Jesus rejoices. Let's read verse 21, "In that same hour he rejoiced in the Holy Spirit and said, "I thank you, Father, Lord of heaven and earth, that you have hidden these things from the wise and understanding and revealed them to little children; yes, Father, for such was your gracious will." Jesus, in verse 21 rejoices in the Holy Spirit and rejoices that the Father's will was done. This rejoicing is exceedingly glad rejoicing in the original, the same word used in his mother's response to the angel in Luke 1, "And Mary said, 'My soul magnifies the Lord, and my spirit rejoices in God my Savior.'"

Jesus rejoices at the return of the Seventy-Two. We need to see Jesus rejoicing with those who are rejoicing because we often think of Jesus as one who fulfills the prophecy that he "is a man of sorrows and acquainted with grief" from Isaiah 53. Jesus indeed had many sorrows, suffered much opposition, and suffered death at the hands of those who despised him. And yet, here, in Luke 10, we clearly see Jesus rejoicing exceedingly. Luke 19. We remember the mission of Jesus in Luke in this summary verse, Jesus, "the Son of Man, came to seek and to save the lost" in Luke 19:10.

Now let's turn to Luke 15. Jesus is telling these parables to tax collectors and sinners. The Pharisees grumbled about Jesus eating with tax collectors and sinners. And the tax collectors and sinners listened to Jesus while the Pharisees scorned him. In Luke 15, we have three parables of the lost sheep, the lost coin, and the lost son. In the first one, one of 100 sheep wanders away and needs rescuing.

Look at verses 4-6 (ESV):

> *What man of you, having a hundred sheep, if he has lost one of them, does not leave the ninety-nine in the open country, and go after the one that is lost, until he finds it? And when he has found it, he lays it on his shoulders, rejoicing. And*

when he comes home, he calls together his friends and his neighbors, saying to them, 'Rejoice with me, for I have found my sheep that was lost.'

There is also rejoicing with the other two parables of the Lost Coin and the Prodigal Son.

For those of us who are encouragers, rejoicing with those who rejoice comes more easily. we are joyful at others' answers to prayers, blessings, and good news. We would have gone to the party to celebrate the prodigal son's return. For those of us who have trouble rejoicing with those who rejoice, there might be some heart and soul work that could help us. If we hear good news and our default is jealousy or anger, or we think that we deserve better than we have received, we can hear the father's words to the elder brother in Luke 15:31 (NIV), "You have always been with me and all that I have is yours."

Here is an excerpt from a poem in the Vineyard Institute "Heroic Leadership" Class. It is a soul-searching poem about dying to self. Just one of the paragraphs. "When you can see your brother prosper and have his needs met, and can honestly rejoice with him in spirit and feel no envy, nor question God, while your own needs are far greater and in desperate circumstances, that is dying to self."[44]

We, who have this hope in us, do not grieve like those without hope. We know that one day we will see Jesus and have our sorrows turned into joy when we see him face to face. In the meantime, there are losses. There are sorrows. There are unfair circumstances and devastations. And there is a time for lament. Lament is a word that we will consider. A short definition of lament. A sincere complaint about circumstances. Martha and Mary lamented to Jesus in John 11, "If only you had been here, our brother would not have died." Lament is a way to petition God for relief from suffering and pain. There are Psalms of Lament and prayers of lament. An entire book in the Old Testament is the Lamentations of Jeremiah, when the people were taken into exile. Someone who is weeping may have a sincere lament.

Looking back at Job. Now we are going to look at an account in the Old Testament of the life of Job. Turn there with me. Job 1:1-3 (NIV),

In the land of Uz, there lived a man whose name was Job. This man was blameless and upright; he feared God and shunned evil. He had seven sons and three daughters, and he owned seven thousand sheep, three thousand camels, five

---

[44] https://www.scribd.com/doc/34441785/Dying-to-Self-Poem.

> *hundred yoke of oxen and five hundred donkeys, and had a large number of*
> *servants. He was the greatest man among all the people of the East."*

Job had a beautiful life, a blessed life, a prosperous life, a righteous life. He rejoiced in the Lord's provision and offered sacrifices to the Lord. And then some devastations happen to Job. he loses his way of life. The servants, livestock, and children. What Job does not see is behind the scenes. There is a court of heaven, and God gives Satan permission to take away Job's prosperity and to cause devastation to Job's household. Job 1:8 (NIV), "Have you considered my servant Job? There is no one on earth like him; he is blameless and upright, a man who fears God and shuns evil." Messengers came and announced to Job the loss of oxen, donkeys, sheep, servants, camels, and sons and daughters were all gone, wiped out, and the four corners of his house collapsed, too. Verses 20-22:

> *At this, Job got up and tore his robe and shaved his head. Then he fell to the*
> *ground in worship and said: "Naked I came from my mother's womb, and naked*
> *I will depart. The Lord gave, and the Lord has taken away; may the name of*
> *the Lord be praised." In all this, Job did not sin by charging God with*
> *wrongdoing.*

In the next chapter, the scene in the court of heaven repeats, and God gives Satan permission to touch Job's health and body, and Job has sores all over his body. He is scraping himself with broken pottery. Job 2:7-10:

> *So Satan went out from the presence of the Lord and afflicted Job with painful*
> *sores from the soles of his feet to the crown of his head. Then Job took a piece of*
> *broken pottery and scraped himself with it as he sat among the ashes. His wife*
> *said to him, "Are you still maintaining your integrity? Curse God and die!" He*
> *replied, "You are talking like a foolish woman. Shall we accept good from God,*
> *and not trouble?" In all this, Job did not sin in what he said.*

Calamity. What happens when we hear of calamities in the world? We might pray. We might donate food, water, clothing, and funds to reputable organizations. We might go on mission trips to assist. For example, after Hurricane Katrina in 2005, teams went. In 2010 we sent a team from the church that planted us to Haiti for assistance with construction and rebuilding. This year, many healthcare workers assisted in various cities that were hardest hit by the virus that caused the pandemic.

Job's friends. Now Job had friends, and they heard about his troubles and adversities, and so they came much like we would respond if we hear that one of our friends or neighbors has suffered calamity. Job 2:11, 13:

When Job's three friends, Eliphaz the Temanite, Bildad the Shuhite and Zophar the Naamathite, heard about all the troubles that had come upon him, they set out from their homes and met together by agreement to go and sympathize with him and comfort him. Then they sat on the ground with him for seven days and seven nights. No one said a word to him, because they saw how great his suffering was.

Silence. Sitting in silence is sitting in solidarity. Sitting in silence is being with a person in pain, grief, and loss. Sitting in silence was the custom in those days and is still practiced in many cultures today.

Assumptions. Job's friends made assumptions as to why Job was suffering this devastation. They decided to speak instead of maintaining their silence. And we have a series of speeches in which Job's friends accused him of sinning and told him that is why he was suffering. Their assumptions became accusations. Accusations are painful and add devastation on top of the suffering that is already there.

Three friends with speeches-Eliphaz Eliphaz speaks in Chapter 4, "the innocent prosper." Look at Chapter 4, verse 7. "Remember: who that was innocent ever perished?" Eliphaz also speaks in Chapters 15 and 22. Bildad. Bildad speaks in Chapter 8. "Job should repent." Look at verses 2 and 3, "How long will you say these things, and the words of your mouth be a great wind? Does God pervert justice? Or does the Almighty pervert the right?" Bildad also speaks in Chapters 18 and 25. Zophar. Zophar speaks in Chapter 11. "You deserve worse. Your guilt deserves punishment." Look at verses 5-6. "But oh, that God would speak and open his lips to you, and that he would tell you the secrets of wisdom! For he is manifold in understanding. Know then that God exacts of you less than your guilt deserves." Zophar also speaks in Chapter 20.

Job's Lament. Job 10:1-3, 18-22:

I loathe my very life; therefore, I will give free rein to my complaint and speak out in the bitterness of my soul. I say to God: Do not declare me guilty but tell me what charges you have against me. Does it please you to oppress me, to spurn the work of your hands, while you smile on the plans of the wicked? (Skipping to verses 18-22), "Why then did you bring me out of the womb? I wish I had died before any eye saw me. If only I had never come into being or had been carried straight from the womb to the grave! Are not my few days almost over? Turn away from me so I can have a moment's joy before I go to the place of no return, to the land of gloom and utter darkness, to the land of deepest night, of utter darkness and disorder, where even the light is like darkness."

Miserable Comforters in Job 16:2. After Job has listened to Eliphaz, Bildad, and Zophar, and Job is quite upset with their speeches and accusations. He called them miserable comforters. In Chapter 16 (before there are even more speeches). Look at Job 16:2 (NASB) "I have heard many such things; Sorry comforters are you all." And, I wonder if Job felt betrayed to have friends who would come and sit with him and help him think he was not alone in this devastation. And then to turn on him, accuse him, and tell him why he was suffering. That sounds like a betrayal to me—miserable comforters.

So many Losses. Throughout history, nations and people groups have experienced losses and devastations. The current pandemic has affected countries around the world. So many losses, to name only some. Lost wages and businesses: Loss through fires and loss through floods and weather events. Loss of health, loss of life, and loved ones are gone. And you can add many more losses to this list.

Grief. Grief is the word we use to describe pain and loss. Grief is experienced in different ways. Grief lasts longer for some than for others. It is easy to look up practical ways to help someone who is grieving. To mention a few: Listen. Invite them to share stories. Expect that there are many ways to grieve. It is okay to say, "I do not know what to say." It is okay to say, "I want you to know I am here for you." Some things we SAY. Some things we PRAY. Ministry of Presence, non-anxious and compassionate presence. Story from chaplaincy with listening and not trying to fix a person. It's Friday. We still have to get through Holy Saturday before Resurrection Sunday. Learn not to be too quick to move a person from grief to joy.

Lament at lack of Comforters. Job was not the only one who could not find good comforters. Psalm 69:20 (A Psalm of David) David could not find comforters. "Reproach has broken my heart and I am so sick. And I looked for sympathy, but there was none, And for comforters, but I found none." The writer of Ecclesiastes could not find comforters. Ecc 4:1, "Then I looked again at all the acts of oppression which were being done under the sun. And behold I saw the tears of the oppressed and that they had no one to comfort them; and on the side of their oppressors was power, but they had no one to comfort them."

And there are verses throughout scripture that promise comfort. It is a blessing to hear the words of comfort from the Lord. Isaiah 40:1 "Comfort, comfort my people, says your God." Isaiah 49:13 "Shout for joy, you heavens; rejoice, you earth; burst into song, you mountains! For the Lord comforts his people and will have compassion on his afflicted ones." Isaiah 66:13 "As one whom his mother comforts, so I will comfort you; And you will be comforted in Jerusalem." Psalm 30:5, "Weeping may linger for the night but joy comes in the morning." Psalm 30:11, "You have turned my mourning into dancing you have taken off my sackcloth and clothed me with joy." God is called the "God of All Comfort" in 2 Cor 1:3-4, "Blessed be the God and Father of our Lord Jesus Christ, the Father of mercies and God of all comfort, who comforts us in all our affliction, so that we may be able to comfort those who are in any affliction, with the comfort with which we ourselves are comforted by God." Jesus in Matthew 5:4 in the Beatitudes, "Blessed are those who mourn, for they shall be comforted."

We are to comfort. We are to comfort with the comfort we have received. Empathy, sympathy, ministry of presence. Loss of loved ones. If you have lost loved ones you miss, you know about grief. I have had losses this year and so have some of you. I know what it is to grieve and have good comforters who have supported me in several grief and loss situations. And they have also been there in times of rejoicing.

Prophetic hope. And we do grieve, and we grieve not as those who have no hope. So even though we mourn now, there is an end to mourning. Our hope is in the Lord. Our hope is in God's unfailing love. Our hope is beyond this world. We have eternal life through Jesus Christ, our Lord. We know that one day all of our tears will be gone. Wiped away. These two verses from Revelation 7:17, "For the Lamb at the center of the throne will be their shepherd; 'he will lead them to springs of living water.' 'And God will wipe away every tear from their eyes.'" Revelation 21:4, 'He will wipe every tear from their eyes. There will be no more death' or mourning or crying or pain, for the old order of things has passed away."

Application. We can offer the hope we have to others along the way through the ministry of presence by listening to stories of the person who has suffered loss and in practical ways for those who have lost homes, businesses, employment, and finances for those who have practical needs. We can share what we have. We do not need to rejoice alone.

We do not need to weep alone. We can invite our friends and family, coworkers, classmates, and colleagues to rejoice and weep with us. When we see them (our friends, family members, coworkers, classmates, and colleagues) celebrating or weeping, we can offer the ministry of presence. Lesson from Job. If we do not have words, it is better to be quiet than to be miserable comforters. We do not need to have the right words to say. We need the presence of the God of All Comfort with us and God's love through us.

Re-presenting Jesus. As Jesus grieved over Jerusalem and wanted to gather her as a hen gathers her chicks. As Jesus wept with those who were weeping at the tomb of Lazarus. As Jesus ate/had table fellowship with tax collectors and sinners. As Jesus rejoiced when the seventy returned with testimonies of how they had healed the sick and cast out demons in the name of Jesus. Even so. Jesus gave us the great commission to go into all the world and preach the good news, making disciples, teaching what he commanded. We promise that the presence of Jesus will go with us as we are His ambassadors, as we let our love be genuine, as we bless those who curse us and persecute us, and rejoice with those who rejoice and weep with those who weep.

Ministry Time. We are here for you if you want us to pray with you and for you today. Or sometime in the future when you are listening online. You can contact me or any of us on the team, and we will be honored to pray with you and for you. On the website, we have a place where you can submit prayer requests and other contact information.

Closing Prayer: Heavenly Father, We thank You today for sending Jesus, Your only begotten Son, who knew how to rejoice and weep. Grant us hearts of love and compassion so that we may have what we need to rejoice with those who rejoice and weep with those who weep. In Jesus' Name. Amen.

Restoration of Peter (in 1st Person)
John 21:15

April 3, 2016

John 21:15 (CEV) *"When Jesus and his disciples had finished eating, he asked, "Simon son of John, do you love me more than the others do?"*

Opening Prayer: Today, Lord. Meet us in Scripture and in the recalling of the account of how You met Your disciples and revealed Yourself to them. Teach us what You would have us understand today. Amen.

Introduction: One of the practices of reading Scripture is sitting with the text and imagining what sounds and smells and words were like in the Bible. So, as I sat with the text in John 21, I pondered. Somewhere in the sermon preparation, I wondered what it would be like to hear the words from Jesus, *"Do you love me?"* What would it have been like to hear it from Peter's point of view? Most of this is taken directly from scripture in John 21 and John 18 with splashes of Luke 5, Luke 9, and the denial and resurrection accounts from the 4 Gospels, Matt, Mark, Luke, and John. I know I do not look like Peter. But listen to his voice.

It was clear the night that we went fishing in Galilee. We, the disciples of Jesus, were gathered together when I said I was going fishing. The sons of Zebedee, Thomas, Nathaniel, and two others said they would join me. This is what we used to do for our work before we followed Jesus. We got into the boat and set out a good distance from the shore. We fished all night and caught nothing. Sometimes you win, and sometimes you lose in fishing. In life, we tried, but our nets were empty. We were hungry. In the early morning light, there was someone on the shore who called to us, "Children, you DO NOT have any fish, do you?"

What kind of question was that? After all, we were good fishermen. Why would this man on the shore ask us for fish like we did not have any? We said, "No." and then he said, "Cast your net on the right-hand side of the boat and you will find a catch." Now, this is starting to sound familiar. I remember a time when I first met Jesus. If you want to look it up, it was recorded in Luke 5 at the Lake of Gennesaret or the sea of Galilee. When we were cleaning our nets, and Jesus got into my boat and asked me to put out to sea a little way. He did this to teach the crowds that were coming to hear Him. And then, after Jesus finished teaching, He asked me to put out into the deep water and let down our nets for a catch. I told Him we had fished all night and had caught nothing. But, at His word, I would do as He said and let down the nets. When we had done this, our nets had so many fish that our nets began to break, and we signaled our partners, James and John, in the other boat for them to come and help us. And our partners, James and John, the sons of Zebedee, came and filled both of the boats, so that the boats began to sink.8."But when I saw that, I fell down at Jesus' feet, saying, "Go away from me Lord, for I am a sinful man!" *I* said this because my companions and I were so amazed at the tremendous catch of fish. And Jesus said to me, "Do not fear, from now on you will be catching men."11 So, when we had brought our boats to land, we left everything and followed Him.

That catch of fish and the invitation to follow Him was the time when we first started following Jesus. That was maybe about three years ago before he was crucified. And Now. Now, since He was crucified, we have seen Him alive. He appeared to us since His resurrection. And now this man on the shore said to us, "Cast the net on the right-hand side of the boat and you will find a catch." So, we cast, and then we were not able to haul it in because of the great number of fish. 7 That is when my friend and fishing partner, John, said to me, "It is the Lord."

So when John recognized Him and told me that it was the Lord, I put my outer garment on because it just got in the way when I was fishing. And then I threw myself into the sea. I did not need to walk on water. Swimming would be just fine. 8 But the other disciples came in the little boat, because they were not far from the land, only about one hundred yards away, dragging the net full of fish. 9 So when my friends and I got to shore, we saw a charcoal fire already laid and fish placed on it, and bread..10 Jesus said to us, "Bring some of the fish which you have now caught." 11 So I went up by myself and drew the net to land, full of large fish. I counted the fish. There were a hundred and fifty-three fish, and although there were so many, the net was not torn. When we first met Jesus, the nets were breaking with the catch. Now, none of the fish we had caught were lost, although there were 153 fish. And I counted. Not one was lost.

12 then Jesus said to us, "Come and have breakfast." None of us ventured to question Him, "Who are You?" since we knew that it was the Lord.13 Jesus came and took the bread and gave it to us, and the fish likewise. We were all with Him on the night that He was betrayed by Judas. When He ate the Passover with us and gave us bread and wine. Now, here He was cooking fish and bread and offering to feed us again with some of the fish we had

caught in this catch. 14 Here Jesus is, appearing to us again after He was raised from the dead. And we were eyewitnesses. We were there, eating at the charcoal fire, when Jesus asked me if I loved Him. He looked right at me and asked, "Do you love Me?" Now I am in the midst of a flashback. (to John 18 and Luke 22).

It was at another charcoal fire the night He was arrested, when I stood at that fire and warmed my hands. I was standing and warming myself. Then those standing at the fire asked me, "You are not also one of His disciples, are you?" I denied it and said, "I am not." Just earlier when we were in the garden, Jesus had said I am He. Here I am saying I am not. Oh. Here Jesus is claiming to be Jesus, the one they are seeking. And I am denying that I am one of His disciples by saying the words, I am NOT. John 18. We were just in the garden earlier when Judas, who was betraying Jesus, came. Judas knew the place, for Jesus had often met there with us, with His disciples.3 Judas had received the Roman cohort and officers from the chief priests and the Pharisees, and they came there with lanterns and torches and weapons. 4 So Jesus, knowing all the things that were coming upon Him, went forth and said to them, "Whom do you seek?"

John 18.5 They answered Him, "Jesus the Nazarene." He said to them, "I am He." And Judas also, who was betraying Him, was standing with them. 6 So when Jesus said to them, "I am He," they drew back and fell to the ground.7 Therefore He again asked them, "Whom do you seek?" And they said, "Jesus the Nazarene." 8 Jesus answered, "I told you that I am He; so if you seek Me, let these go their way." This was to fulfill the word which Jesus spoke, "Of those whom You have given Me I lost not one."

Did you hear that? Of those you have given me, I have lost not one. And here we had a catch of 153 fish, and not one was lost. The net was held together so that none of the fish were lost. Jesus said He would make us fishers of men if we followed him. What if all of those we fished for were found and not lost? And yet I was the one who said I AM NOT when they asked me if I were his follower. How could I have said, I AM NOT? How could I have said, I AM NOT when Jesus said I AM He? Where was my faith when Jesus was arrested? When He had asked us to watch and pray. And then found us sleeping. Where was my faith.? I thought I was ready to follow Him. Even I wondered. How could I have said I NEVER knew Him? Luke 9. I remember the day we went up on the mountain to pray with Jesus. The day of his transfiguration. It was like this. 28 Jesus took along John and James and me, and Jesus went up on the mountain to pray. 29 And while He was praying, the appearance of His face became different, and His clothing became white and gleaming. 30 And behold, two men were talking with Him; and they were Moses and Elijah, 31 who, appearing in glory, were speaking of His departure which He was about to accomplish at Jerusalem. 32 Now my companions and I had been overcome with sleep; but when we were fully awake, we saw His glory and the two men standing with Him. 33 And as these were leaving Him, I was the one who said to Jesus, "Master, it is good for us to be here; let us make three tabernacles: one for You, and one for Moses, and one for Elijah"—not realizing what I was saying. 34 While I was saying this, a cloud formed and began to overshadow us; and we were afraid as we entered the cloud. 35 Then a voice came out of the cloud, saying, "This is My Son, My Chosen One; listen to Him!" 36 And when the voice had spoken, Jesus was found alone. And we kept silent, and we reported to no one in those days any of the things which we had seen.

Luke 22:28 Just earlier, before Jesus was arrested, after supper. We had an argument about who was the greatest. And Jesus said, "You are those who have stood by Me in My trials; 29 and just as My Father has granted Me a kingdom, I grant you 30 that you may eat and drink at My table in My kingdom, and you will sit on thrones judging the twelve tribes of Israel. But then Jesus looked at me and said, 31"Simon, Simon, behold, Satan has demanded permission to sift you like wheat; 32 but I have prayed for you, that your faith may not fail; and you, when once you have turned again, [once you have repented. Once you have been restored.] strengthen your brothers." 33 But I said to Him, "Lord, with You I am ready to go both to prison and to death!" 34 And He said, "I say to you, Peter, the rooster will not crow today until you have denied three times that you know Me." He looked at me and told me what would happen. He looked at me and said He had prayed for me.

And then it happened. There we were in the garden in John 18:10 When they came to arrest Jesus.10 Then, I took my sword and drew it and struck the high priest's servant and cut off his right ear; and the servant's name was Malchus. 11 So Jesus said to me, "Put the sword into the sheath; the cup which the Father has given Me, shall I not drink it?" (And in our friend Luke's account he shares that) Jesus then restored the ear to Malchus and healed his ear. Of course, He did. Of course, Jesus would heal Malchus. He was the Christ, the Son of the Living God. I had said it with my own mouth when He was in conversation with us one day.

Luke 9:18-22:

> *And it happened that while Jesus was praying alone, that we disciples were with Him, and He questioned us, saying, "Who do the people say that I am?"19*

Some disciples answered and said, "John the Baptist, and others say Elijah; but others, that one of the prophets of old has risen again." 20 And He said to us, "But who do you say that I am?" And I answered and said, "The Christ of God." 21 But He warned us and instructed us not to tell this to anyone, 22 saying, "The Son of Man must suffer many things and be rejected by the elders and chief priests and scribes and be killed and be raised up on the third day."

It was not long after that, when Jesus had said some hard things, many of His followers went away. John 6:67-69, "So Jesus said to us the twelve, "You do not want to go away also, do you?" 68 I answered Him, "Lord, to whom shall we go? You have words of eternal life. 69 We have believed and have come to know that You are the Holy One of God."

So, when Jesus was arrested and led away from the garden to the house of the high priest, and I was there, and I followed at a distance. Now let's go back to the part of the story where I was warming my hands at the charcoal fire when Jesus was brought to the house of the high priest. Luke 22: 55-60:

After they had kindled a charcoal fire in the middle of the courtyard and had sat down together, I was sitting among them. 56 And a servant-girl, seeing me as I sat in the firelight and looking intently at me said, "This man was with Him too." 57 But I denied it, saying, "Woman, I do not know Him." 58 A little later, another saw me and said, "You are one of them too!" But I said, "Man, I am not!" 59 After about an hour had passed, another man began to insist, saying, "Certainly this man also was with Him, for he is a Galilean too." 60 But I said, "Man, I do not know what you are talking about."

As a note, in John's account, One of the servants of the high priest, being a relative of the one whose ear I cut off, said, "Did I not see you in the garden with Him?" 27 I denied it again, and immediately a rooster crowed. And I remembered the word of the Lord, how He had told me, "Before a rooster crows today, you will deny Me three times." Immediately, while I was still speaking, a rooster crowed.

Back to Luke 22. 61 The Lord turned and looked at me. He looked at me. I was warming my hands, but I had kept my eyes in the direction of where I could see Jesus. And then it happened. He looked at me. There was such a gaze. A look that went right through me. I knew He saw me. I knew that He knew what I had said. How I disavowed even knowing Him. He looked at me. The rooster had crowed. 62 And I went out and wept bitterly.

Let me tell you now that sometimes we need that look from Jesus to help us weep bitterly. But the story does not end with me weeping bitterly. Maybe some of you have lived a life devoted to Jesus, always following Him. Always loving Him. Always serving him. With all of your heart and all of your strength. Or maybe some of you are like me. Maybe you feel like you have let Jesus down. Disappointed Jesus. Disappointed yourself. You are sorry. You are ashamed. You need a look from Jesus. A look of love. A look of forgiveness. A look of restoration hope. No wonder, after fishing all night and then seeing this marvelous catch of fish. When I heard it was the Lord, I just got out of the boat and swam to shore. I just had to be with Him. I just knew I needed to be with Him. I had been there on the day of His resurrection. I saw the empty tomb with my own eyes. I saw Jesus with my own eyes when He appeared to us. I just had to get to shore.

Such love this Jesus had. Such love. The angel in the tomb told Mary Magdalene to go tell his disciples *and Peter* that He was alive. He said my name. He wanted me to know.12 And I got up and ran to the tomb; stooping and looking in, and I saw the linen wrappings only; and I went away to my home, marveling at what had happened. John is the only one who records this breakfast scene at the shore in John 21. 15 So when we had finished breakfast, Jesus called me by the name I had been given at birth. He said to me, "Simon, son of John, do you love Me more than these?" I answered and said to Him, "Yes, Lord; You know that I love You." He said to me, "Tend My lambs." Here He is asking me if I love Him more than these. I was with Him when He was transfigured. He invited me. I was with Him for the miracles. I was with Him to teach the crowds, cast out demons, and heal the sick.

And now Jesus is looking at me again and asking me if I love Him with self-sacrificial love, an agape love that bears all things, believes all things, always hopes. And I could not tell him that I would die for him. How could I tell Him I would die for Him when I had just failed Him so? My big mouth got in the way when I had said even if others forsake you, I won't forsake you. So, I answered Him that I love Him like I love a brother. 16 Jesus said to me again a second time, "Simon, son of John, do you love Me?" I said to Him, "Yes, Lord; You know that I love You," still answering him that I loved him like a brother. Jesus said to me, "Shepherd My sheep." And then, Jesus asked me a third time, but this time He used the word for brotherly love that I had used. 17 Jesus said to me the third time, "Simon, son of John, do you love Me?" I was grieved because He said to me the third time, "Do you love Me?" And I said to Him, "Lord, You know all things; You know that I love You." Jesus said to me, "Tend My sheep." I had denied Him three times, and he asked me if I loved Him three times.

Here we were in a conversation about sheep. I remember when Jesus told us this parable in Luke 15:3 saying, 4 "What man among you, if he has a hundred sheep and has lost one of them, does not leave the ninety-nine in the open pasture and go after the one which is lost until he finds it? 5 When he has found it, he lays it on his shoulders, rejoicing.6 And when he comes home, he calls together his friends and his neighbors, saying to them, 'Rejoice with me, for I have found my sheep which was lost!' 7 I tell you that in the same way, there will be more joy in heaven over one sinner who repents than over ninety-nine righteous persons who need no repentance. (Luke 15) and now here I am, the sheep that needed to be restored, and Jesus has come for me.

(Back to John 21) 18 "Truly, truly, I say to you, when you were younger, you used to gird yourself and walk wherever you wished; but when you grow old, you will stretch out your hands and someone else will gird you, and bring you where you do not wish to go." 19 Now this He said, signifying by what kind of death I would glorify God. And when He had spoken this, Jesus said to me, "Follow Me!" 20 And then I turned around. Jesus had just reinstated me, and yet I turned around and saw the disciple whom Jesus loved. I saw John. Following us. The John who also had leaned back on His bosom at the supper and said, "Lord, who is the one who betrays You?" 21 So then when I saw John, I said to Jesus, "Lord, and what about this man?" 22 Jesus said to me, "If I want him to remain until I come, what is that to you? You follow Me!" 23 Therefore this saying went out among the brethren that that disciple, John, would not die; yet Jesus did not say to me that he would not die, but only, "If I want him to remain until I come, what is that to you?" It was my calling to follow Jesus and not compare myself to John or any of the other followers.

Later on, my friend the Apostle Paul wrote in his epistle to the Galatians that if any person was overtaken in a fault, we should restore that person in the spirit of gentleness. Well, I can tell you that Jesus was gentle with me. And I can tell you that He will be that way with you. If you need restoration today, just look at Jesus, and turn your eyes towards Jesus. Look full in His wonderful face. See His look of love. See Him searching your soul to the depths. Nothing can separate you from His love if you want to accept His love. His love is high and deep and wide and long. His love will reach you right where you are.

Just look at me. Look at what Christ's love did for me. It reached me. I was looking at him while I was warming myself at the fire, and He looked at me. I saw the look. I knew I had done wrong. It was such a look of love and forgiveness it melted my stony heart. It melted me. I went and wept bitterly.

I was so sorry for my sin. But Jesus did not leave me. Jesus did not forsake me. Jesus loved me enough to die for me. Enough to cook fish for me, to feed me, to ask me three times if I loved Him. I had denied Him three times. I told Him I loved him like a brother. And He told me to feed His lambs. To feed His sheep, to tend to His sheep. They are HIS sheep. Not my sheep. His. I wondered about John. Jesus did not want me to compare myself to John. Jesus just called me to follow Him. The call to follow Jesus. Again.

So then, I went on to feed His sheep. The sheep of His pasture. The ones who would believe in His name, in His life, in His promises. I was there when we were all gathered in Jerusalem, and we heard the sound of a mighty rushing wind. And I got up and preached and saw many repent and be baptized and added to the church. The lame man at the Gate Beautiful was healed in the name of Jesus. I refused to stop preaching in the name of Jesus. I preached to the Gentiles when Cornelius sent for me. And I watched them come into the kingdom of God and be baptized with the Holy Spirit. I was jailed, and an angel let me out of prison. I eventually died for the cause of Christ under the reign of Nero. It has been reported that I asked to be crucified upside down.

One day I will meet you, and I will want to hear your story. The story of how Jesus met you, how you were changed, how you left everything to follow Him. And how you were forgiven and restored. If Jesus knew I would be sifted like wheat and he encouraged me with the words, "But I have prayed for you," How much more is Jesus praying for you right now so that your faith will not fail? I stumbled, and Jesus restored me. How much more will He be ready now to restore you? If you want Him to. If He looked at you now and asked, "Do You Love Me?" What would your answer be?

Ministry Time. Jesus is ready to meet with you today. Some of His followers are here to pray with you and to introduce you to Him. To pray for your restoration if you feel like you have disappointed Him. For those listening online, write to or call us, and we will pray with you and for you. As the music plays, come for prayer.

Closing Prayer. Lord Jesus, We thank You for forgiving us, for choosing us, for loving us, for restoring us, for empowering us, for calling us to continue to do the good works You have already prepared for us to do. We love You, Lord. Hear our prayer, see our tears. Look upon us with Your penetrating gaze. Thank You for what You are about to do in us and through us, for Your glory and the fame of Your name, Jesus. Amen.

Instructions: Write on a card the names of those persons or initials of persons who need to be restored. Those who might have walked away from their passion for Jesus. Those who might feel that they have disappointed Jesus. We are going to take the time to pray for them. And if you select to turn in your cards, we will pray for those you have listed this week. Gather in groups of 3 or 4, and let's take a few minutes to ask God to offer opportunities for repentance and restoration to these persons.

Road to Emmaus
Luke 24:13-16

April 8, 2018

Luke 24:13-16 (NRSV), *"That very day two of them were going to a village named Emmaus, about seven miles from Jerusalem, and they were talking with each other about all these things that had happened. While they were talking and discussing together Jesus himself drew near and went with them. But their eyes were kept from recognizing him."*

Opening Prayer: O Lord, come and meet us today and walk with us as we travel on this road with you. In Jesus' name, Amen.

Introduction: Hidden and Revealed. Watching a rerun of Undercover Boss where the boss is disguised and then goes undercover to find out what their employees are experiencing. And then the moment comes for #Boss Reveal. And the boss lets the employees know how they have impressed the boss and usually rewards the good employees somehow. It is a hiddenness revelation theme show. The employees are surprised to learn that they have been working with their boss—the company's owner. A television show is trivial compared to what we are studying today. It is a shadow of the theme of hiddenness and revelation.

Shocking events. If we have lived long enough, we can remember events that shook us, shook the world, and forever changed the way we see things. For my parents' generation, the Great Depression marked them. The Wall Street crash in 1929 led to lean times in the 1930s. The December 7th, 1941, bombing of Pearl Harbor led to greater US involvement in WWII. 1950-1953 the Korean Conflict with 2 million lives lost. 1964-1973 the Draft Lottery for Viet Nam conscripted 2.2 million. For some, the Viet Nam war indelibly affected them or their family members. The assassination of President John F. Kennedy on Nov 22, 1963. The assassination of Rev. Dr. Martin Luther King, Jr April 4, 1968. For some younger ones, the Twin Towers going down in New York was monumental. I remember the churches filling up that night of September 11, 2001.

Shocking School shootings have rocked communities here in the US. The death of a child. The death of a spouse. The death of a parent. A cancer diagnosis. A fire, a flood, an earthquake. Shocking things rock our world and the way we see life. We are shocked and shook. I have realized that none of us knows what a day will bring. Name a shocking event in your life. For me, it was the sudden and life-threatening illness of my husband, who was laughing and joking in the morning one day four and a half years ago and on a ventilator with multiple system organ failures before nightfall. That led us to a three-month hospitalization with recovery miracles along the way. When events and circumstances rattle us and throw us off balance, we often turn to our friends. We talk with them. We try to make sense of things. We try to figure out why or what just happened. And how we are going to live now that we are sad and disappointed and grieving. Our understanding can become clouded. Talking it out with a friend and talking it out with God in prayer can help us.

Our Scripture today takes us to a scene that happened on the day Jesus was raised from the dead. The drama unfolds, and we, the readers, know more about what is happening than the disciples. We get an inside glimpse as we watch the account unfold. We know the end of the story before they do. Two disciples are walking along, and they are talking about all of the events that had just happened in Jerusalem. One is named Cleopas, and we do not know the name of the other. They had seen Jesus go to Jerusalem. They had seen Jesus flogged, they had seen Jesus crucified, and they had seen Jesus die. They knew his body was taken down and buried Disciples on the road. They knew what the women who went to the tomb had told them. They had heard that the tomb was empty. They had heard that angels appeared to the women and said that Jesus was not there but had risen. And then, a stranger joins the conversation. Their eyes are prevented from recognizing this stranger. Turn with me in the Scriptures to Luke 24, the 3rd gospel. Matthew, Mark, Luke. Before John. And Chapter 24 Last week was Easter Sunday, and we heard a wonderful message about the resurrection and how we are invited to receive the good news of the gospel. Our text officially starts in verse 13, but we need to look at what happened just before we get there. Let's start at verse 4. for those listening online. We have some slides of scriptures and artist depictions on the screen today. I may comment on a couple of slides.

Paintings. Here is a famous picture from 1877, a copy I remember seeing in my grandmother's house and my pastor's study. The Swiss painter, Robert Zund, loved oak trees and painted them into this piece of scenery even though trees might not have overshadowed the Road to Emmaus.[45] The shadow was over the eyes of the disciples. They could not see that it was Jesus. They did

---

[45] "Road to Emmaus,"
.https://www.allartclassic.com/pictures_zoom.php?p_number=883&p=&number=ZUN001.

not recognize him as he physically appeared to them. Photo Here is a photograph of the road away from Jerusalem. We do not know precisely where Emmaus is, but it is about seven miles away from Jerusalem. But this photo is titled Road to Emmaus. It is barren and devoid of foliage. On this day, the like it would be sun is shining, and it just looks like a hot walk out of Jerusalem. Artistic depictions in Road to Emmaus images. Slides of artistic depictions offer windows into what the artist perceives in the account. If we were to imagine this biblical narrative, what would we see? "Christ on the Road to Emmaus" in Flanders, 1640s. This painting is by the Antwerp artist Hans Jordaens, III.[46] Luke 24:4-7:

> *While they were perplexed about this, behold, two men stood by them in dazzling apparel. And as they were frightened and bowed their faces to the ground, the men said to them, "Why do you seek the living among the dead? He is not here, but has risen. Remember how he told you, while he was still in Galilee, that the Son of Man must be delivered into the hands of sinful men and be crucified and on the third day rise.*

Comment: The Women. The women were not expecting a resurrection. They are perplexed. Heaven visits earth with the angels. Two men in gleaming clothes. Why do you look for the living among the dead? Remember how he told you? The Son of Man must be delivered into the hands of sinful men, be crucified, and on the third day be raised again. Angels remind them of verses we now find in Luke 9:22, Luke 18:22-23, and Luke 24:8-11. And they remembered his words, and returning from the tomb, told all these things to the eleven and all the rest. Now it was Mary Magdalene, Joanna, and Mary, the mother of James and the other women, who told these things to the apostles, but these words seemed to them an idle tale, and they did not believe them. Comment: The women tell the disciples. The women are convinced that Jesus has risen, and they tell the disciples.

The disciples did not believe at first. They needed to understand and realize the reality of the resurrection, not just in the words of a sentence but in the implications of what it will mean for their lives. Comment "all the rest." In verse 9, "and all the rest." "And returning these things from the tomb, they told all the eleven and to ALL THE REST. This is the first hint of the disciples that were going to walk toward Emmaus. They were included in the "all the rest," as we shall see. Luke 24:13-16 (NRSV), That very day, two of them were going to a village named Emmaus, about seven miles from

---

[46] "Road to Emmaus,".https://commons.wikimedia.org/wiki/File:Jan_Wildens_-_Landscape_with_Christ_and_his_Disciples_on_the_Road_to_Emmaus_-_WGA25745.jpg.

Jerusalem, and they were talking with each other about all these things that had happened. While they were talking and discussing together, Jesus himself drew near and went with them. But their eyes were kept from recognizing him.

An aspect of hiddenness. In this account, in Luke, we are told that the disciples were prevented from recognizing Jesus. Sometimes God allows things to be hidden from people we know and from us and love, and we could speculate about the reasons for this. We can learn to trust God to know what it is best for us to know and when it is best for us to know it. Luke 24:17, And he said to them, "What is this conversation that you are holding with each other as you walk?" And they stood still, looking sad. Comment: What is this conversation?

Notice verse 17. Jesus entered the conversation with a question. What is this conversation you are having? They were trying to process what had just happened, and they were talking with one another, looking sad when this stranger appeared along the way. Comment: grief.

When someone we are close to dies, we remember certain things about them. We tell stories at funerals or memorial services, and we remember through the eyes of grief. Some persons are magnified, and others are diminished in the eyes of grief. While they were taking an outer journey toward Emmaus, they were also taking an inner journey trying to process all that had happened. Their hope had been buried in the tomb, and now the body was not there. Luke 24:18-21:

> *Then one of them, named Cleopas, answered him, "Are you the only visitor to Jerusalem who does not know the things that have happened there in these days? "And he said to them, "What things?" And they said to him, "Concerning Jesus of Nazareth, a man who was a prophet mighty in deed and word before God and all the people, and how our chief priests and rulers delivered him up to be condemned to death, and crucified him. But we had hoped that he was the one to redeem Israel." "What things?"*

Notice verse 19, "What things?" Jesus invited them to tell him what they were talking about, from the way they understood it, from their perspective. They were incredulous. How could this stranger NOT know what had been happening in Jerusalem? Has there been ANYONE who did not know what had happened? And so, they began to tell this stranger what they had understood and what a quandary they were in. And they were sad. Expressing their emotions. A prophet. They have heard, but they do not yet believe that

Jesus is the Messiah. Notice verse 21 "We had hoped that he was the one to redeem Israel." When they are talking to the stranger on the road, they say that Jesus was a prophet. They do not say that Jesus was God or the Messiah of God.

We HAD hoped. (Past perfect tense). Verse 19 He was a prophet. In their devastation, they remembered him in a diminished way. And today, in various world religions, so many in this world see Jesus as ONLY a prophet. I submit to you today that MERELY seeing Jesus as a prophet who died is not good news. It is not the gospel. Luke 24:21b-24:

> *Yes, and besides all this, it is now the third day since these things happened. Moreover, some women of our company amazed us. They were at the tomb early in the morning, and when they did not find his body, they came back saying that they had even seen a vision of angels, who said that he was alive. Some of those who were with us went to the tomb and found it just as the women had said, but him they did not see."*

Him, they did not see. They heard the words but did not have the revelation. Luke 24:25. And he said to them, "O foolish ones, and slow of heart to believe all that the prophets have spoken!" "Slow of heart." Literally, this is bradycardia, and the only place this is used in scripture is this "slow of heart." Luke 24:26-27, "Was it not necessary that the Christ should suffer these things and enter into his glory?" And beginning with Moses and all the Prophets, he interpreted to them in all the Scriptures the things concerning himself" And beginning with Moses. Here the resurrected Jesus invites the disciples on the road to understanding the metanarrative of the Scriptures.

From the books of Moses and the prophets and the writings, how the big picture of salvation is foretold and foreshadowed and fulfilled in Jesus. Jesus was a prophet without honor in his own country. But Jesus is more than a prophet. Jesus is God. Jesus said, "If you have seen me, you have seen the father." John 3:13-15 English Standard Version (ESV). "No one has ascended into heaven except he who descended from heaven, the Son of Man. And as Moses lifted up the serpent in the wilderness, so must the Son of Man be lifted up, that whoever believes in him may have eternal life."

Daniel 7:13-14 Messianic. The Son of Man Is Given Dominion,

> *I saw in the night visions, and behold, with the clouds of heaven there came one like a son of man, and he came to the Ancient of Days and was presented before him. And to him was given dominion and glory and a kingdom, that all peoples, nations, and languages should serve him; his dominion is an everlasting dominion, which shall not pass away, and his kingdom one that shall not be destroyed.*

Isaiah 53:7-12:

> *He was oppressed, and he was afflicted, yet he opened not his mouth; like a lamb that is led to the slaughter, and like a sheep that before its shearers is silent, so he opened not his mouth. By oppression and judgment he was taken away; and as for his generation, who considered that he was cut off out of the land of the living, stricken for the transgression of my people? And they made his grave with the wicked and with a rich man in his death, although he had done no violence, and there was no deceit in his mouth. Yet it was the will of the LORD to crush him; he has put him to grief; when his soul makes an offering for guilt, he shall see his offspring; he shall prolong his days; the will of the LORD shall prosper in his hand. Out of the anguish of his soul he shall see and be satisfied; by his knowledge shall the righteous one, my servant, make many to be accounted righteous, and he shall bear their iniquities. Therefore I will divide him a portion with the many, and he shall divide the spoil with the strong, because he poured out his soul to death and was numbered with the transgressors; yet he bore the sin of many, and makes intercession for the transgressors.*

Luke 1:32-33 prophecy, "He will be great and will be called the Son of the Most High, and the Lord God will give to him the throne of his ancestor David. 33 He will reign over the house of Jacob forever, and of his kingdom there will be no end." We could spend years studying how Jesus fulfilled the prophecies and how specifically and particularly they were fulfilled. Luke 24:28-31:

> *So they drew near to the village to which they were going. He acted as if he were going farther, but they urged him strongly, saying, "Stay with us, for it is toward evening and the day is now far spent." So he went in to stay with them. When he was at table with them, he took the bread and blessed and broke it and gave it to them.*

And their eyes were opened, and they recognized him. And he vanished from their sight. Suddenly what they had heard the women say, what they had heard Jesus say, What was to them formerly just "hearsay," became "Say, here! Here is the good news! Hear the good news. We saw him. We recognized him in the breaking of the bread. We were there when he offered thanks to his father and broke the bread. By the time we realized who he was, he was gone from our sight." Eyes opened. Luke 24:31, "Then their eyes were opened, and they knew Him, and He vanished from their sight." (Read "Gone From My Sight" poem by Henry Van Dyke[47]).

---

[47] "Gone from My Sight," https://allpoetry.com/gone-from-my-sight.

Luke 24:32-35, They said to each other, "Did not our hearts burn within us while he talked to us on the road, while he opened to us the Scriptures?" And they rose that same hour and returned to Jerusalem. And they found the eleven and those who were with them gathered together, saying, "The Lord has risen indeed, and has appeared to Simon!" Then they told what had happened on the road and how he was known to them in the breaking of the bread after Jesus disappeared. Notice. They did not stay in the room after Jesus vanished. Once their eyes were open, they became witnesses, credible witnesses. Once they had a revelation, once they had the AHA moment. Once they were transformed, once they were convinced, they were compelled to act. Open our eyes, Lord. Song. "Open our eyes, Lord. We want to see Jesus, to reach out and touch him."[48]

This is what happened to the Emmaus disciples. Our eyes were opened, and now we see. Our hearts were burning on the road when he opened the scriptures to us and explained how the messiah must suffer. Enlighten in Ephesians 1:17-18. "the spirit of wisdom and revelation in the knowledge of him, having the eyes of your hearts enlightened, that you may know what the hope to which he has called you is, what are the riches of his glorious inheritance in the saints." Luke 24:36-43:

> *As they were talking about these things, Jesus himself stood among them, and said to them, "Peace to you!" But they were startled and frightened and thought they saw a spirit. And he said to them, "Why are you troubled, and why do doubts arise in your hearts? See my hands and my feet, that it is I myself Touch me, and see. For a spirit does not have flesh and bones as you see that I have." And when he had said this, he showed them his hands and his feet. And while they still disbelieved for joy and were marveling, he said to them, "Have you anything here to eat?" They gave him a piece of broiled fish, and he took it and ate before them.*

Comment Jerusalem in Verses36-43 When they got to Jerusalem to the eleven, Jesus appeared and spoke peace to them. Jesus quelled their fears and corroborated their story and asked them to wait in Jerusalem. And the second volume, the book of Acts, goes into more detail about waiting in Jerusalem until they received the Promise and received power from on high. Luke 24:44-49:

> *Then he said to them, "These are my words that I spoke to you while I was still with you, that everything written about me in the Law of Moses and the Prophets and the Psalms must be fulfilled." Then he opened their minds to understand the*

Scriptures, and said to them, "Thus it is written, that the Christ should suffer and on the third day rise from the dead, and that repentance for the forgiveness of sins should be proclaimed in his name to all nations, beginning from Jerusalem. You are witnesses of these things. And behold, I am sending the promise of my Father upon you. But stay in the city until you are clothed with power from on high."

Luke 24:44-45 Open Scripture. Notice again. Luke 24:44 Then He said to them, "These are the words which I spoke to you while I was still with you, that all things must be fulfilled which were written in the Law of Moses and the prophets and the psalms concerning Me." Luke 24:45 And He opened their understanding that they might comprehend the Scriptures. Burn within. Remember Luke 24:32, "And they said to one another, 'did not our heart burn within us while He talked with us on the road, and while He opened the Scriptures to us?" Burning hearts. Our hearts were burning, but now our eyes are open, and we need to testify. We need to be witnesses. We need to tell someone that Jesus is alive. So they went to Jerusalem to describe what they had seen and heard. And what they now believed. Jesus is not only a prophet who was crucified. Jesus is the messiah who needed to suffer for the people's sins and rise again victorious over death.

John Wesley in the Aldersgate meeting May 24, 1738. Heart Strangely Warmed. Burning hearts society. We need a burning heart's revival in our day. Keith Green, "Oh Lord, you're beautiful. Please light the fire that once burned bright and clear."[49] Brian Doerksen, "Light the fire again. Don't let my love grow cold. I'm calling out."[50]

Blindness. We could be walking with Jesus and not knowing it. We mentioned 2 Cor 4:4 last week, where the god of this age has blinded minds. The god of this age has blinded the minds of unbelievers, so they cannot see the light of the gospel that displays the glory of Christ, who is the image of God. Three Rs for the message today. Revealed through scripture and revealed through the breaking of the bread. Recognized. Outwardly hidden/inwardly revealed. Responded to go and tell, share the good news, and share the revelation.

Revealed. Recognized. Responded. Unless we have a revelation. Unless we have a revelation, our eyes will not see. Unless we have a revelation, we will

---

[49] "Oh Lord You're Beautiful,"
https://www.lyrics.com/lyric/1375475/Keith+Green/Oh+Lord%2C+You%27re+Beautiful.
[50] "Light the Fire Again,"
https://www.azlyrics.com/lyrics/briandoerksen/lightthefireagain.html

hear reports. We might even listen to accounts of those who have had a transformation in their lives. We can HEAR good news without BELIEVING it. Meeting the Way on the Road Jesus is the Way. John 14:6 Jesus calls himself "The Way, the Truth, and the Life. He meets these disciples in these three areas. He meets them along the road, along their way, and became for them the Way to recognize Him and the power of his resurrection. He reveals the Truth. Beginning with Moses, he teaches the truth of the scriptures concerning the messiah who must come and suffer and become the Passover Lamb. They recognize he is alive. He met them and gave them life. Their hearts were burning. They were awakened and alive to hope and joy and peace and good news.

When they were walking AWAY from Jerusalem, they met The Way, Jesus, who is the Way, the Truth, and the Life, on the way to Emmaus. They were walking away when they met the Way on the Road. Jesus showed them the Way from the scriptures. They met the Way in the breaking of the bread. They went AWAY from Emmaus to become followers of the Way on the Way to Jerusalem. It is possible. Listening to Jesus and still not knowing. It is possible to hear the gospel and still not believe it. It is possible to come to church and not be a Christian. It is possible to know the good news, to know the truth, and to act on it. Suddenly they got it. And suddenly, God can turn around situations that seem impossible with aha moments. In the breaking of the bread, they received nourishment for their body and their soul. They Shared their happiness and good news and walked back to Jerusalem. Jesus appeared to many Each of the gospels records the appearances of the resurrected Jesus.

And then consider this wonderful passage from 1 Cor 15,

> *For I delivered to you as of first importance what I also received: that Christ died for our sins in accordance with the Scriptures, that he was buried, that he was raised on the third day in accordance with the Scriptures, and that he appeared to Cephas, then to the twelve. Then he appeared to more than five hundred brothers at one time, most of whom are still alive, though some have fallen asleep. Then he appeared to James, then to all the apostles. Last of all, as to one untimely born, he appeared also to me. For I am the least of the apostles, unworthy to be called an apostle, because I persecuted the church of God. But by the grace of God I am what I am, and his grace toward me was not in vain. On the contrary, I worked harder than any of them, though it was not I, but the grace of God that is with me. Whether then it was I or they, so we preach and so you believed.*

How should we then pray? Ephesians 1. For a spirit of wisdom and revelation in the knowledge of Christ. How should we then live? Realize that unless Jesus is revealed to us, Jesus can be present with us, and we do not perceive it. Realize that unless Jesus is revealed to our friends and family members, they could be on the road with Jesus and not perceive it. Allow for grace. Allow for God to be gracious in the timing of revelation. Allow for God's timing and God's Holy Spirit to awaken cold hearts. To cause a holy burning in the hearts of those we love. Pray to that end.

Anointed words have power when they are full of the power of the Holy Spirit. We need to be ready to give a reason for the hope in us. God is still revealing Jesus. The presence of God can be so strong in a conversation, a worship song, a piece of scenery, a walk along the beach, or a prayer meeting. God uses various means to reveal Jesus to us. We could read Scripture and meditate on it, and suddenly we see something we have never seen before. We hear a whisper we have never heard before.

Sometimes a sermon. God uses scripture, dreams, visions, fellowship, and the gathering of believers to reveal God's purposes to awaken us to something that had previously been hidden from our eyes. Sometimes God uses a sermon to invite us to see Jesus in a new way. As we leave here, pray that God will reveal Jesus to us. Pray for those who have not yet realized the gospel because the gospel has been veiled. Pray that we will, and our families and friends will keep growing. Keep being changed, from glory to glory.

Resurrection. Even the faithful followers and disciples of Jesus needed to be convinced of what His resurrection meant. The Emmaus travelers knew about the reports of the empty tomb, the angelic messages, and the testimony of the women and the disciples. This could be happening today to our friends. Something happens, and they are trying to process it. Something stumbles them, and they are stuck, Whatever road we are on. We have an opportunity to meet the One who is the Way on the Road in our particular journey of life. We will invite you to a time of prayer for one another A ministry time in which we will pray for a deeper understanding of Jesus and a revelation for us and those we love. As I close in prayer if you are listening online and want to talk to someone about knowing Jesus or you want prayer. Find the prayer request button on the website or the contact us button, and we would be happy to pray with you and for you.

Closing Prayer. O, dear Father, Your son, our Lord Jesus Christ, revealed himself to his sad and hopeless disciples on the Road to Emmaus. Some of us here have places in our hearts that are sad and hopeless today. We need a burning heart revelation of the living and resurrected Lord today. By the power of Your Holy Spirit, come. Open our eyes. Awaken our hearts, come in Your manifest presence. Do in us what needs to be done in our hearts and minds so that You can do through us what You desire for us to do. Open our ears to hear You speak to us. Open our hearts to feel Your love, Your great love. In the name of Jesus, we pray, Amen.

Shiphrah and Puah: Two Hebrew Midwives
Exodus 1:15-17

Mother's Day, May 8, 2022

Exodus 1:15-17 (NRSV) *"The king of Egypt said to the Hebrew midwives, one of whom was named Shiphrah and the other Puah, 'When you act as midwives to the Hebrew women and see them on the birthstool, if it is a son, kill him, but if it is a daughter, she shall live.' But the midwives feared God; they did not do as the king of Egypt commanded them, but they let the boys live."*

Let us start with prayer: Today, O Lord, meet us here. Meet us in our hearts, minds, and bodies, in the core of our being. Give us ears to hear what You are saying to us, Lord, and how You are inviting us to join you in the world, You have provided for us in which to live. In Jesus's name. Amen.

Introduction: In the summer of 2013, some of my colleagues and I participated in a Doctor of Ministry class taught by my friend and colleague, Dr. Denise Massey. This class was on Coaching for Spiritual Growth. She explained that in the ministry of coaching, the name "coach" derives from the stagecoach days. The stagecoach driver drove a route from here to there. The stagecoach driver picked up passengers who wanted to go from one city to another city, and the driver was responsible for going from here to there. You ride in the stagecoach and get from one city to the destination city. The coaching ministry asks the clients, "where do you want to go?" Where is there? And then coaches help the clients get from here to there. And what obstacles do you foresee in the way from here to there? Then, coaches help with a plan to start the journey from here to there, and then as obstacles come along, coaches help clients find ways to navigate the occurring obstacles.

Let's pause and segue to our scriptures. As we turn to the Scriptures this morning for our sermon, we have been in a sermon series from Hebrews 11 about faith and the Hall of Heroes of the Faith for several months. We have looked at several heroes, from Abel to Enoch to Noah to Abraham to Isaac and Jacob. Hebrews 11 does not name our heroes, but we will find their names in the Bible. Last week, Karen preached about Jacob and his journey from one who stole blessings to one who distributed blessings. This morning, we can anchor our two heroes with Hebrews 11:1,."Now faith is confidence in what we hope for and assurance about what we do not see. 2 This is what the ancients were commended for." And verse 6, "And without faith, it is impossible to please God, because anyone who comes to him must believe that he exists and that he rewards those who earnestly seek him."

Today's scripture concerns two heroes, Shiphrah and Puah, the Hebrew midwives. Their chronology happens between the lives of Joseph and Moses. Next week, the sermon is about the faith of one of Jacob's sons, Joseph. Then, about Moses' faith in two weeks. Before we get to our scripture lesson in Exodus 1 with our two heroes today, Shiphrah and Puah, we will talk a little about midwives in Scripture in Genesis. In Genesis, we have the accounts of midwives attending the births of Benjamin, Jacob's son, and Perez and Zerah, Judah's twin sons. Turn left from Exodus 1 and go with me to Genesis 38. On the way to Genesis 38, I will mention that Genesis 35 records the account of a midwife helping Jacob's wife Rachel give birth to Benjamin, and then Rachel did not live to care for Benjamin, Joseph's youngest brother. Now, look with me at Genesis 38. Here, Tamar is in labor with twins, and the father of the twins is Judah, one of the other sons of Jacob. Verses 27-30:

> *When the time of her delivery came, there were twins in her womb. 28 While she was in labor, one put out a hand, and the midwife took and bound on his hand a crimson thread, saying, "This one came out first." 29 But just then he drew back his hand and out came his brother, and she said, "What a breach you have made for yourself!" Therefore he was named Perez. 30 Afterward his brother came out with the crimson thread on his hand, and he was named Zerah.*

Just a note here: Jacob, Judah, and Perez, with his mother Tamar are ancestors of Jesus and are listed in the gospel of Matthew Chapter 1. We will go there a little bit later.

Now Let's Talk A Bit About The Function Of Midwives: The midwives help and assist at the birth of a child. Midwives help women give birth, but the midwives do not raise the children once the children are born. They may stay for a while to help the mothers, and then mothers raise the children. Midwives care for mothers. Mothers are the ones who give birth to babies. After midwives deliver babies, they move on to other mothers who are ready to give birth to babies. Men did not do this work for much of history. In the journal of Medical Humanities, Dr. Laura Kaplan wrote an article in 2012 entitled "Changes in childbirth in the United States from 1750-1950." In America, it was the 1760s before men were invited to help birthing babies, largely because of the new inventions of forceps and anesthesia. In the 1800s, the medical model of women having babies delivered by doctors in hospitals and maternity wards became more popular. Birthing hospitals started in the early 1900s with the promise of medication for twilight sleep to produce painless childbirth through medication. As an aside, Allen was my birthing coach. He was not a midwife. He was a great coach, though. For thousands of years, it was women who helped women with birthing babies. Maybe you know some babies who were born under the care of midwives. My mom was born at home with the assistance of a midwife. Two of my granddaughters had midwives attending their birth. Midwives have been needed for thousands of years and continue to be employed and requested by moms giving birth all across the world.

We Have The Names Of Two Midwives who were heroes In Exodus, Chapter 1. Turn with me to Exodus Chapter 1. We find today's heroes in verses 15-21. Read with me. Exodus, Chapter 1. I am reading from the New Revised Standard Version this morning.

> *The king of Egypt said to the Hebrew midwives, one of whom was named Shiphrah and the other Puah, 16 "When you act as midwives to the Hebrew women and see them on the birthstool, if it is a son, kill him, but if it is a daughter, she shall live." 17 But the midwives feared God; they did not do as the king of Egypt commanded them, but they let the boys live. 18 So the king of Egypt summoned the midwives and said to them, "Why have you done this and allowed the boys to live?" 19 The midwives said to Pharaoh, "Because the Hebrew women are not like the Egyptian women, for they are vigorous and give birth before the midwife comes to them." 20 So God dealt well with the midwives, and the people multiplied and became very strong. 21 And because the midwives feared God, he gave them families.*

Notice: Here, We See Two Midwives who were called into a conversation with Pharaoh. This Pharoah had devised a wicked plan to exterminate the boy babies. Boy babies could grow up to fight in wars and overthrow Pharoah's kingdom. By this time, the Hebrews had multiplied exponentially. God had promised Abraham seed from his loins that would be as numerous as the stars in the sky. The Hebrews who had settled in Goshen during the famine in Canaan were multiplying, and Pharoah started enslaving them and using them to construct buildings.

Go back with me a few verses in Exodus Chapter 1 verse 8, "Now a new king arose over Egypt who did not know Joseph." (Remember, Next week we will hear about Joseph). By this time, in verse 8, Joseph is forgotten, and a new king, a new Pharoah, is in power. Verse 9 "He said to his people, "Look, the Israelite people are more numerous and more powerful than we.

Notice: This new king is distinguishing between the Israelite people and the people of Egypt.

He Is Making The Israelites OTHER THAN. They are more numerous than we. So he hatches a despotic plan. now Verse 10, "Come, let us deal shrewdly with them, or they will increase and, in the event of war, join our enemies and fight against us and escape from the land." Notice: This king, this Pharoah, is setting up an argument that says we need to do something with these foreigners, these OTHER people. We need to do something shrewdly. If we do nothing preemptively, they will increase and join our enemies to fight against us and escape.

Verses 11-12, "Therefore, they (the Egyptians) set taskmasters over them (the Israelites) to oppress them with forced labor. They built supply cities, Pithom and Rameses, for Pharaoh. 12 But the more they were oppressed, the more they multiplied and spread, so that the Egyptians came to dread the Israelites." Notice: Here, we see that failure is the immediate result of the oppression of the Israelites. "The more they were oppressed, the more they multiplied and spread" (Exod 1:12). Verses 13 and 14, "The Egyptians subjected the Israelites to hard servitude 14 and made their lives bitter with hard servitude in mortar and bricks and in every kind of field labor." They (the Egyptians) were ruthless in all the tasks that they imposed on them (the Israelites)." What do we see here? For the Egyptians to identify with the king and be loyal to the king to be "the king's people," then they needed to deal shrewdly with the Israelites, to make them OTHER. The Egyptians would have a reason to oppress them, subjugate them, and make the Israelites' lives difficult. And so, for loyalty to the king, the Pharoah, the Israelites became the targeted group for oppression. The Egyptians oppressed the Israelites with hard labor and ruthless tasks.

Now, Enter The Scene With Two Midwives Named Shiphrah And Puah. In Smith's Bible Dictionary, Shiphrah means "brightness," and Puah's name means "splendid." With the population multiplying, there were babies born quite frequently. What Was Pharoah's Request of the Hebrew midwives, the midwives who attended to the birth of the Hebrew children? Allow the girls to live but kill all the boys. What just happened here? A government official, Pharoah, gave the midwives a direct command to carry out an order that would severely affect the population of the Hebrews. If there are no boys, they will not grow up to be men. Men will not be there to reproduce children. With no children, the people will die off. It might take a couple of generations, but populations need both boys and girls to flourish. It is one thing for men to go off to war and fight and die in battle. It is quite another thing for the men to be cut off at birth and not allowed to live at all. The question: What will Shiphrah and Puah do? Will they follow the orders of the Pharoah and carry out the annihilation plot for the baby boys born? No.

Shiphrah And Puah Allow The Baby Boys To Live. They disobeyed a direct command from the Pharoah. They believed that they were obeying God in allowing these boys to live. See Verse 17, "But the midwives feared God; they did not do as the king of Egypt commanded them, but they let the boys live." This is not a fear of God in the dread of God or terror of God kind of way of seeing God as the Divine Punisher. The God-fearers were those who worshiped God and honored God and God's commands more than the contradictory commands of earthly human leaders. This "fearing" God is reverentially obeying God, this God who holds much more power and authority than the Pharoah and counting the cost for their disobedience to Pharoah. If the boys live, eventually, Pharoah will notice. There could be consequences. Shiphrah and Puah chose to disobey Pharoah to their own peril rather than carry out the Pharoah's plan to kill all of the boy babies at birth. The midwives were willing to suffer the consequences of the wrath of Pharoah rather than disobey God, the giver of life, the Creator. The one who promised this family to Abraham, Isaac, and Jacob.

Civil Disobedience is the term used to describe those who choose to break the lesser law for obedience to a higher law. If we look back in the history of nations around the world, there have been many occasions where persons rose up and disobeyed laws and protested against injustice to change the rules. In several places in the Bible, we will not take time to mention today, civil disobedience happens. One of the places in the New Testament we will mention is with Peter and John, Jesus' disciples, now apostles, sent ones, who were ordered not to preach this Jesus message anymore. We will look at Acts 4 and Acts 5 if you want to turn there. Acts 4:18, So they called them (the "they" is in verse 5). Their rulers, elders, and scribes assembled in Jerusalem, 6 with Annas the high priest, Caiaphas, John, and Alexander, and all who were of the high-priestly family).and ordered them (Peter and John) not to speak or teach at all in the name of Jesus. 19 But Peter and John answered them, "Whether it is right in God's sight to listen to you rather than to God, you must judge; 20 for we cannot keep from speaking about what we have seen and heard." In Acts 5:27-32:

> *When they had brought them, they had them stand before the council. The high priest questioned them, 28 saying, "We gave you strict orders not to teach in this name, yet here you have filled Jerusalem with your teaching, and you are determined to bring this man's blood on us." 29 But Peter and the apostles answered, "We must obey God rather than any human authority. 30 The God*

of our ancestors raised up Jesus, whom you had killed by hanging him on a tree. 31 God exalted him at his right hand as Leader and Savior that he might give repentance to Israel and forgiveness of sins. 32 And we are witnesses to these things, and so is the Holy Spirit whom God has given to those who obey him."

So, the apostles disobeyed the religious leaders who had them imprisoned for preaching Jesus and Peter, and the apostles answered in Acts 5:29, "We must obey God rather than any human authority." And yet governments are given to us for reasons. In the New Testament, we have commands to obey those in authority in governments because governments are given to us for our good. Romans 13:1, "Let every person be subject to the governing authorities, for there is no authority except from God, and those authorities that exist have been instituted by God. Therefore whoever resists authority resists what God has appointed, and those who resist will incur judgment. For rulers are not a terror to good conduct but to bad."

Laws have a purpose for the good of society and the community. Just whimsically disregarding the rules and the reasons they are there leads to people doing what they think is right in their own eyes, leading to anarchy. Battles have been fought against injustice in several military wars in our lifetimes. In this country, people have protested and won court cases for causes of civil rights, disability rights, gender rights, reproductive rights, prison reform, educational reform, healthcare reform, police reform, immigration reform, and a host of concerns, including environmental impacts of mining and polluting the earth. Laws and legislation go through processes of implementation. What compels folks to civil disobedience for godly causes is complicated. If you believe the Holy Spirit is inspiring you to fight injustice, that may be the case. Invite wise counsel into your situation. Prayer and discernment will help you with wisdom on possible ways to affect change in your community. You may have something in you that says, "this is unjust. I need to fight for this cause." It may be the Holy Spirit leading you to do something. Pay attention and share your heart in this matter of perceived injustice with a trusted friend. Some countries have authoritarian leadership that sets all the rules, and anyone who tries to protest will be arrested, jailed, and could lose their life. The consequences of disobedience to rulers and rules could cost our lives, but we have to obey God's laws and commands.

God's requirement of us to follow Jesus wherever it leads us could cost us our lives. We could be persecuted to death. Some of our brothers and sisters in hostile environments to Christians risk their lives to preach Jesus, serve Jesus, and follow Jesus. Back to Shiphrah and Puah. Advocates for Civil Disobedience cite this pair and hail them as the first exemplars to practice civil disobedience in the Bible. When Pharoah calls them to report why all these baby boys are alive, they tell a story to explain. 19 The midwives said to Pharoah, "Because the Hebrew women are not like the Egyptian women, for they are vigorous and give birth before the midwife comes to them." Shiphrah and Puah tell the Pharoah that the Hebrew women are just too fast at giving birth, and the midwives cannot get to the birthing stools before the Hebrew women have given birth and are back to work. Shiphrah and Puah either literally took their time tending to the Hebrew moms in labor, or they gave a shrewd excuse that the Hebrew moms were very fast in having children. 19 The midwives said to Pharoah, "Because the Hebrew women are not like the Egyptian women, for they are vigorous and give birth before the midwife comes to them." Remember that men were not involved in birthing babies. Pharoah did not punish the midwives.

Now Turn With Me To Matthew 1, The First Gospel In The New Testament. In the genealogy of Jesus, we can read in Matthew Chapter 1:2-6:

> *Abraham was the father of Isaac, and Isaac the father of Jacob, and Jacob the father of Judah and his brothers, 3 and Judah the father of Perez and Zerah by Tamar, and Perez the father of Hezron, and Hezron the father of Aram, 4 and Aram the father of Aminadab, and Aminadab the father of Nahshon, and Nahshon the father of Salmon, 5 and Salmon the father of Boaz by Rahab, and Boaz the father of Obed by Ruth, and Obed the father of Jesse, 6 and Jesse the father of King David.*

(And the genealogy list goes on). Notice in Matthew 1 verse 3 that Hezron, the grandson of Judah, is included in the list of the 70 people in Jacob's family during the famine and migration to Egypt (Gen 46:12). So, Hezron lived during the first stage of the 430 years of slavery in Egypt. Amminadab's son Nahshon appears as a leader of the sons of Judah during the journey in the wilderness after the Exodus (Num 2:3, 10:14). Nahshon could have been of the last generation of slavery in Egypt.

The genealogy of Jesus Christ records only four generations-Hezron, Aram, Amminadab, and Nahshon (Matt 1:3-4) - for the 430 years of slavery in Egypt. And so I wonder. Could it be that Shiphrah and Puah preserved the life of Amminadab or Nahshon of the ancestors of Jesus when these midwives allowed the boy babies to live? (Just wondering). And what was the reward for Shiphrah and Puah? Verses 20 and 21, "So God dealt well with the midwives, and the people multiplied and became very strong. And because the midwives feared God, he gave them families." God rewarded the midwives and gave them households of their own. We might need to have the courage of the midwives in Exodus 1, to stand against injustice and be willing to suffer the consequences of mandates that are against God's design, commandments, and kingdom coming here on earth as it is in heaven.

In Wars, the Military personnel are given direct commands and are to follow the direct commands explicitly. BUT, there have come to be exceptions to following orders. For instance, In the war crimes court in Nurenberg after WWII, persons who exterminated the Jewish people in concentration camps were found guilty of war crimes. They could not receive protection by saying, "I was just following orders." War crimes are happening in our world today, now. Persons committing annihilation of populations will have to give an account to God for their actions. Here is a quote from the Exodus Commentary in the Wesleyan Tradition, "The church hears in this text the challenge to be God's agency to promote life wherever the power of death is at work in our world. In particular, the church needs to be Shiphrah and Puah, daring to rescue children who have lost parents and home and who are maimed by war and violence."[51]

We Cannot Blindly Follow Orders That Contradict The Heart Of God. We may not have the power to change the laws directly, but we can do our part to act indirectly. To pray, protest, write letters, vote, and support the causes for which Jesus advocated. Jesus brought good news to the poor, the marginalized, and the disenfranchised. He took the persons that the society of his day regarded as unworthy and brought dignity and worth to them. Just as the midwives help mothers get from pregnancy through the birthing process, they move on. So, spiritual midwives assist in helping believers give birth to what God has been growing in hearts and lives. Spiritual midwives encourage, coach, advise, listen, support, and assist in bringing forth, and then they move on to another ministry that is about to be birthed. They come alongside folks who are pregnant with ideas and offer practical assistance. We may have experiences with spiritual midwives, coaches, and encouragers. Encouragers are like midwives in that encouragers come alongside persons who are carrying God's dream inside of them. Encouragers are like coaches who come alongside and help us bring dreams to life. It is not about the credit of the midwives, coaches, or encouragers.

What Is Being Born Belongs To God. We must be born from above. We must follow Jesus and see where he leads us. Midwives in the kingdom of God help birth into the earth what God wants to do here. When God wants to do something, God gives the ideas and the prayers to people who will pray

---

[51] The Foundry Publishing. NBBC, Exodus: A Commentary in the Wesleyan Tradition, The Foundry Publishing, 2018.

until they see the prayers answered. Ones who pray and intercede are like midwives who approach the throne room in the heavenly realms and ask Jesus, the king of glory, to rule and reign in this area or that area. When we pray and intercede, we are following Jesus's command to pray to the Lord of the harvest to send workers into the harvest field. Jesus instructed the disciples to pray and not give up. Ask, seek, knock, and the door will open.

Where are we, as a community of believers, called to stand against injustice? Where are we noticing someone who is in power and who is not acting with the heart of God? Who is acting justly? Who can we support? Prayers and conversation continue. Today is Mother's Day and Mother's Day is a complicated holiday. Some of us have mothers who are still living. Some of us have mothers who have died. Some of us have wanted to be mothers, and it has not happened. Some are single mothers, stepmothers, adoptive mothers, and foster mothers. So many moms live through challenges with their children, from little ones to grown ones. We all have mothers, whether or not we have them with us today.

Ministry Time. You may want to talk and pray with someone today before you leave. You are welcome to come up front here for prayer or find someone to pray with you near where you are seated. And if you are here today and you are not a mom, but you have a prayer need, please find someone to pray with you today. Some of us will be up front here and others will pray with you close to where you are seated. If you are listening online, we have ways on our website for you to reach out to us for prayer. And now I will close the service with the benediction. And remember, we are here for you. We love you and would love to pray with you and for you.

Benediction: God Bless You And Keep You. May the Lord give you increase, both you and your children. May you be blessed by the Lord, who made heaven and earth. May The Lord bless you and keep you. May His face shine upon you and be gracious to you. The Lord turn His face toward you, And give you peace.

This Same Jesus
Acts 1:11

April 26, 2020

Acts 1:11 (NIV), *"Men of Galilee,"* they said, *"why do you stand here looking into the sky? This same Jesus, who has been taken from you into heaven, will come back in the same way you have seen him go into heaven."*

Opening Prayer. Holy Father, Lord Jesus, Holy Spirit. There is a song that says Give me Jesus. In the morning, when I rise, in the morning, when I rise, in the morning, when I rise, give me Jesus. Refrain: Give me Jesus. Give me Jesus, you may have all this world, give me Jesus. Today, Lord, come. We need you, Jesus. Come here this morning. We would see Jesus. Let us see Jesus and hear Your word for us today that we might know you, love you, and serve you with the lives and gifts you have given us, In Jesus' name, Amen.

Introduction. We are in the Eastertide time of the church calendar. Eastertide is the time between the resurrection and Pentecost Sunday. This year, Pentecost Sunday is on May 31st. Pentecost, is derived from the Greek meaning 50 and is celebrated fifty days after Easter Sunday. Pentecost commemorates the descent of the Holy Spirit upon the Apostles and other followers of Jesus Christ while they were in Jerusalem celebrating the feast of weeks (Acts 2:1–31). If we look back into the Hebrew Bible, we see that First fruits is the beginning of the barley harvest and Pentecost (or the feast of weeks) is the celebration of the beginning of the wheat harvest. Since it was always 50 days after First fruits, and since 50 days equals seven weeks, it always came a "week of weeks" later. Therefore, they either called it the Feast of Harvest or the Feast of Weeks.

During Eastertide Season, we have the resurrection. The tomb is empty the graveclothes are there, folded, in the tomb and no one is in the graveclothes. Men in white announce, "He is not here; He is risen as he said" We have the post-resurrection appearances. We have the ascension. We have the days between the ascension and Pentecost when Jesus told his followers to wait in Jerusalem until they received the gift of the Holy Spirit, roughly nine or ten days between his ascension and Pentecost.

Our scripture for today is Acts 1 (NIV):

In my former book, Theophilus, I wrote about all that Jesus began to do and to teach 2 until the day he was taken up to heaven, after giving instructions through the Holy Spirit to the apostles he had chosen. 3 After his suffering, he presented himself to them and gave many convincing proofs that he was alive. He appeared to them over a period of forty days and spoke about the kingdom of God. 4 On one occasion, while he was eating with them, he gave them this command: "Do not leave Jerusalem, but wait for the gift my Father promised, which you have heard me speak about. 5 For John baptized with water, but in a few days you will be baptized with the Holy Spirit." 6 Then they gathered around him and asked him, "Lord, are you at this time going to restore the kingdom to Israel?" 7 He said to them: "It is not for you to know the times or dates the Father has set by his own authority. 8 But you will receive power when the Holy Spirit comes on you; and you will be my witnesses in Jerusalem, and in all Judea and Samaria, and to the ends of the earth." 9 After he said this, he was taken up before their very eyes, and a cloud hid him from their sight. 10 They were looking intently up into the sky as he was going, when suddenly two men dressed in white stood beside them. 11 "Men of Galilee," they said, "why do you stand here looking into the sky? This same Jesus, who has been taken from you into heaven, will come back in the same way you have seen him go into heaven."

Taken up before their very eyes notice v. 9, "After he said this, he was taken up before their very eyes, and a cloud hid him from their sight." Jesus went up into the clouds and the clouds hid him from their sight. Clouds are very high up in the air from where we are. If we are in an airplane, we fly high up above the clouds. Jesus vanished into the clouds.

The disciples were watching. The ones who gathered with Jesus and saw him go up into the air were watching and watching and staring up into the sky. Jesus was gone from their sight. Look at vv. 10-11 This same Jesus will come back. 10 They were looking intently up into the sky as he was going, when suddenly two men dressed in white stood beside them. 11 "Men of Galilee," they said, "why do you stand here looking into the sky? This same Jesus, who has been taken from you into heaven, will come back in the same way you have seen him go into heaven." This Same Jesus will come back. Our sermon today is entitled THIS SAME JESUS.

Passion Play. Maybe some of us have attended a performance of the Passion Play. At the end, the character who plays Jesus stands in the middle of the stage, and the crew attaches wires to his belt or a connection at his back so that they can safely lift him up and out of sight. Jesus goes up and up into the rafters, and the persons on stage look up as he disappears and vanishes from view. In the scripture, a cloud hides him. There are no wires lifting Jesus.

Jesus has risen from the dead. Jesus ascends into the sky. No wires. No jet pack. No mechanical assistance. Jesus goes up.

Hot air balloon. I had a little glimpse of going up and up myself. For Valentine's Day, this year, Allen and I went up in a hot air balloon in Albuquerque. We got up before sunrise and were ready to take off. We had a pilot with us, and the three of us went up high over the river, the Rio Grande. I was just fine being a little high up, and then the pilot told us we were going up higher. Higher? We were already far up, and yet we went higher. It was so quiet up there in the sky. It was amazing to ascend and float high up in the air. If I were there, I just know. I would be amazed if I were there in the account of Jesus ascending into the sky. I would wonder where Jesus went. Where did Jesus go? He was with us, and now Jesus just started going up and up and up, and I cannot see him. All the way to the clouds. High up. Wow! Jesus is high up in the clouds. I have never seen a bird fly that high.

Before Airplanes. This ascension happened before airplanes. Before hot air balloons. Before the space program. Space X. Maybe some of you have been to Houston or Cape Canaveral to witness the space shuttle taking off. I have been to Cape Canaveral in Florida when the SpaceX rocket is launched into the sky. There is a countdown. And there is a lot of burning fuel to build up enough power to thrust a rocket into space. When the rocket takes off, it goes very high and fades away, disappears, and vanishes.

No Rocket Booster. Pick Me up, Dad. Jesus did not need a rocket booster. Jesus did not need an airplane. Jesus did not need a hot air balloon. Jesus did not need wires. Jesus just went up. Here is what I imagine. I imagine he lifted his hands like a child reaches up for Daddy's arms. Pick me up, Dad. Pick me up. And that day, Jesus went up. Jesus was received back in heaven. Jesus, who came down from heaven to be born as Mary's child, is lifted up from the earth.

Lifted on a Cross-Lifted into the Sky. We remember that Just about 40 days earlier, Jesus was lifted up on a cross. Jesus was nailed to a cross and lifted up at Golgotha, the place of the skull. Jesus hung there between two thieves, between heaven and earth, and said, "It is finished." The work that the Father sent Jesus to do was finished. The sacrifice was offered for sin. Jesus laid down his life. He was crucified. If I be lifted up (on a cross), Jesus talked about being lifted up. Once in John 3:13-15 (with Nicodemus):

> *No one has ever gone into heaven except the one who came from heaven—the Son of Man. 14 Just as Moses lifted up the SERPENT (snake) in the*

wilderness, so the Son of Man must be lifted up, 15 that everyone who believes may have eternal life in him."

And once, when he was talking about his death with the crowd standing there in John 12:32, "And I, when I am lifted up from the earth, will draw all people to myself." 33 He said this to show the kind of death he was going to die." Lifted on a cross-Now lifted into the sky. Ascend. Ascension. This Same Jesus. Here they were looking intently up into the sky as he was going when suddenly two men dressed in white stood beside them. 11 "Men of Galilee," they said, "why do you stand here looking into the sky? THIS SAME JESUS, who has been taken from you into heaven, will come back in the same way you have seen him go into heaven." Not gone forever. Not gone forever, just gone for now. This same Jesus will come back again.

Redundancy-Tautology. Saying the same thing twice in different words is generally considered a fault of style. When I am editing for some of the seminary students, the grammar program highlights the redundancy—the tautology. The program wants the writer to be concise. This SAME Jesus. In other versions, they remove the tautology. Some versions say This Jesus. Some say, Jesus. The NIV, King James, and New King James all say This SAME, Jesus. And I like the sound of it.

This SAME Jesus is what we need today. Tell it again. When my grandchildren were younger, and they could not read for themselves, I used to read stories to them. When I reached the end of the story, I would hear, "Grandma, read it again! Again? Okay, again. "Tell me the story of Jesus. Write on my heart every word. Tell me the story most precious. Sweetest that ever was heard." (Look up the history of hymn 1880) Fannie Crosby was blind from 6 weeks after birth and lost the only child she gave birth to as an infant. Knew Jesus. Tell me the story of Jesus. BIBLE VERSE: Acts 5:42, "And every day, in the temple and from house to house, they did not cease teaching and preaching that the Christ is Jesus." Tell me the story of Jesus— Yes. Yes, Jesus loves me. When I was a little girl, we sang hymns from the hymn book in church. One of the hymns I learned was Jesus loves me. The chorus has the same message over and over. Yes. Jesus Loves me. Yes, Jesus loves me. Yes, Jesus loves me. The Bible tells me so. The message is still true today. We want to hear it over and over. Yes, Jesus loves me.

This Same Jesus who was taken into Heaven will return—looking back to Isaiah. I have been reading Isaiah devotionally for a few weeks now. It is a LONG book. 66 chapters. Isaiah lived in the 8th century before Christ. So many of the prophecies of Isaiah point to the Messiah. And looking back with our gospels in hand, we can see THIS SAME JESUS prophesied in Isaiah and other prophets, too. Just a few from Isaiah here. Isaiah 9.

> *But in the future he will honor Galilee of the nations, by the Way of the Sea, beyond the Jordan The people walking in darkness have seen a great light; on those living in the land of deep darkness a light has dawned. You have enlarged the nation and increased their joy; they rejoice before you as people rejoice at the harvest, as warriors rejoice when dividing the plunder. For to us a child is born, to us a son is given, and the government will be on his shoulders. And he will be called Wonderful Counselor, Mighty God, Everlasting Father, Prince of Peace. Of the greatness of his government and peace there will be no end. He will reign on David's throne and over his kingdom, establishing and upholding it with justice and righteousness from that time on and forever. The zeal of the Lord Almighty will accomplish this.*

Isaiah 11 The Branch From Jesse

> *A shoot will come up from the stump of Jesse; from his roots a Branch will bear fruit. The Spirit of the Lord will rest on him, the Spirit of wisdom and of understanding, the Spirit of counsel and of might, the Spirit of the knowledge and fear of the Lord and he will delight in the fear of the Lord. He will not judge by what he sees with his eyes or decide by what he hears with his ears; but with righteousness he will judge the needy, with justice he will give decisions for the poor of the earth. He will strike the earth with the rod of his mouth; with the breath of his lips he will slay the wicked. Righteousness will be his belt and faithfulness the sash around his waist."*

Isaiah 40, A voice of one calling: "In the wilderness prepare the way for the Lord; make straight in the desert a highway for our God. Every valley shall be raised up, every mountain and hill made low; the rough ground shall become level, the rugged places a plain. And the glory of the Lord will be revealed, and all people will see it together. For the mouth of the Lord has spoken." And so many more. Isaiah 53, Isaiah 60, 61, and So many more.

And then, when we get to the New Testament, we see Isaiah there, too. Isaiah in the NT Isaiah is referred to in Matthew, Mark, Luke, John, Acts, and Romans. Wow. Here are just a couple from Luke. Because the writer of Acts also wrote the Gospel of Luke, referred to as the former treatise at the beginning of Acts 1. Isaiah in Luke. Luke 3:4 As it is written in the book of the words of Isaiah the prophet: "A voice of one calling in the wilderness, 'Prepare the way for the Lord, make straight paths for him." Luke 4:17-21:

And the scroll of the prophet Isaiah was handed to him. Unrolling it, he found the place where it is written: "The Spirit of the Lord is on me, because he has anointed me to proclaim good news to the poor. He has sent me to proclaim freedom for the prisoners and recovery of sight for the blind, to set the oppressed free, to proclaim the year of the Lord's favor." Then he rolled up the scroll, gave it back to the attendant and sat down. The eyes of everyone in the synagogue were fastened on him. He began by saying to them, "Today this scripture is fulfilled in your hearing."

This Same Jesus. In the Gospels. Matthew's Gospel. This same Jesus is Immanuel, God with us. This same Jesus was taken to Egypt to flee the wrath of Herod and fulfilled the prophecy, "Out of Egypt I called my Son." This same Jesus is the one who taught the Sermon on the Mount. The beatitudes, the Lord's Prayer. This same Jesus called the disciples and said, "follow me." This same Jesus taught parables about the kingdom of God. This same Jesus taught about the signs of the times at the end of times. Mark's Gospel. John (the Baptist) wore clothing made of camel's hair, with a leather belt around his waist, and he ate locusts and wild honey. And this was his message: "After me comes the one more powerful than I, the straps of whose sandals I am not worthy to stoop down and untie. I baptize you with water, but he will baptize you with the Holy Spirit." This same Jesus does many miracles and moves immediately and straightway.

Luke's Gospel. This same Jesus healed the sick, cast out demons, and restored sight to the blind. This same Jesus welcomed tax collectors and sinners. This same Jesus taught us to pray, "Our Father in Heaven, hallowed be your name." This same Jesus broke bread and blessed it and invited us to do this in remembrance of him. John's Gospel. This same Jesus is the Word who was in the beginning, who was made flesh and dwelt among us. This same Jesus said, "I Am." I am the light of the world. I am the door. I am the Good Shepherd. I am the way, the truth, the life, the bread of life, the vine. This same Jesus washed the disciple's feet. This same Jesus is the one who offered up his life for his friends. This same Jesus who said it was good that he would go away. This same Jesus said It would be better if he went away because he would send the Holy Spirit.

Greater Things. This same Jesus said that greater things would we do. John 14:12, "Very truly I tell you, whoever believes in me will do the works I have been doing, and they will do even greater things than these, because I am going to the Father." This same Jesus appeared to Mary at the tomb and called her by name. This same Jesus. The books could not contain all that he said and did. John 20:30-31. "Jesus performed many other signs in the presence of his disciples, which are not recorded in this book. But these are written that you may believe that Jesus is the Messiah, the Son of God, and that by believing you may have life in his name." Jesus was returning to God. John 13:3 "Jesus knew that the Father had put all things under his power, and that he had come from God and was returning to God;" This was the night that Jesus took the towel and basin and washed the feet of the disciples. Jesus told them he would be leaving. John 14:3, "I go to prepare a place for you. And if I go, I will come again and receive you unto myself that where I am there you may be also." Jesus spent time preparing them for his departure. And promised to come back again.

Coming Back To Earth-Return. Remember when Peter was asking Jesus, What about him? What about John? John 21:22, Jesus answered, "If I want him to remain alive until I return, what is that to you? You must follow me." Jesus will be returning in glory. Several verses in Matthew. Matthew 16:27, "For the Son of Man is going to come in his Father's glory with his angels, and then he will reward each person according to what they have done." At the renewal of all things. Matthew 19:28, Jesus said to them, "Truly I tell you, at the renewal of all things, when the Son of Man sits on his glorious throne, you who have followed me will also sit on twelve thrones, judging the twelve tribes of Israel.

Coming In The Clouds Of Heaven. Matthew 24:30, "Then will appear the sign of the Son of Man in heaven. And then all the peoples of the earth will mourn when they see the Son of Man coming on the clouds of heaven, with power and great glory." Sitting at the right hand and coming in the clouds. In Matthew 26:64, "You have said so," Jesus replied. "But I say to all of you: From now on you will see the Son of Man sitting at the right hand of the Mighty One and coming on the clouds of heaven." In Luke 17:24, "For the Son of Man in his day will be like the lightning, which flashes and lights up the sky from one end to the other." Luke 21:27, "At that time they will see the Son of Man coming in a cloud with power and great glory." Luke 22:69, "But from now on, the Son of Man will be seated at the right hand of the mighty God."

Let's look at the end of each of the Gospels. Our Commission. Matthew 28:16-20:

> *Then the eleven disciples went to Galilee, to the mountain where Jesus had told them to go. When they saw him, they worshiped him; but some doubted. Then Jesus came to them and said, "All authority in heaven and on earth has been given to me. Therefore go and make disciples of all nations, baptizing them in the name of the Father and of the Son and of the Holy Spirit, and teaching them*

to obey everything I have commanded you. And surely I am with you always, to the very end of the age."

Mark 16:19-20. "After the Lord Jesus had spoken to them, he was taken up into heaven and he sat at the right hand of God. Then the disciples went out and preached everywhere, and the Lord worked with them and confirmed his word by the signs that accompanied it."

Luke 24: 50-53 "When he had led them out to the vicinity of Bethany, he lifted up his hands and blessed them. While he was blessing them, he left them and was taken up into heaven. Then they worshiped him and returned to Jerusalem with great joy. And they stayed continually at the temple, praising God." Look at John 20:17-18:

> *Jesus said, "Do not hold on to me, for I have not yet ascended to the Father. Go instead to my brothers and tell them, 'I am ascending to my Father and your Father, to my God and your God.'" Mary Magdalene went to the disciples with the news: "I have seen the Lord!" And she told them that he had said these things to her."*

Jesus Appears to His Disciples. Starting in John 20:19-23:

> *On the evening of that first day of the week, when the disciples were together, with the doors locked for fear of the Jewish leaders, Jesus came and stood among them and said, "Peace be with you!" After he said this, he showed them his hands and side. The disciples were overjoyed when they saw the Lord. Again, Jesus said, "Peace be with you! As the Father has sent me, I am sending you." And with that he breathed on them and said, "Receive the Holy Spirit. If you forgive anyone's sins, their sins are forgiven; if you do not forgive them, they are not forgiven.*

This Jesus in Acts. Peter's Sermon Acts 2:22 "Fellow Israelites, listen to this: Jesus of Nazareth was a man accredited by God to you by miracles, wonders and signs, which God did among you through him, as you yourselves know." Acts 2:32 "God has raised this Jesus to life, and we are all witnesses of it." Acts 2:36 "Therefore let all Israel be assured of this: God has made this Jesus, whom you crucified, both Lord and Messiah." Acts 6:14 accusation against Stephen by false witnesses. "For we have heard him say that this Jesus of Nazareth will destroy this place and change the customs Moses handed down to us." Paul in Athens explaining and proving that the Messiah had to suffer and rise from the dead. Acts 17:3, "This Jesus I am proclaiming to you is the Messiah," he said.

Come Down from Heaven.1 Thessalonians 4:7-12: "For the Lord himself will come down from heaven, with a loud command, with the voice of the archangel and with the trumpet call of God, and the dead in Christ will rise first." And 2 Peter 3:8-12,

> *"But do not forget this one thing, dear friends: With the Lord a day is like a thousand years, and a thousand years are like a day. 9 The Lord is not slow in keeping his promise, as some understand slowness. Instead he is patient with you, not wanting anyone to perish, but everyone to come to repentance. 10 But the day of the Lord will come like a thief. The heavens will disappear with a roar; the elements will be destroyed by fire, and the earth and everything done in it will be laid bare. 11 Since everything will be destroyed in this way, what kind of people ought you to be? You ought to live holy and godly lives 12 as you look forward to the day of God and speed its coming."*

Revelation of Jesus Christ. Chapter 1:12-17:

> *I turned around to see the voice that was speaking to me. And when I turned I saw seven golden lampstands, 13 and among the lampstands was someone like a son of man, dressed in a robe reaching down to his feet and with a golden sash around his chest. 14 The hair on his head was white like wool, as white as snow, and his eyes were like blazing fire. 15 His feet were like bronze glowing in a furnace, and his voice was like the sound of rushing waters. 16 In his right hand he held seven stars, and coming out of his mouth was a sharp, double-edged sword. His face was like the sun shining in all its brilliance. 17 When I saw him, I fell at his feet as though dead. Then he placed his right hand on me and said: "Do not be afraid. I am the First and the Last. 18 I am the Living One; I was dead, and now look, I am alive for ever and ever!*

Go back to Acts 1 verse 3. "After his suffering, he presented himself to them and gave many convincing proofs that he was alive." He appeared to them over a period of forty days and spoke about the kingdom of God. Many infallible proofs. Witnesses. We believe the witnesses. What do witnesses do? They tell what they have seen and heard. What happens when we are witnesses in court? The judge wants our testimony. What we have seen and heard. What did you see? What did you hear? Legal evidence from eyewitnesses. These followers were eyewitnesses of his resurrection. These followers did not keep it a secret what they saw and what they heard.

Appearances and Thomas. In these days, we need this same Jesus. In these days of uncertainty, we need this same Jesus. The disciples saw this same Jesus after he rose from the dead. He appeared to them and taught them and prepared them even after his resurrection so that they were certain that this person who appeared in their midst was this same Jesus. They were willing to be witnesses of Jesus's life and resurrection because they saw him, they touched him, they were witnesses of the empty tomb, the nail prints in his hands and feet, and the wound on his side. This same Jesus is the one that Doubting Thomas said, "My Lord and My God."

The Book of Acts is the Gospel of the Holy Spirit. The Book of Acts starts with the resurrected Jesus showing himself to witnesses for 40 days. And eating with them and teaching them and instructing them and preparing them for his departure. The Book of Acts offers us glimpses into the early church. Offers us the coming of the Spirit at Pentecost. Offers us the persecution, early martyrs, and scattering of the church. Offers us the conversion of Saul the persecuting Pharisee into Paul the Apostle. The welcoming of Gentile Christians as the kingdom of God spreads beyond into Judea, Samaria, and the ends of the earth. The council of the church at Jerusalem, the missionary journeys of Paul and his companions. When we read Acts, there are "we" passages of we went here, and we traveled there. The book of Acts stops before the death of Peter, before the death of Paul. The timeline for Acts is after the resurrection of Jesus until the early 60s. The Apostle Paul is preaching the gospel as the book of Acts closes.

There we see, at the end of the book of Acts, that the gospel is being preached in an unhindered way. Acts 28: 28-31 (NASB):

> *Therefore let it be known to you that this salvation of God has been sent to the Gentiles; they will also listen." [When he had spoken these words, the Jews departed, having a great dispute among themselves.] And he stayed two full years in his own rented quarters and was welcoming all who came to him, preaching the kingdom of God and teaching concerning the Lord Jesus Christ with all openness, unhindered.*

The good news of Jesus Christ CANNOT BE HINDERED by imprisonment, perils, persecutions, famines, or plagues. The good news of Jesus Christ has come to us through the witness of the church, through the witness of the scriptures, and through the continuing witness of the signs, wonders, and miracles. And just as the prophecies of the Old Testament were fulfilled in Jesus Christ, the promises of Jesus are being fulfilled now and will yet be fulfilled. The angels said. THIS SAME JESUS will return.

Memory Verse. Acts 1:8 *But You Will Receive Power.* Ponder this verse. Memorize it. Think about it. *"But you will receive power when the Holy Spirit comes on you; and you will be my witnesses in Jerusalem, and in all Judea and Samaria, and to the ends of the earth."*

This Same Jesus Prays For Us. Hebrews 7:25 "Therefore he is able to save completely those who come to God through him, because he always lives to intercede for them." We receive power from the Holy Spirit to be witnesses in our Judea, Samaria, and to the ends of the earth, wherever the Lord sends us. As we go in the power of the Holy Spirit, We go in the power of this Same Jesus who promised the Holy Spirit to live in us, to minister through us, to help us to be witnesses, to help us to teach and make disciples of all nations, to pray for us.

When? When the world is shaking, We need this same Jesus. When the pandemic is spreading. We need this same Jesus. In the hot spots all over the world. Of suffering, famine, persecution, and sickness. When we are tired of sheltering-in-place, We need this same Jesus. When healthcare workers and first responders, and essential services workers are overwhelmed, We need this same Jesus. When life is crushing us, We need this same Jesus. When we are feeling overwhelmed, We need this same Jesus. When we do not know if we will see tomorrow, We need this same Jesus. When everything is uncertain, We need this same Jesus. We need this firm foundation. We need to be rooted and grounded in love. We need to stand, to stand firm, to be unwavering, to have faith that perseveres to the end.

Who can give us this faith? This same Jesus. This same Jesus gives us love for one another. This same Jesus helps us to forgive one another. This same Jesus is our message. The world needs this same Jesus. Spiritual hunger is arising. I am going to close in prayer. If you need specific prayer today, If you need specific prayer this week, Reach out to us. We will pray with you.

Closing Prayer. O Lord Our God. We come to You because You invite us to come. Jesus, You said if any of us were weary and heavy laden, we could come to You, and You would give us rest. Today, Lord, some of us want to lay our heavy burdens down. We want to cast our cares on You because You care for us. We want to invite You to renew our minds, heal our bodies, and save our souls. Lord, we need You. You see exactly where we need You. Come, Holy Spirit. Come in Your Power, Come and reign in us. Have Your way, O Lord. Lead us, guide us, and direct us in the journey ahead. In Jesus' Name, Amen.

www.ingramcontent.com/pod-product-compliance
Lightning Source LLC
Chambersburg PA
CBHW051004140626
46546CB00016B/274